7 th E

POST OFFICE JOBS

The Ultimate 473 Postal Exam Study Guide and Job Finder

Apply For Post Office Jobs

Pass the 473 Postal Exam

Explore ALL Job Options

DENNIS V. DAMP

ISBN Print: 978-0-943641-34-8
ISBN Ebook: 978-0-943641-35-5
ISSN: 1947-6671

BOOKHAVEN PRESS LLC
302 Scenic Court
Moon Township, PA 15108
http://bookhavenpress.com and http://postalwork.net

Cover design by George Foster
Editing by Nancy Ledgerwood and Dennis V. Damp Jr.

Printed in the United States of America

Disclaimer of All Warranties and Liabilities

This book provides information on post office employment and preparing for the 473 postal exam. It is sold with the understanding that the publisher and author are not engaged in rendering legal, general counseling, or other professional services. If expert assistance is required, the services of a competent professional should be sought. The author and publisher make no warranties, either expressed or implied, with respect to the information contained herein. The author and publisher shall not be liable for any incidental or consequential damages in connection with, or arising out of, the use of material in this book. This book and its companion web site at www.postalwork.net are not affiliated with or endorsed by the U.S. Postal Service.

Publisher's Cataloging-In-Publication Data
(Prepared by The Donohue Group, Inc.)

Names: Damp, Dennis V.
Title: Post Office jobs : the ultimate 473 postal exam study guide and job
    finder / Dennis V. Damp.
Description: 7th edition. | Moon Township, PA : Bookhaven Press LLC, 2018.
    | "Apply for Post Office Jobs, Pass the 473 Postal Exam, Explore ALL
    Job Options." | Includes bibliographical references and index.
Identifiers: ISBN 9780943641348 (print) | ISBN 9780943641355 (ebook)
Subjects: LCSH: Postal service--Vocational guidance--United States. |
    Postal service--United States--Employees. | Postal service--United
    States--Examinations, questions, etc. | Postal service--United States--
    Examinations--Study guides. | LCGFT: Examinations. | Study guides. |
    BISAC: BUSINESS & ECONOMICS / Careers / Job Hunting. | STUDY AIDS /
    Tests (Other) | REFERENCE / Questions & Answers.
Classification: LCC HE6499 .D18 2018 (print) | LCC HE6499 (ebook) | DDC
383/.4973/023--dc23

Distributed to the trade by Midpoint Trade Books, 27 West 20th Street, Suite 1102, New York, NY 10011, 212-616-2020, http://midpointtrade.com.

Table of Contents

Chapter Six

Chapter Seven

Preface

The U.S. Postal Service employs 644,000 workers and generated $69.7 billion dollars in revenue in 2017. They paid their employees over $1.8 billion dollars every payday! Over 149 billion pieces of mail were delivered last year, serving 157 million delivery points every delivery day. On a typical day, postal workers travel over 4 million miles and 3.6 million people visit their website.

Over the past three years, the postal service increased employment by 4 percent and streamlined operations. Even with billions in revenue, there are challenges ahead and they continue to reduce costs and reorganizing to improve operational efficiency.

The postal service has remained a reliable employment option, even under these challenging conditions, for those who know how to apply for job vacancies and prepare for postal exams. Additional opportunities will be created as those who are at or beyond retirement age opt to retire. Each day 10,000 baby boomers turn age 65 and this trend is projected to continue for another 12 years. Hiring will be driven by retirements and the need to maintain staffing throughout their extensive network that includes 31,000 Post Offices, 4,000 contract Postal Units, Community Post Offices, and Village Offices.

The revised seventh edition provides an overview of what is available, including many jobs that don't require written tests and how to apply for them. A comprehensive 473/473E study guide provides helpful test-taking strategies that could dramatically improve many applicant's exam scores. Seven other sample postal exams for maintenance, clerical, technician, and other major occupations are included in this new edition.

Most limit their job search to mail carrier and clerk positions and are unaware of the many other career opportunities that the postal service offers. Even with mail carriers and clerks making up over 50% of the workforce, the postal service still employs hundreds of thousands in other occupations. They employ

30,000 building and equipment maintenance workers, 5,000 vehicle maintenance employees, thousands of motor vehicle operators, postal inspectors, accountants, administrative staff, human resource personnel, and professionals across a broad spectrum of fields.

Post Office Jobs is the only post office career guide that includes a comprehensive 473/473E exam study guide, sample exam questions for 7 other careers, and job descriptions for the top 24 occupations. It provides guidance on how to explore alternative civil service occupations and includes a chapter on how to apply for postal inspector positions. Nancy Ledgerwood, our editor, worked for the postal service for 22 years. She provided an insider's perspective of their eCareer recruiting system and testing processes.

Postal employees are interviewed prior to appointment by the selecting official. Chapter Six provides sample questions and detailed guidance on how to successfully handle these often nerve-racking face-to-face encounters.

Professional and administrative occupations do not require written examinations. Your background, work experience and education determine your eligibility for the job. You'll learn how to locate vacancies and apply for these positions nationwide. Appendix B describes how to prepare your resume and includes examples of Knowledge, Skills & Abilities (KSA) statements that must be submitted with your application for many of the corporate positions.

Appendix C provides an updated list of Customer Service District Offices that you can contact for test results and to learn when jobs will be advertised in your area. Many who apply for and take postal exams misplace their paperwork and do not know who to contact. These offices can direct you to the right department when you have questions or have to reschedule an exam.

Visit www.postalwork.net, the companion web site for the new seventh edition, for up-to-date guidance on postal service job options including direct links to the postal service's recruiting site. Also visit www.federaljobs.net to explore related civil service jobs. These sites include extensive assistance for job seekers and cover many topics for people interested in exploring all federal careers.

If you are seeking a job with the postal service, you should also be aware of postal employment and testing scams that charge excessive fees. The postal service does not charge application fees and no one can guarantee you a postal or federal job. All jobs are filled competitively.

The average annual pay and benefits for all postal employees was $77,000 in 2017. The largest postal service pay system is predominantly for bargaining unit employees. There is also an Executive Administrative Schedule (EAS) for non-bargaining unit members where pay ranges from $25,619 up to an authorized maximum of $129,792.

If you're looking for good pay with excellent benefits, explore the postal service job market. Use this book's resources, including the Job Hunter's Checklist in Appendix A, to begin your personal job search.

Chapter One
The U.S. Postal Service

Thousands apply each year for postal jobs, and those who understand the hiring process and study for entrance exams – when required – will dramatically improve their chances. The postal service never charges fees to take an exam or to apply for jobs. Don't be misled by ads that offer postal employment and charge a fee for their services. You will find all you need in this book, its companion website at www.postalwork.net, and on the official USPS website listed below.

The postal service employs over 644,000 workers spending $72.4 billion to fund operations in 2017 while paying $1.8 billion in salaries and benefits every two weeks to employees. They employ workers in 300 occupations for positions at 35,000 post offices, branches, and stations throughout the United States. Thousands of postal workers are hired yearly to backfill for retirements, transfers, deaths, and to replace employees who choose to leave for other reasons. They also hire tens of thousands of casual temporary workers for peak mail periods including the holiday rush every year.

Starting pay in 2018 for city carrier assistants was $16.78 per hour, $35,019 per year. Assistant rural carriers earn $17.78 per hour, mail handler assistants $15.46 per hour, and mail processing clerks start at $16.98 per hour. Tractor trailer operators salary range is from $21.44 to $29.44 per hour while automotive technicians salary range is from $43,880 to $58,888 annually.[1] Mail processing, clerk, and delivery workers are initially hired as supplemental workers with temporary appointments and typically work 40 or more hours per week.

Adding benefits, overtime, and premiums, the average annual compensation rate for all employees was $77,000 in 2018.

www.postalwork.net
http://about.usps.com/careers/welcome.htm

---

[1] Beginning salary figures obtained from various national 2018 Post Office job announcements.

The average pay and benefits for all postal employees was $77,000 per year in 2018.[2] The largest postal service pay system is predominantly for bargaining unit employees and 90% of career employees are covered by collective bargaining agreements. There is also an Executive Administrative Schedule (EAS) for non-bargaining unit members, divided into 26 grades, with pay ranging from $25,619 up to an authorized maximum of $129,792.

Applicants apply for job vacancies online. Under the postal service's eCareer recruiting program the *"473 Delivery, Distribution and Retail Exam,"* the exam that all mail carriers, clerks, and mail handlers must pass, is divided into two parts. The first part is an unproctored online assessment (473E). If you pass the initial online assessment with a score of 70 or higher you will be scheduled for a 473 proctored test. The proctored exams are contracted out to local testing facilities that provide greater access for applicants.

BENEFITS

Postal employees receive the same general benefits provided to federal employees for the most part. However, USPS employees health care bi-weekly premiums are considerably less than what the competitive civil service must pay.

Vacation and Sick Leave

All employees receive: 10 paid holidays, 13 days of vacation for the first three years, 20 days of vacation with three to fifteen years service, and after fifteen years, 26 days. Additionally, 13 sick days are accrued each year regardless of length of service. Military time counts toward benefits. If you have three years of military service, you begin with four weeks paid vacation and three years toward retirement.

Health Benefits and Life Insurance

Medical health plans and the Federal Employees' Group Life Insurance (FEGLI) programs are available to all employees. The medical plan is an employee-employer contribution system and includes HMO and Blue Cross and Blue Shield programs. There are hundreds of plans to choose from. The FEGLI program offers low-cost term life insurance for the employee and basic coverage for the family. FEGLI offers up to five times the employee's salary in death benefits.

---

[2] Comprehensive Financial Statement on Postal Operations, 2018 — USPS

One of the primary benefits of postal service employment is the satisfaction you experience from working in a challenging and rewarding position. Positions are available with the level of responsibility and authority that you desire.

Retirement

There are three components to the Federal Employees Retirement System (FERS). Retirees receive a fixed annuity based on the number of years served, typically 1% of an employee's high three years average earnings for each year of service, Social Security, and there is an employee contribution system that is fashioned after a 401k defined contribution plan.

Employees can contribute into a *THRIFT savings 401k plan*. The government matches contributions up to 5 percent. Contributions are tax deferred and reduce your taxable income by the amount contributed. The retirement benefit is determined by the amount that has accumulated during the employee's career. This includes the interest earned and capital gains realized from the retirement fund. Go to www.federalretirement.net to learn more about the FERS retirement system

There are many withdrawal options, including lump sum and various fixed-term annuities. The contribution plan payout is in addition to the Social Security and fixed annuity benefits that you will be eligible for at retirement. Postal workers pay considerably less for their health benefits than competitive federal Civil Service employees due to their negotiated union contracts.

EMPLOYEE CLASSIFICATIONS

Initial appointments are either casual or transitional (temporary) or Part-Time Flexible (Career). Hourly rates for Part-Time Flexible employees vary depending upon the position's rate schedule. Some positions are filled full-time, such as the Maintenance (Custodial) classification.

- Full-Time and Part-Time Flexible (career) employees compose the *Regular Work Force*. This category includes security guards. Part-time flexible employees are scheduled to work fewer than 40 hours per week and they must be available for flexible work hours as assigned. Part-time flexible employees are paid by the hour. Hourly rates vary from $15.30 for PS Grade 3 Step JJ to $35.87 for PS Grade 11 step P.

- A *Supplemental Work Force* is needed by the postal service for peak mail periods and offers casual mail handler positions for 360 calendar days. During Christmas an additional 21 days of employment can be offered to supplemental work force employees. City carrier assistants, mail handler assistants, and postal support employees (clerks) can be hired for a period of 360 calendar days and may be rehired after a break in service.

Entrance exams are not required for casual clerk or postmaster relief positions. These positions cannot be converted to full-time positions. However, you will be able to apply for future job vacancies and take the 473 Postal Exam in your area when they are advertised. Many, if not the majority of, postal workers today start out in casual or transitional positions and eventually apply for the job, pass the exam, and get hired.

College students may be considered for casual (temporary) employment with the postal service during the summer months. Tests are not required and appointments cannot lead to a career position. Apply early for summer work. Contact post offices in your area no later than February for summer employment applications. Casual temporary positions are also advertised on the postal service's employment and job listing website at www.usps.com/employment.

QUALIFICATION REQUIREMENTS

Various standards from age restrictions to physical requirements must be met before you can take one of the postal service exams.

Age Limit

You must be at least eighteen to apply. Certain conditions allow applicants as young as sixteen to apply. Carrier positions, requiring driving, are limited to age 18 or older. High school graduates or individuals who terminated high school education for sufficient reason are permitted to apply at age 16.

Entrance Exams

Clerks, carriers, rural carriers, and other mail-handling job applicants must pass the 473E and 473 entrance exams. Specialties such as mechanic, electronic technician, machinist, and trades must also take and pass a proctored test. The overall rating is based on the test results and your qualifying work experience and education. Professionals and certain administrative positions don't require an entrance exam. They are rated and hired strictly on their prior work experience and education.

The **473 Major Entry Level Jobs Exam** covers the following positions:

- ✔ City Carrier
- ✔ City Carrier Assistant
- ✔ General Clerk
- ✔ Mail Handler
- ✔ Postal Support
- ✔ Rural Carrier
- ✔ Sales and Service Associate

This exam, previously referred to as the *473 Battery Examination,* covers the vast majority of entry-level hiring.

Custodial positions are reserved for veteran preference eligibles by federal law. The USPS also requires *motor vehicle operators*, *tractor trailer operators*, and highly skilled maintenance positions such as *building equipment mechanic, electronics technicians, and general mechanics* to pass entrance exams.

Maintenance mechanics must take the 955 test for their speciality and electronics technicians must complete the same exam's electronics technician group section. The 955 test replaced the 931 and 932 exams that were previously used. An exams list is provided on page 23 and Chapter Four presents sample tests for a seven major occupations other than the 473 exam.

A comprehensive sample *473 and 473E Examination* is provided in Chapter Five. Study tips are included and the test-taking strategies that can help you achieve as high a score as possible.

The 473 examination and completion of forms requires approximately three hours and fifteen minutes to complete. The first half of the exam, the 473-E, is completed online when you apply and a second proctored exam is taken at a local testing facility. Applicants that score between 80% and 100% will be called sooner than lower graded applicants and they have a better chance of being hired.

Citizenship

Applicants do not have to be U.S. citizens. If you have permanent alien resident status in the United States of America or owe allegiance to the United States of America you can apply for postal service jobs.

Physical Requirements

Physical requirements are determined by the job. Carriers must be able to lift a 70-pound mail sack and all applicants must be able to efficiently perform assigned duties. Eyesight and hearing tests are required. Applicants must have at least 20/40 vision in the good eye and no worse than 20/100 in the other eye. Eyeglasses are permitted.

State Driver's License

Applicants must have a valid state driver's license for positions that require motor vehicle operation. A safe driving record is required and a postal service road test is administered for the type of vehicle that you will operate.

DRUG TESTING (SUBSTANCE ABUSE)

The postal service maintains a comprehensive program to ensure a drug-free workplace. A qualification for postal employment is to be drug free and this qualification is determined through the use of a urinalysis drug screen. When you are determined to be in the area of consideration for employment, you will be scheduled for a drug screening test.

APPLICATION PROCEDURES

All Vacancies

All applications are processed online and after you register write down your user name, password, and email address. Keep this information handy. You will need it to check on your application and to apply for other jobs. Once you register, apply for a job, and take an exam you will receive a *"Candidate ID Number."* You are able to apply for other jobs requiring the same exam without retesting if you enter this number when you start a new application. Write this information in the margin of this workbook so you will have it available when needed.

A position announcement is provided for each job vacancy that applicants must read carefully.

> When you search for jobs click on a vacancy of interest in your area and **print a copy of the announcement for future reference.** Many forgo doing this and regret it later. There is essential information that you may need to apply. You will also find a contact email address or phone number to call if you have problems applying or need to reschedule an exam.

Positions Requiring Entrance Examinations

When a vacancy exists the postal service advertises the job on its website and you apply for a specific job that will be filled within four to six weeks of the job announcement's closing date.

To apply for postal positions, first visit www.postalwork.net/jobs.htm, this book's companion web site, and review the step-by-step instructions with helpful hints on how to apply for post office jobs on the official website. This site shows screen shots of the official application pages with instructions to help you successfully navigate the *eCareer* application system. Don't get sidetracked by major private-sector jobs board ads. The postal service seldom advertises on any of the large online jobs boards, and if it does you are linked directly to their official web site to apply at no cost.

> There are many postal job scams online and in newspaper classifieds that list toll-free numbers and charge fees up to $100 or more for exam study guides. The application process is free to all who apply and this book provides a comprehensive 473 exam study guide in Chapter Five.

Apply online at http://about.usps.com/careers/welcome.htm. Most libraries offer online access if you don't have a computer at home. Job opportunities are also advertised at local post offices, in national and local newspapers, journals, and periodicals. Read the caution notice above prior to calling a toll-free number.

A passing score of 70 percent or better is required for your name to be added to the register. The highest-rated applicants will be called to complete additional paperwork, take a drug screening test, and an interview. Your score determines your placement on the list.

Apply for each job separately and to improve your chances, apply for all positions that you meet the basic qualifications. To determine your eligibility read the *position announcement* that is provided for each job vacancy. Your exam results are valid for several years provided you have your Candidate ID Number (formerly called the Exam History Code) when you apply for other jobs.

Positions That Don't Require Entrance Exams

Generally professional and administrative occupations don't require written exams. Typically they are announced (advertised) first within the postal service and postal employees who meet the job qualifications may apply for these openings. If there aren't any qualified internal applicants, then the postal service advertises the vacancies to the general public and they accept résumés and applications for rating. All applicants must pass an entrance examination and/or an evaluation process to be considered for a job. Corporate positions that don't require entrance exams are covered in Appendix B.

It may be advantageous for job applicants seeking entry-level professional and administrative positions to take the 473 Exam to get their foot in the door. Once hired, as vacancies open in their specialty such as accounting, budget, and engineering, they will have first crack at the jobs through internal postal service job announcements. You can view the diverse lists of job advertisements online at their career center. There are lists of jobs reserved for current postal employees only. Once you get your foot in the door you can bid on these restricted announcements, and the experience that you will gain from the entry-level position will help you better understand the postal system.

Realistically, many professional jobs won't be filled internally. Few postal clerks and non-professional employees will have law degrees, engineering credentials or doctorates, for example. Visit the employment website to explore all the available jobs, and review the job classifications list in Chapter Ten.

These job openings will be advertised on the USPS website. You should also contact local Customer Service and Sales District (CSSD) personnel offices listed in Appendix C to identify upcoming job vacancies for your specialty. You can also call your local CSSD office's human resources or staffing department for assistance if you lose your paperwork and need them to direct you to the proper office.

You will be rated on a point system (maximum of 100 points) plus veterans preference points if applicable, even without a written test. Therefore, your résumé and *Application for Employment* and online submission must include all key information such as degrees, training, credentials, and detailed work experience. Only the top candidates will generally be referred to the selecting official for consideration.

I suggest compiling your résumé and application offline first and spend quality time drafting your work experiences, collecting the required employment and education history, and spell and grammar check your application. Then, and only after thorough review, copy and paste it into the online résumé builder. Make sure you capture all required information. If you omit key information your application may be rejected, and at the very least you stand to lose points.

Corporate applicants need to spend quality time compiling their résumé and application. You will find Chapter Six in *The Book of U.S. Government Jobs* very helpful. This book takes applicants step-by-step through the process from evaluating the job announcement to compiling work histories and Knowledge, Skills & Abilities (KSAs) statements. This book's companion website at www.federaljobs.net will also prove helpful.

VETERANS PREFERENCE

Veterans receive five or ten point preference. Those with a 10% or greater compensable service-connected disability are placed at the top of the register in the order of their scores. All other eligibles are listed below the disabled veterans group in rank order. The Veterans Preference Act applies to all postal service positions. Refer to Chapter Seven for detailed information on veterans preference.

Custodial exams for the position of cleaner, custodian, and custodial laborer are exclusively for veterans and present employees. These jobs are open only to veterans preference candidates.

PAY SCALES

The Postal Service (PS) pay scale for bargaining unit employees and the Executive and Administrative Schedule (EAS) pay scale for non-bargaining unit employees are presented in this chapter.

Special pay scales are also used for rural letter carriers, city carriers, mail handlers, and others. Pay scales for most of the major occupations are available online at www.postalwork.net/pay_scales_.htm.

The postal service also pays extra compensation, overtime, and night shift differential to workers. A Cost of Living Adjustment (COLA) is added to the base salary of employees at the rate of one cent per hour for each .4 point increase in the Consumer Price Index. You will find General Schedule federal pay schedules posted on www.federaljobs.net.

POSTAL SERVICE (PS) Full Time Annual Rates (3/8/2018)

Steps	\multicolumn{9}{c}{Grades}

Steps	3	4	5	6	7	8	9	10	11
JJ	30,598	31,943							
II	31,691	33,026							
HH	32,784	34,109							
GG	33,877	35,192							
FF	34,970	36,275	38,573	40,852	43,135	43,880			
EE	36,063	37,358	39,593	41,814	44,045	44,818			
DD	37,156	38,441	40,613	42,776	44,955	45,756			
CC	38,249	39,524	41,633	43,738	45,865	46,694			
BB	39,342	40,607	42,653	44,700	46,775	47,632			
AA	40,435	41,690	43,673	45,662	47,685	48,570			
A	41,528	42,773	44,693	46,624	48,595	49,508			
B	42,621	43,856	45,713	47,586	49,505	50,446			
C	43,714	44,939	46,733	48,548	50,415	51,384			
D	44,807	46,022	47,753	49,510	51,325	52,322	56,378	59,839	61,140
E	45,900	47,105	48,773	50,472	52,235	53,260	57,080	60,673	62,023
F	46,993	48,188	49,793	51,434	53,145	54,198	57,782	61,507	62,906
G	48,086	49,271	50,813	52,396	54,055	55,136	58,484	62,341	63,789
H	49,179	50,354	51,833	53,358	54,965	56,074	569,186	63,175	64,672
I	50,272	51,437	52,835	54,320	55,875	57,012	59,888	64,009	65,555
J	51,365	53,520	53,873	55,282	56,785	57,950	60,590	64,843	66,438
K	52,458	53,603	54,893	56,244	57,695	58,888	61,292	65,677	67,321
L	53,551	54,686	55,913	57,206	58,605	59,826	61,994	66,511	68,204
M	54,644	55,769	56,933	58,168	59,515	60,764	62,696	67,345	69,087
N	55,737	56,852	57,953	59,130	60,425	61,702	63,498	68,179	69,970
O	56,965	57,935	58,973	60,092	61,335	62,640	64,100	69,013	70,853
P							64,802	69,847	71,736

Step Increases BB-P are awarded on time in service and range from 24 weeks to 96 weeks between increases.

EXECUTIVE & ADMINISTRATIVE STEP SCHEDULE (EAS) 2018

Grade	Min / Max	Grade	Min / Max	Grade	Min / Max
1	$25,619 / $33,101	11	$38,042 / $57,134	21	$61,046 / $98,188
2	$26,457 / $34,186	12	$39,867 / $58,876	22	$64,843 / $106,415
3	$27,327 / $35,310	13	$41,726 / $62,669	23	$68,378 / $112,213
4	$28,430 / $36,735	14	$43,904 / $65,954	24	$71,764 / $117,767
5	$29,377 / $37,959	15	$46,309 / $69,551	25	$75,332 / $123,627
6	$30,439 / $39,330	16	$48,360 / $77,785	26	$79,090 / $129,792
7	$31,683 / $40,939	17	$50,507 / $81,234		
8	$32,954 / $42,579	18	$52,724 / $84,802		
9	$34,242 / $44,243	19	$55,221 / $88,821		
10	$35,504 / $45,876	20	$58,217 / $93,639		

THE LARGEST
POSTAL OCCUPATIONS

Occupation

Accounting Specialist / Tech
Address Management Specialist
Auto Technician
Auto Technician (Lead)
Bldg. Equipment Mechanic
Bulk Mail Technician
Carrier City
Carrier (Temporary Relief)
Carrier Technician
Casual Temporary
Clerk Special Delivery Services
Criminal Investigators
Customer Service Analyst
Data Collection Technician
Data Conversion Operator
Distributions Windows & Markup Clerk
Electronics Technician
Flat Sorting Machine Operator
Human Resource Specialists
Laborer Custodial, Custodian
Mail Handler/Tech/Operator
Mail Processing Clerk
Mail Processing Machine Operators
Maintenance Support Clerk/Tech
Maintenance Mechanic & MPE
Motor Vehicle Operator
Parcel Post Dist-Machine
PM/Relief/Replacement
Postal Inspector
Postal Police
Postmaster
Review Clerk
Rural Carrier Associates
Rural Delivery Carriers
Sales Services Associates
Secretary
T&A Payroll Clerks
Tractor Trailer Operator
Training Technicians
Transitional Employee

Source: Employee Master File/RDL/OCCLIST/ Occupation Code Listing (2017)

Chapter Two
The Hiring Process

The postal service uses their **eCareer** application system to advertise internal and new hire vacancies. All applicants apply for a specific job vacancy. Applicants typically know within two to six weeks of the job announcement's closing date whether or not they are being considered for the position. Thousands apply yearly and their online application system collects background information, education, and work history when you first apply. This information is saved in your personal online profile and can be reused to apply for other postal positions.

Applicants who pass the exam with a score of 70 or higher are added in rank order to a hiring list for each vacancy. The Postal Service selection committee works their way down the list until the best qualified candidate is initially identified. If the applicant makes it through the interview and passes the medical assessment an offer may follow.

When I was researching a previous edition of this book I applied for a mail carrier position in Ohio. I took and passed the 473 exam and received a notice of rating. A letter arrived from their human resource department months later requesting that I report for an interview. I didn't go to the interview since my only purpose was to understand the application and testing process so that I could relay that information to my readers.

The majority of positions, approximately 80 percent of all postal jobs, require passing an exam. Most tested positions are for city and rural carriers, mail processing specialists, mail handlers, sales, service, and distribution associates. Exams are also required for vehicle operators, mechanics, electronics technicians and others. A list of tested occupations is on page 23, and sample examinations are presented in Chapter Four. Chapter Five includes a comprehensive study guide for the 473E / 473 Exam that is required for most mail handling positions.

The majority of positions, approximately 80 percent of all postal jobs, require passing a postal exam.

The remaining twenty percent of jobs, mostly corporate positions, don't require a written entrance exam. Your work experience, education, and accomplishments are evaluated to determine your eligibility for the position. These jobs require that applicants prepare a detailed professional *postal style résumé* which is considerably different from a standard one-page private sector résumé. More information on this application process is included in Appendix B.

The U.S. Postal Service is an Equal Opportunity Employer. Hiring and advancement in the postal service is based on qualifications and performance regardless of race, color, creed, religion, sex, age, national origin, or disability. Permanent alien residents and those who owe allegiance to the United States can apply for postal service jobs.

Postal installation managers are generally appointing officials and are delegated the authority to fill vacancies by transfer, reassignment, reinstatement of a former federal or postal employee, promotion, or from a current job announcement register. Regardless of the recruitment source, applicants must meet the position's qualifications, including passing the appropriate examination if required. Examinations are internet and computer based or a *rated application process* such as that used for professional positions.

EMPLOYEE CLASSIFICATIONS

There are two employee classifications for the largest tested occupational group, the Regular and Supplemental Work Force. The regular work force includes full-time, part-time flexible, and part-time regular pay schedules. Most new hires except technicians, professionals, and other corporate employees start as part-time flexibles. Part-time flexibles are not guaranteed 40 hours per week but generally work five to six days per week and will be required to work up to 50 hours per week during peak periods.

The postal service's hiring process is composed of the following parts, the suitability component is separated into sub groups as specified below:[1]

- Recruitment / Job announcement
- Examinations (if required)
- Suitability review
    - The applicant's work history
    - Criminal conviction history[2]
    - Personal interviews (see Chapter Seven)
    - Medical assessment
- Selection

---

[1] Reference the U.S. Postal Service's Self-Instruction Module.

[2] Suitability screening, evaluation activities continue after you are hired.

RECRUITMENT OPTIONS

Noncompetitive *(Internal Hiring)*

Noncompetitive hiring for current employees and select groups may include reassignment, a change to lower level, or a promotion from a lower level, the reinstatement of eligible former postal or federal employees, or the transfer of career or career-conditional employees from other federal agencies.

Additionally, the options exist for the noncompetitive appointment of veterans with thirty percent or more disabilities, or noncompetitive appointment of Veterans' Readjustment Appointment (VRA) eligibles. Regardless of the choice of action, the appointee must meet the qualification standards of the position, including the examination requirement, if any. Noncompetitive hiring options also include the postal service's program for employment of persons with severe disabilities.[3]

Competitive *(External Hiring)*

Job vacancies are announced to the public and entrance examinations administered when necessary to meet the staffing needs of the postal service. During the period the job announcement is open, persons who meet the qualifications stated in the job announcement may apply. For age and citizenship eligibility, applicants do not have to meet these requirements at the time of application if they will become eligible during the time their ratings are on the register. When the job announcement is closed, applications are no longer accepted unless the applications are covered by one of the exceptions due to military service and other situations. Selections are made from a register of eligibles composed of scores on the basis of an examination or a rated application examination. If veterans' preference is claimed, the basic scores are increased by 5 or 10 points.

Scores are converted to ratings on a scale of 100. Scores lower than passing are given ratings of ineligible. Claimed veterans' preference points are added only to eligible ratings.

A rated application examination is an evaluation of an application and résumé that will be scored on a scale of 100 based on your work experience, education, certifications and special skills. About 20 percent of postal jobs, mostly non-bargaining unit and corporate jobs, don't require an online test. However, your application will be evaluated against the job announcement's required duties and specialized experience. Applicants must tailor their application and postal style résumé to the job announcement to achieve the highest score possible and improve their chances of being called for an interview. Additional information on how to tailor your application to the job announcement is including in Appendix B.

---

[3] Excerpts from Handbook EL-312, Updated With Postal Bulletin Revisions

Advertising Job Vacancies

The postal service uses many avenues to advertise job vacancies, depending on the labor pool in each area. They typically post vacancy announcements in postal facility lobbies, on the website, and in federal, state, and municipal buildings open to the public. They may also:

- Send press releases to newspapers and other periodicals, including those directed toward women, minorities, veterans, and people with disabilities.

- Supply information to public and nonprofit employment services and to other social service agencies, veterans' organizations, state employment agencies, and organizations that represent special emphasis groups.

- Use public service advertisements or spots on radio or television to reach the members of the community.

- Advertise on the Internet.

- Partner with appropriate State Employment and Job Service Offices to promote maximum publicity of recruitment efforts and to increase the pool of qualified applicants through the employment service network.

- Conduct and participate in job fairs, open houses, or other recruitment activities to reach the community.

Positions Restricted to Applicants Eligible for Veterans' Preference

Certain positions are restricted to applicants eligible for veterans' preference under the Veterans' Preference Act of 1944. This rule applies only to appointments from external recruitment sources (whether competitive or noncompetitive). The following are restricted positions in the postal service:[4]

- Building maintenance custodian
- Custodian laborer
- Custodian
- Elevator operator
- Laborer custodial
- Window cleaner

Applicants who are not entitled to veterans' preference may be considered for positions restricted to preference eligibles only when preference eligibles are not available for appointment.

---

[4] Postal Handbook EL-312, Section 232.52

EXAMINATIONS

The majority of applicants must pass an entrance test, with mail carriers, clerks, and mail handlers – the largest group – taking the 473 examination. The examinations help identify applicants that meet pre-established qualification requirements for filling vacant positions. Examinations measure or evaluate knowledge, skills, and abilities to predict probable future work performance. Passing examination scores are between 70 and 100. Applicants will be advised when applying for jobs whether or not a written examination is required. Most complete at least part of the exam online. A monitored exam will be scheduled at a local testing facility within 14 days from the date you apply. You are given 14 days to complete your application and assessments, and most do this online.

A list of exams follows, and you will find sample exams in Chapter 4 for the 630/630E (Postal Police), 710/720/725/730 (Clerical Abilities), 714 (Data Conversion), 741/744 (Accounting), 943 (Auto Mechanic), 741 (Accounting Technician), and 955 (Mechanical and Electrical Skills) exams. A comprehensive 473 exam study guide is offered in Chapter 5. The postal service also sends an Assessment Information Package to applicants when they apply via an e-mail attachment.

The eCareer application process is administered online. Applicants develop a Candidate Profile and establish a user name and password when they first apply that is used when applying for all other jobs.

NOTE: Annotate your user name, password, and the email address you applied under on a copy of the job announcement for future reference. You may need this information to reschedule and exam or to contact the Postal Service for assistance.

Examination List: (Partial List)

Exam #	Exam Title	Occupational Groups
473	473-473E Postal Exam	Carriers, Mail Handlers, Clerks
630	Postal Police Officer	Police Officer
710	Clerical Abilities	Secretary, Clerks, Admin.
712/713	CBT Ver 2.0	Typing Test
714	Computer Based Test	Data Entry
715	715 Ver 2.0	Data Entry
744	Accounting Tech	Accounting Technicians
807	Defensive Driving Course	Drivers
916	Custodial Maintenance	Custodian and Laborer
931	General Maintenance	Most Maintenance Positions
941	Automotive Technician	Automotive Technicians
943	Automotive Mechanic	Automotive Mechanics
955	Mechanical & Electronics	Mechanics and Technicians

REGISTERS

Registers are lists containing applicant names and other information, including an examination rating and/or results of an evaluation process. The names of applicants who pass an entrance examination and/or evaluation process are placed on the register in numerical score order. That is why it's important for applicants to score as high as possible on their entrance exams. Passing grades are between 70 and 100; however, the higher your score the better chance you have of being called for an interview.

Eligible applicants are ranked on a register according to final ratings (including veterans preference points – see Chapter 7) and divided into two groups. The first group is made up of veterans who have a compensable service-connected disability. The second group is made up of everyone else.

An alternative recruitment source, called the general application file, can be used to fill temporary positions when it isn't feasible to announce an examination. A general application file is comparable to a one-time use or temporary register. Because no examination is given and to comply with the provisions of veteran preference, applicants must be considered for employment by priority groups. Persons entitled to 10-point veteran preference who have a compensable service-connected disability are placed ahead of all other persons entitled to veteran preference and then placed ahead of all other applicants on the list.

> Under the old recruitment system, large registers were maintained for each major metropolitan area and used to hire for a period of from one to three years. Now, registers are compiled for each job vacancy as they occur.

SUITABILITY

Applicants are screened and evaluated to determine their overall suitability for postal employment prior to selection. This evaluation includes a review of:

- ✔ The applicant's work history
- ✔ Criminal conviction history
- ✔ Personal interviews (See Chapter Seven)
- ✔ Medical assessment

Medical assessment occurs after the job offer. The Rehabilitation Act of 1973 prohibits the postal service from inquiring into an applicant's medical suitability until a bona fide job offer is made. Medical assessment is done after selecting an applicant who has met all other suitability requirements.

After an applicant is hired, a career employee's job performance is evaluated during the probationary period. Fingerprints are submitted for a special agency check to ensure that there is no derogatory information about the individual that has not been discovered in the screening process. Thorough screening is done to ensure that individuals who do not meet postal service requirements are eliminated from the hiring process.

SELECTION

Selection is the process of identifying the best-qualified applicant for employment. Employing officials make selection decisions based on an evaluation of all information obtained during suitability screening. It is important to understand that a decision to select does not guarantee that the applicant will be appointed to the postal service. The applicant's medical assessment, which is completed after selection, or the identification of derogatory information about the applicant, may disqualify the individual before the appointment is effected.

APPOINTMENT

Appointment is the process of placing a selected applicant on the postal service rolls. The appointment is made after suitability is confirmed. Before a selection has been made or the medical assessment scheduled, an interview is scheduled for the applicant. Wherever feasible, the applicant must be given the opportunity to visit the actual job site and to observe working conditions. The selecting official or certified interviewer discusses the following with the eligible candidate:[5]

- Duties of the position.
- Working hours including reporting times, overtime, holidays, and weekends.
- An explanation of the Equal Employment Opportunity and Affirmative Action policy.
- Required dress code.

---

[5] Postal Handbook EL-312, Section 621.1

GETTING IN THE FRONT DOOR

Getting in the door is half the battle. If you are qualified in other occupations and there are currently no openings, apply for positions that require the 473 exam for entry level positions such as Postal Clerks and Mail Carriers to get in the door. You can also apply for related occupations that you meet the qualifications for. The postal service generally advertises jobs in-house first to offer qualified workers opportunities for advancement. If the position can't be filled in-house, they advertise the job to the general public. You will have the opportunity to bid on other jobs if you have the qualifications and a good track record.

Another option is to apply for supplemental work as a casual or transitional part time employee. The postal service hires many casual workers to assist with mail-delivery during peak periods, and hires transitional employees to backfill for career carrier positions. You don't have to pass an exam to be hired, and if you do well in the position you will be able to take the 473 exam when permanent positions open up. Many current employees start out as supplemental workers. Casuals can work two 89-day employment terms and 21 days during the Christmas holiday each year and transitional employees can work up to one year to backfill for letter carriers. Also consider applying for rural carrier positions in your area.

Supplemental workers earn a fair wage, and you will get exposure to what the postal service has to offer. These jobs are demanding and have flexible schedules and often require long hours on short notice.

There are two things to aim at in life: first, to get what you want; and after that to enjoy it. Only the wisest of people achieve the second.
— **Logan Smith**

INTERVIEWS

The postal service conducts interviews as part of the suitability recruitment process. You need to be prepared for these interviews. There are generally a good number of high scoring applicants, and the selecting official will use the interview process to determine the best candidate for the job. Refer to Chapter Six for guidance on how to prepare for interviews.

Chapter Three
What Jobs Are Available

This chapter describes the nature of work, working conditions, training, qualifications, employment, job outlook, and average earnings potential for postal workers. You will also find occupational descriptions for the most common postal service jobs. A list of occupations with more than 400 employees is on page 18 of Chapter One.

View job vacancies at http://www.about.usps.com/careers/welcome.htm. Additional guidance, updates, and related web links are available on this book's companion web site at www.postalwork.net. Use the *Job Hunters Checklist* in Appendix A to take you step-by-step through the postal service's job search, testing, and application process.

Postal recruitment notices may also be advertised in national and local newspapers, publications, journals, and periodicals. If there are no vacancies listed on the sites mentioned above, contact postmasters and mail facilities in your area to find out when they intend to recruit. Otherwise you will have to visit these sites frequently to check for new job postings.

To expand your employment options explore related occupations with the federal civil service as discussed in Chapter 10. Visit http://federaljobs.net/ to search for federal jobs by occupation or agency. This site also provides links to 141 federal recruiting web sites and consolidated, federal, state government, and private sector job listings.

> *Our business in life is not to get ahead of others, but to get ahead of ourselves — to break our own records, to outstrip our yesterdays by our today.*
>
> **Susan B. Johnson**

IMPROVING YOUR CHANCES

The more contacts you make, the greater your chances. **Don't get lost in the process.** Too many job seekers pin all their hopes on one effort. They apply for one job, then forget about the process until they receive a reply. Post office jobs are highly competitive. The more positions you apply for the better your chances. There are also jobs that don't require entrance exams. Visit the USPS website to explore all occupations. A list of exams is located on page 23.

The interviewing techniques presented in Chapter Six will help you prepare for the suitability screening process discussed in Chapter Two. Prepare and practice for the interview. The postal service requires that each individual be interviewed prior to making an offer of appointment. Its purpose is to verify your education, job history, and specialized skills, and clarify reasons for leaving previous jobs. You may have the highest score but that doesn't mean you automatically get the job. The interview and medical qualifications including a drug test is what the selecting official uses to make the final decision.

Take time to thoroughly complete your job application online when you register and use the sample PS Form 2591, available on www.postalwork.net, as a guide for completing your online application. All applications must be submitted online and you will have to enter all of the information that is on the PS Form 2591 into your online application. The form is only used as a guide.

Collect all the data requested on this form and compile your work histories and education on your desktop prior to starting your online application. You can copy and paste your work histories into the online résumé builder after registering. This will save time when you actually apply. Online applications time out after 30 minutes without any activity.

You aren't locked into the first job or location that you are originally selected for. Once hired, you'll have opportunities to bid for jobs in-house. Post offices, general mail facilities, and district offices are located throughout the country. You will be able to apply for jobs at other locations including future promotions or to enter a related or new career field. There are over 35,000 postal facilities nationwide.

POSTAL SERVICE WORKERS

Nature of Work

Each week, the U.S. Postal Service delivers billions of pieces of mail, including letters, bills, advertisements, and packages, through heat, snow, or rain. To do this in an efficient and timely manner, the postal service employs about 644,000 individuals who process, sort, and deliver mail and packages as well as provide customer services and supplies in post offices. Most postal service workers are clerks, mail carriers, or mail sorters, processors, and processing machine operators. Postal clerks wait on customers at post offices, whereas mail sorters, processors, and processing machine operators sort incoming and outgoing mail at post offices and mail processing centers. Mail carriers deliver mail to urban and rural residences and businesses throughout the United States.[1]

Postal service clerks, also known as window clerks, sell stamps, money orders, postal stationery, and mailing envelopes and boxes in post offices throughout the country. Today they even sell greeting cards and collectible stamp albums. They also weigh packages to determine postage and check that packages are in satisfactory condition for mailing. These clerks register, certify, and insure mail and answer questions about postage rates, post office boxes, mailing restrictions, and other postal matters. Window clerks also help customers file claims for damaged packages.

Postal service mail sorters, processors, and processing machine operators prepare incoming and outgoing mail for distribution at post offices and at mail processing centers. These workers are commonly referred to as mail handlers, distribution clerks, mail processors, or mail processing clerks. They load and unload postal trucks and move mail around a mail processing center with forklifts, small electric tractors, or hand-pushed carts. They also load and operate mail processing, sorting, and canceling machinery.

Postal service mail carriers deliver mail, once it has been processed and sorted, to residences and businesses in cities, towns, and rural areas. Although carriers are classified by their type of route—either city or rural—the duties of city and rural carriers are similar. Most travel established routes, delivering and collecting mail. Mail carriers start work at the post office early in the morning, when they arrange the mail in delivery sequence. Automated equipment has reduced the time that carriers need to sort the mail, causing them to spend more of their time delivering it.

Mail carriers cover their routes on foot, by vehicle, or a combination of both. On foot, they carry a heavy load of mail in a satchel or push it on a cart. In most urban and rural areas, they use a car or small truck. Although the postal service provides vehicles to city carriers, most rural carriers must use their own automobiles, for whose use they are reimbursed. Deliveries are made

---

[1] Bureau of Labor Statistics, U.S. Department of Labor, *Occupational Outlook Handbook*

house-to-house, to roadside mailboxes, and to large buildings such as offices or apartments, which generally have all of their tenants' mailboxes in one location.

Besides delivering and collecting mail, carriers collect money for postage-due and COD (cash-on-delivery) fees and obtain signed receipts for registered, certified, and insured mail. If a customer is not home, the carrier leaves a notice that tells where special mail is being held. After completing their routes, carriers return to the post office with mail gathered from homes, businesses, and sometimes street collection boxes, and turn in the mail, receipts, and money collected during the day.

Some city carriers may have specialized duties such as delivering only parcels or picking up mail from mail collection boxes. In contrast to city carriers, rural carriers provide a wider range of postal services, in addition to delivering and picking up mail. For example, rural carriers may sell stamps and money orders and register, certify, and insure parcels and letters. All carriers, however, must be able to answer customers questions about postal regulations and services and provide change-of-address cards and other postal forms when requested.

Work Environment

Window clerks usually work in the public portion of post offices. They have a variety of duties and frequent contact with the public, but they rarely work at night. However, they may have to deal with upset customers, stand for long periods, and be held accountable for an assigned stock of stamps and funds. Depending on the size of the post office, they also may be required to sort mail.

Despite the use of automated equipment, the work of mail sorters, processors, and processing machine operators can be physically demanding. Workers may have to move heavy sacks of mail around a mail processing center. These workers usually are on their feet, reaching for sacks and trays of mail or placing packages and bundles into sacks and trays. Processing mail can be tiring and tedious. Many sorters, processors, and machine operators work at night or on weekends, because most large post offices process mail around the clock, and the largest volume of mail is sorted during the evening and night shifts. Workers can experience stress as they process mail under tight production deadlines and quotas.

Most carriers begin work early in the morning—those with routes in a business district can start as early as 4 a.m. Overtime hours are frequently required for urban carriers. Carriers spend most of their time outdoors, delivering mail in all kinds of weather and face many natural hazards. They must deal with extreme temperatures, wet and icy roads and sidewalks, and even dog bites. Serious injuries are often due to the nature of the work, which requires repetitive movements, as well as constant lifting and bending. These types of repetitive injuries occur to the employee's joints and muscles and can include carpal tunnel syndrome.

Training, Other Qualifications, and Advancement

Education and training

There are no specific education requirements to become a postal service worker; however, all applicants must have a good command of the English language. Upon being hired, new postal service workers are trained on the job by experienced workers. Many post offices offer classroom instruction on safety and defensive driving. Workers receive additional instruction when new equipment or procedures are introduced. In these cases, workers usually are trained by another postal employee or a training specialist.

Other qualifications

Postal service workers must be at least 18 years old. They must be U.S. citizens or have been granted permanent resident-alien status in the United States, and males must have registered with the Selective Service upon reaching age 18.

Most applicants must pass a written examination that measures speed and accuracy at checking names and numbers and the ability to memorize mail distribution procedures. Job seekers should visit the postal service's web site or contact local mail processing centers where they wish to work to determine when job vacancies are anticipated. You can also call the district offices listed in Appendix C. Applicants who pass the exam are listed in order of their examination scores. Five points are added to the score of an honorably discharged veteran, and 10 points are added to the score of a veteran who was wounded in combat or is disabled. The appointing officer chooses one of the top three applicants on the job vacancy list. Applicants must reapply for other job vacancies as they occur.

When accepted, applicants must pass a physical examination and drug test, and may be asked to show that they can lift and handle mail sacks weighing 70 pounds. Applicants for mail carrier positions must have a driver's license, a good driving record, and must receive a passing grade on a road test.

Postal clerks and mail carriers should be courteous and tactful when dealing with the public, especially when answering questions or receiving complaints. A good memory and the ability to read rapidly and accurately are important. Good interpersonal skills are important, particularly for mail clerks and mail carriers who deal closely with the public.

Advancement

Postal service workers often begin on a part-time, flexible basis and become regular or full time in order of seniority, as vacancies occur. Full-time workers may bid for preferred assignments, such as the day shift or a high-level nonsupervisory position. Carriers can look forward to obtaining preferred routes as their seniority increases. Postal service workers can advance to supervisory positions on a competitive basis.

Employment

The U.S. Postal Service employs approximately 79,000 clerks, 316,700 mail carriers, 106,700 mail sorters / processors, 7,000 motor vehicle operators, 30,000 building and equipment maintenance personnel, 120,000 non-career employees, and 4,300 professional administration and technical positions in 2017. Most of them worked full time. Postal clerks typically provide window service at post office branches. Many mail sorters, processors, and processing machine operators sort mail at major metropolitan post offices; others work at mail processing centers. The majority of mail carriers work in cities and suburbs; others work in rural areas.

Postal service workers are classified as casual, part-time flexible, part-time regular, or full time. Casuals are hired for 360 days to help process and deliver mail during peak mailing or vacation periods. Part-time flexible workers do not have a regular work schedule or weekly guarantee of hours but are called as the need arises. Part-time regulars have a set work schedule of fewer than 40 hours per week, often replacing regular full-time workers on their scheduled days off. Full-time postal employees work a 40-hour week over a 5-day period.

Job Outlook

Overall employment of postal service workers is projected to decline 13 percent from 2016 to 2026. Automated sorting systems, cluster mailboxes, and tight budgets are expected to adversely affect employment. Employment changes, however, will vary by specialty.

Employment of postal service clerks is projected to decline 12 percent from 2016 to 2026. Employment may be adversely affected by the decline in First-Class Mail volume caused by the continued increase in the use of automated and electronic bill pay and email.

Employment of postal service mail carriers is projected to decline 12 percent from 2016 to 2026. The use of automated "delivery point sequencing" systems that sort letter mail directly reduces the amount of time that carriers spend on mail sorting.

The amount of time carriers save on sorting letter mail and flat mail will allow them to increase the size of their routes, which should reduce the need to hire more carriers. In addition, the postal service is moving toward more centralized mail delivery, such as the use of cluster mailboxes, to cut down on the number of door-to-door deliveries.

Employment of postal service mail sorters, processors, and processing machine operators is projected to decline 16 percent from 2016 to 2026. The postal service will likely need fewer workers because new mail sorting technology can read text and automatically sort, forward, and process mail. The greater use of online services to pay bills and the increased use of email should also reduce the need for sorting and processing workers.

Job prospects

Those seeking jobs as postal service workers can expect to encounter keen competition. The number of applicants usually exceeds the number of job openings because of the occupation's low entry requirements and attractive wages and benefits.

Employment and schedules in the postal service fluctuate with the demand for its services. When mail volume is high, full-time employees work overtime, part-time workers get additional hours, and casual workers may be hired. When mail volume is low, overtime is curtailed, part-timers work fewer hours, and casual workers are discharged.

Despite declining employment, the need to replace workers who retire will result in some job openings. However, strong competition can be expected as the number of applicants typically exceeds the number of available positions.

Earnings

The median annual wage for postal service workers was $57,260 in May 2017. The median wage is the wage at which half the workers in an occupation earned more than that amount and half earned less. The lowest 10 percent earned less than $33,430, and the highest 10 percent earned more than $59,860. Median annual wages for postal service occupations in May 2017 were as follows:

$57,000 for postal service mail carriers

$58,550 for postal service clerks

$57,260 for postal service mail sorters, processors, and processing machine operators

The average pay plus benefits for all postal employees was $77,000 per year in 2018. Generous benefits, including a defined benefit retirement plan and 401 K Thrift Plan, attract many applicants for available job vacancies.

Most postal service workers are employed full time. However, overtime is sometimes required, particularly during the holiday season. Because mail is delivered 6 days a week, many postal service workers must work on Saturdays.

Sources of Additional Information

Review Chapter Four and Five for specific exam information and visit http://about.usps.com/careers/welcome.htm to register and apply for vacancies. Also visit www.postalwork.net, the companion web site for this book, for additional information and updates. Explore http://federaljobs.net to find links to 141 federal agency personnel recruiting offices and for guidance on how to locate related jobs in the competitive federal civil service.

NOTE: The above occupational description was excerpted from the Bureau of Labor Statistics, U.S. Department of Labor, Occupational Outlook Handbook , Postal Service Workers. The content was amended with updated information that was compiled in 2018.

MAJOR OCCUPATIONS

The following occupational descriptions are provided for a variety of postal jobs. You will find job descriptions for 24 of the more common occupations in Chapter Eight that you can review along with the following to evaluate which occupations would be best suited for you. The occupations reviewed in this chapter include:

- Custodian and Custodial Laborer
- Data Conversion Operator
- Maintenance Positions
- Vehicle Operator / Tractor-Trailer Operator
- Processing, Distribution & Delivery
- City Carrier & Clerk / Rural Carrier
- Distribution Clerk, Machine & Flat Sorting Machine Operators
- Mail Handler
- Mail Processor
- Automated Mark Up Clerk

Custodian and Custodial Laborer

Note: These positions are restricted to veteran preference eligibles.

The Job

Custodian duties include manual cleaning, housekeeping, and buildings and grounds maintenance. Custodial laborers perform manual labor in connection with the maintenance and cleaning of the buildings and grounds. All positions may include irregular hours.

General Qualifications

All applicants will be required to take a written examination. The examination and completion of forms will require approximately one hour and 30 minutes.

Custodial positions require prolonged standing, walking, climbing, bending, reaching, and stooping. Employees must lift and carry heavy objects on level surfaces, on ladders and/or stairways. Custodial positions may require the use of hand tools and power cleaning equipment.

A qualification for postal employment is to be drug-free. This is determined through the use of a urinalysis drug screen. Applicants who qualify on the examination and are in the area of consideration for employment will be scheduled for the drug test.

Applicants must have vision of 20/40 (Snellen) in one eye and the ability to read without strain printed material the size of typewritten characters; glasses permitted.

Selection Process

A minimum score of 70 points (exclusive of Veteran Preference) on the examination places the applicant's name on a list of eligibles for two years. Names are placed on the hiring list according to the score on the examination.

Data Conversion Operator

The Job

Data conversion operators extract information from source documents, transfer that information to computer input forms, and enter data using a keyboard.

General Qualifications

All applicants will be required to take a written examination. The examination and completion of forms will require approximately two hours.

Applicants must have six months or equivalent of clerical or office machine operating experience, preferably on a data conversion machine. Typing is required.

A qualification for postal employment is to be drug-free. This is determined through the use of a urinalysis drug screen. Applicants who qualify on the examination and are in the area of consideration for employment will be scheduled for the drug-test.

Applicants must have vision of 20/40 (Snellen) in one eye and the ability to read without strain, printed material the size of typewritten characters, corrective lenses permitted. The ability to distinguish basic colors and shades is desirable.

Applicants must be able to hear the conversational voice; hearing aids permitted.

Selection Process

Applicants must first attain a minimum score of 70 points (exclusive of Veteran Preference) on the written examination. The applicants names are then placed, by score, on a hiring list of eligibles for a period of two years. Applicants who qualify on the examination and are in the area of consideration for employment will be scheduled for a job-simulated typing performance test.

Maintenance Positions

The Job

Maintenance positions require highly skilled and experienced individuals. All applicants must meet the Knowledge, Skills, and Abilities (KSAs) listed on the job description.

General Qualifications

All applicants will be required to pass a three-hour written examination, complete a Candidate Supplemental Application booklet, and successfully complete an interview.

A qualification for postal employment is to be drug-free. This is determined through the use of a urinalysis drug screen. Applicants who qualify on the examination and are in the area of consideration for employment will be scheduled for the drug test.

Maintenance positions require prolonged standing, walking, climbing, bending, reaching and stooping. Employees must lift and carry heavy objects on level surfaces, on ladders and/or stairways.

For positions requiring driving, applicants must have a valid state driver's license and a safe driving record. They must be able to obtain a Government Motor Vehicle Operator's Identification Card. Applicants may be required to qualify on industrial powered lifting equipment.

Applicants must have vision of 20/40 (Snellen) in one eye and the ability to read without strain, printed material the size of typewritten characters; glasses permitted. The ability to distinguish basic colors and shades is required.

Selection Process

Applicants must first attain a minimum score of 70 points (exclusive of Veteran Preference) on the written examination. They must then complete a Candidate Supplemental Application booklet and successfully complete an interview. The applicants names are then placed, by score, on a hiring list of eligibles for a period of two years.

Vehicle Operator/ Tractor-trailer Operator

The Job

Motor vehicle operators operate mail trucks to pick up and transport mail in bulk. Tractor-trailer operators operate heavy duty tractor-trailers either in over-the-road service, city shuttle service or trailer operations. May include irregular hours.

General Qualifications

Applicants for motor vehicle operator and tractor-trailer operator positions must have at least two years of driving experience, with at least one year of full-time experience (or equivalent) driving at least a seven-ton capacity truck or 24-passenger bus.

For tractor-trailer operators, at least six months of the truck driving experience must be with tractor-trailers. Only driving experience in the United States, its possessions, territories, or in any United States military installation worldwide will be considered.

At the time of appointment, applicants must have a valid commercial driver's license, with air brakes certification, for the type(s) of vehicle(s) used on the job from the state in which they live. After being hired, applicants must be able to obtain the appropriate certification to operate specific postal vehicles.

Applicants will be required to pass a two-hour and 30-minute written examination and must also complete forms detailing their employment history, driving record, and other qualifying factors, to demonstrate possession of the following abilities: 1) Ability to drive trucks safely. 2) Ability to drive under local conditions. 3) Ability to follow instructions and prepare trip and other reports.

A qualification for postal employment is to be drug-free. This is determined through the use of a urinalysis drug-screen. Applicants who qualify on the examination, and are in the area of consideration for employment, will be scheduled for the drug test.

Applicants must have a vision of at least 30/30 (Snellen) in one eye and 20/50 (Snellen) in the other eye and the ability to read, without strain, printed material the size of typewritten characters; corrective lenses permitted. Operators must also be able to hear the conversational voice, hearing aids permitted.

Selection

Applicants receive scores based on their examination results and a rating of their qualifications process listed on the U.S. Postal Service's Application for Employment Form, driving record, and supplemental experience statement. The application must contain pertinent information detailed enough to establish that the applicant meets all the requirements listed in this announcement. Applicants must provide full details about the types and weight of vehicles they have driven and the companies for which they worked as well as the length of their experience. A score of 70% (exclusive of Veteran Preference) places the applicant's name on a list of eligibles for two years. Names are placed on the hiring list in the order of their scores.

Processing, Distribution and Delivery Positions

All job vacancies are advertised separately and applicants apply online and to complete required exams. They can bypass the exam if they previously passed the test and have a valid Candidate ID Number. .

General Qualifications

A qualification for postal employment is to be drug-free. This is determined through the use of a urinalysis drug screen. Applicants who qualify on the examination and are in the area of consideration for employment will be scheduled for the drug test. All applicants will be required to take a written examination. The examination and completion of forms will require approximately two hours and fifteen minutes.

The 473 and 473 E exams cover all of the jobs listed below.

Job Titles

City Carrier	**Mail Handler**
City Carrier Assistant	**Mail Handler Assistant**
Clerk	**Mail Processor**
Dist. Clerk, Machine	**Mark up Clerk**
Flat Sorting Mach. Oper.	**Rural Carrier**

City Carrier and Clerk

The Jobs

Clerks work indoors sorting and distributing mail. They may be required to work with the public selling stamps, weighing parcels, and are responsible for all money and stamps. May include irregular hours.

City carriers collect and deliver mail in all kinds of weather, and walk and/or drive on their route.

Carrier and clerk positions require prolonged standing, walking, reaching, and the ability to lift 70 pounds. Carriers are also required to carry a mail bag weighing as much as 35 pounds.

For positions requiring driving, applicants must have a valid state driver's license and a safe driving record. They must be able to obtain a Government Motor Vehicle Operator's Identification Card.

Applicants must have a vision of 20/40 (Snellen) in one eye and the ability to read without strain, printed material the size of typewritten characters; glasses permitted. Clerks working with the public must be able to hear the conversational voice.

Rural Carriers

Rural carriers all begin their career as *Rural Carrier Associates (RCA)*. These positions are part-time, every Saturday and any time the regular carrier needs off work. In most offices, you will have to provide your own vehicle, in which you get paid an *Equipment Maintenance Allowance (EMA)* on top of the hourly wage. The average hourly wage is $17.78 per hour. RCA's do not receive health benefits, but they elect to pay for their own health benefits after one year of employment. RCA's are eligible for annual and sick leave. RCA's are eligible to "bid" on regular rural carrier positions in their office when an opening is available. Sometimes, it can take a long time to become a regular rural carrier. Once you become a regular rural carrier you will begin receiving health benefits, vacation and sick leave, and can contribute to the Thrift Savings 401k Plan. Rural carriers are not paid an hourly wage. The routes are evaluated; this is determined by a yearly mail count and your pay will be based on the evaluation of the route.

In some cities/towns, the rural carrier can drive as much as 100 miles per day. You will have to drive on the right hand side of the vehicle, so you would need an appropriate car. Some offices provide their rural carriers with a postal vehicle, but in most cases you would need your own. As a carrier, you are out in all types of weather; ice, snow, rain, etc. You have to be prepared for any type of weather. Rural carriers usually spend about 2-3 hours in the office casing their mail and 4-5 hours out on the street. Of course, every day is different; it all depends on the mail volume. Mondays and the day after a holiday are usually high volume mail days. If you like driving a vehicle and being outside, this is the job for you.

Distribution Clerk, Machine and Flat Sorting Machine Operators

The Jobs

Distribution clerk, machine and flat sorter machine operators are required to operate machinery which sorts and distributes letters or flats (magazines, over-sized envelopes etc.). Individuals must read address ZIP Codes and enter codes, using special purpose keyboards. Operators must also load and unload the machines, and the job may include irregular hours.

Distribution clerk, machine applicants must pass a vision test and possess the manual dexterity required to operate a two-handed keyboard. Vision requirements are: 20/40 (Snellen) in one eye and at least 20/100 (Snellen) in the other, and the ability to read without strain printed material the size of typewritten characters; corrective lenses permitted.

Flat sorting machine operator applicants must pass a vision test and possess the manual dexterity required to operate a one-handed keyboard. Vision requirements are: 20/30 (Snellen) in one eye and 20/50 (Snellen) in the other; corrective lenses permitted. The ability to distinguish basic colors and shades is desirable.

Mail Handler

The Job

Mail handlers work in an industrial environment. Duties include the loading, unloading and moving of sacks of mail and packages weighing up to 70 pounds. May include irregular hours.

Applicants must be physically able to perform efficiently the duties of the position, which require arduous exertion involving prolonged standing, walking, bending and reaching, and may involve the handling of heavy containers of mail and parcels weighing up to 70 pounds.

Prior to appointment, applicants will be required to pass a test of physical abilities. Applicants must demonstrate they can lift and carry up to 70 pounds.

Applicants must have a vision of 20/40 (Snellen) in one eye and the ability to read without strain, printed material the size of typewritten characters; corrective lenses permitted. The ability to distinguish basic colors and shades is desirable.

Mail Processor

The Job

Mail processors are required to stand for prolonged periods of time loading and unloading mail from a variety of automated mail processing equipment. May include irregular hours.

Applicants must have a vision of 20/40 (Snellen) in one eye and the ability to read without strain, printed material the size of typewritten characters; corrective lenses permitted. The ability to distinguish basic colors and shades is desirable.

Automated Mark up Clerk

The Job

Automated mark up clerks enter change of address data into a computer data base, process mail, and perform other clerical functions. May include irregular hours.

Applicants must have six (6) months or equivalent of clerical or office machine operating experience. Typing is required.

Applicants must have a vision of 20/40 (Snellen) in one eye and the ability to read without strain, printed material the size of typewritten characters; corrective lenses permitted. The ability to distinguish basic colors and shades is desirable.

Selection Process

A minimum score of 70 points (exclusive of Veteran Preference) on the examination places the applicant's name on a list of eligibles for two years. Names are placed on the hiring list according to the score on the examination. An applicant who qualifies on the examination and is in the area of consideration for employment for a certain job will be scheduled for job simulated performance exercises or an additional test. Distribution clerk, machine and flat sorter machine operators will be scheduled for dexterity exercises, mail handlers for a strength and stamina test, and automated mark up clerks for a typing test.

Veteran Preference

Veteran preference is granted for employment in the postal service. Those with a 10-percent or greater compensable service-connected disability are placed at the top of the hiring list in the order of their scores. Other eligibles are listed below this group in rank order.

Age Requirement

The general minimum age requirement for positions in the postal service is 18 at the time of appointment or a high school graduate.

Citizenship

All applicants must be citizens of or owe allegiance to the United States of America, or have been granted permanent resident alien status in the United States. Verification is required.

Selective Service

To be eligible for appointment to a position in the postal service, males born after December 31, 1959 must (subject to certain exceptions) be registered with the Selective Service System in accordance with Section 3 of the Military Selective Service Act. Males between 18 and 26 years of age (have not reached their 26th birthday) can register with the Selective Service System at any U.S. Post Office, or consular officer if outside the United States.

OCCUPATIONS LIST
(Partial List)

Craft and Wage per-hour positions:

Administrative Clerk

Auto Mechanic

Blacksmith-Welder

Building Equipment Mechanic

Carpenter

Carrier

Cleaner, Custodian

Data Conversion Operator

Distribution Clerk

Electronic Technician

Elevator Mechanic

Engineman

Fireman

Garageman-Driver

General Mechanic

Letter Box Mechanic

Letter Carrier

Machinist

Mail Handler

Maintenance Mechanic

Mark Up Clerk

Mason

Mechanic Helper

Motor Vehicle Operator

Painter

Plumber

Scale Mechanic

Security Guard

Professional

Accounting Technician

Architect/Engineer

Budget Assistant

Computer Programmer

Computer System Analyst

Electronic Engineer

Transportation Specialist

Industrial Engineer

Technical Writer

Stationary Engineer

Management

Administrative Manager

Labor Relations Representative

Manager-Bulk Mail

Manager-Distribution

Manager-Station/Branch

Postmaster-Branch

Safety Specialist

Supervisor-Accounting

Supervisor-Customer Service

Tour Superintendent

Chapter Four
Post Office Exams

Clerks, carriers, mail handlers, and other job applicants such as postal police, mechanics, electronic technicians, motor vehicle operators, machinists, data conversion operators, accountants, custodians, clerical, and trades must pass a test when applying for jobs. The rating is based on the test results and your qualifying work experience and education. Certain occupations, including many professionals, don't require a written exam. These groups are evaluated under the postal service's *Rated-Application Examinations* process. They are rated and hired through an extensive evaluation of their prior work experience, education, and how well they do on the interview.

Helpful Web Sites:
http://about.usps.com/careers/welcome.htm
www.postalwork.net

Visit www.postalwork.net to review a comprehensive eCareer guide that walks you through the postal service's application process. Then go to the postal service's official site at http://about.usps.com/careers/welcome.htm and select the "search jobs" link. This will take you to the employment section of the website where you can search for all job vacancies in your area. The postal service's job search feature can be confusing so review the guide mentioned above first.

Review Chapters Two and Three to understand the hiring process and what to expect. The postal service changed the application process significantly several years ago. You now apply for specific jobs rather than taking a standardized test that placed you on a local hiring register if you passed with a score of 70 or higher.

All tests, including the 473 and 473E exams, are scheduled when you apply online. You will be asked to register, complete an application, and take an initial online unproctored exam. Online registration takes time because you will basically complete an application and set up your online account. You must register before applying for jobs. Many occupations also require you to take a proctored exam at a testing facility in your area. The postal service will schedule you for the exam, and you have 14 days to complete your application, assessment, and exams from the date you apply.

473 MAJOR-ENTRY LEVEL EXAM

The **New 473 and 473E Exams** cover the following positions:

- ✔ **City Carrier**
- ✔ **Rural Carrier**
- ✔ **Mail Processing Clerk**
- ✔ **Mail Handler**
- ✔ **Sales, Services, and Distribution Associate**

The **473 Delivery, Distribution, and Retail Exam** in the past was often referred to as the 473 Battery Exam. The 473 and 473E exams are used in conjunction with one another. The 473E online assessment is taken when you first register and apply. It assesses personal characteristics and tendencies and the second part evaluates your experience. If you pass the 473E with a 70 or higher you will be scheduled to take the 473 exam at a local testing facility.

Sample exams and test questions are provided in this chapter for several of the most common job occupations except for the *473 / 473E Test*. The 473 exams and completion of forms is covered in Chapter Five with additional practice exams and study tips.

SKILLS TESTS

Ability and skills tests (*performance tests*) are designed to predict future success, both in job training and job performance. The postal service uses these tests to obtain an indication of your potential to learn and perform particular job responsibilities. Skills tests measure specifically what you know about and can perform in a particular job—they test your mastery of tasks. The postal service administers skills tests when it is interested in filling a position with an applicant who knows the basics of the job and can perform job tasks as soon as he or she starts. Some performance tests are: the road test for operators of postal vehicles, the typing test, and the test of strength and stamina for mail handlers.

ROAD TEST EXAMINATION

The initial road test is a systematic way to measure an individual's ability and skill to drive safely and properly under normal operating conditions. This test is an important part of the overall selection process for positions that require motor vehicle operation, and it is also a practical test to determine whether or not an individual is a skilled and safe driver. The test includes items that have been reported as actual causes of accidents and gives special emphasis to the driving deficiencies identified as major causes of postal motor vehicle accidents.

There is a comprehensive table of disqualifications that apply to the Road Test Examination such as:

1. Applicant doesn't have at least two years of documented driving experience.
2. Applicant has had driving permit suspended once (or more) in the last three years, OR twice (or more) in the last five years.
3. Applicant has had driving permit revoked once (or more) in the last five years.

Specific offenses such as reckless driving, hit-and-run offense, or use of drugs also are disqualifying factors. For the purpose of determining disqualifying violations, consider only offenses followed by a conviction.

STUDY HABITS

It's often helpful to study with a partner, someone to read the question and check your responses. It can be a fellow worker, a spouse, or just a good friend.

Try various study routines until you hit a combination that works. Try studying in 20 to 30-minute sessions, with 5-minute breaks in between, or stretch it out to hour intervals. A good study routine will improve your test scores.

TEST-TAKING STRATEGIES

The following strategies will help you improve your grades. Use these strategies on the practice tests in this book and when you take your actual postal service exam. If you practice these techniques now, when you take the postal exam they will become second nature.

✎ Eliminate the answers in multiple-choice questions that make no sense at all. You can often eliminate half of the answers through this method. If you have to guess an answer, you can improve your chances through the process of elimination.

✎ Be skeptical when an answer includes words like "always, never, all, none, generally," or "only." These words can be a trap. Only select an answer with these words in it if you are absolutely sure it is the right answer.

✎ If two answers have opposite meanings, take your time and look closer. Many times one of the two is correct.

✎ Make a mental note for answers that you are unsure about. After completing the remainder of the exam, go back and review these questions and make a final selection. Often, other questions that you've answered will jog your memory.

✎   One word can dramatically change the meaning of a sentence. Read each question word-for-word before answering.

✎   Don't let the test get the best of you. Build your confidence by answering the questions you know first. If the first question you read stumps you, skip it and go on to the next one. When you've completed most of the exam you can go back – if time permits – to the questions that you couldn't answer.

✎   Get plenty of rest the night before the exam.

SAMPLE EXAMS

Sample practice exams are provided to applicants when you apply for jobs. An expanded list of exams is available in Chapter Two on page 23. Postal service sample practice exams are presented in this chapter for the following occupational groups:

- **Exam 630/630E** (Postal Police)
- **Exam 710/720/725/730** - Clerical Battery Exam
- **Exam 714** (Data Conversion Operator)
- **Exam 741/744** (Accounting)
- **Exam 916** (Custodial)
- **Exam 943** Automotive Mechanic, Automotive Technician
- **Exam 955** Mechanical and Electrical Job Skills

The following guidance is excerpted from the postal service's assessment guides. They provide general information on preparing for exams, what to expect in the exam room, reasonable accommodations for qualified disabled applicants, and frequently asked questions that you will find helpful. All who are scheduled for an exam will receive an Assessment Information Package prior to the actual exam date. You should read it thoroughly and come prepared. You will also find several sample exam questions in the assessment package for the exam you are scheduled to take.

Additional sample exam questions follow each exam section that we developed to augment the questions found on the assessment packages. They provide more exposure to similar questions that you will find on the actual exams. Also review the exam test-taking strategies that we have in Chapter Five for the 473 exam. Use these same strategies for any of the postal service's exams.

PREPARING FOR EXAMS

Read all the information in the assessment package that you receive either by email or in regular mail prior to the test. Come to the test physically and mentally prepared. Get a good night's sleep.

On the day of the test, you will need to arrive at the testing center 15 minutes prior to the beginning of your appointment to allow time for the check-in process. Be sure to leave yourself enough time for traffic, finding the test center location, parking, and getting to the exam room.

The assessment is designed to be taken without interruptions or breaks. Please be sure to take care of any personal needs before appointment check-in.

Please bring these items with you to the testing center:

- Government-issued Photo ID
- Assessment site Login ID and Password

If you are more than 15 minutes late for your assessment appointment, you will not be permitted to test.

What to Expect in the Exam Room

Upon arrival, you will be required to present one piece of state or U.S. Federal Government issued photo ID as specified in your appointment confirmation email. If you are a current USPS employee, you may bring your USPS ID badge.

You will not be permitted to take the assessment if you do not present an ID meeting the stated requirements. Personal items are not allowed in the testing room. This includes all electronic devices such as cell phones, pagers, and PDAs. (With some exams such as the 741/744 accounting exam calculators will be provided.) Please do not bring any unnecessary personal items to your assessment appointment as storage may not be available. We also ask that you not have anyone accompany you into the test center as there is not adequate space for visitors.

You will need your Login ID and Password to access the testing website. Please bring this information with you to the testing center. When you are ready to begin, the examiner will provide you with ear plugs or headphones and assist you with logging in to start the test.

The test will be entirely administered and timed by the computer. All of the testing instructions will be provided by the computer. Before the test starts, you will see several practice and instruction screens. These screens explain how to use the computer to take the test and guide you through practice test items.

Other candidates might begin or end their exams at different times. In addition, the proctor is required to monitor the session frequently, so they will be entering and leaving the test room as needed. All reasonable efforts will be taken to keep distractions to a minimum.

At the end of your exam, you will have the opportunity to complete an online exit survey where you can provide feedback regarding your testing experience.

You must check out with the examiner before leaving the Testing Center.

The examiner will not have access to any information related to your assessment results or your next step. You will receive an e-mail message with instructions on how to access your test results.

REASONABLE ACCOMMODATIONS

The United States postal service is obligated under Section 501 of the Rehabilitation Act of 1973, as amended, found in 29 U.S.C. § 791 et seq. to provide accommodations to a qualified applicant with a disability that will enable the individual to have an equal opportunity to participate in the application process and to be considered for a job.

If you have a disability that will require a special testing arrangement, please make your request when scheduling your exam through the assessment website.

You will be asked to specify the nature of the disability and the accommodation needed.

Supporting documentation to verify the existence of a protected disability or the need for accommodation may be required.

The decision on granting reasonable accommodation will be made on a case-by-case basis.

FREQUENTLY ASKED QUESTIONS

How do I schedule my proctored testing appointment?

You can schedule yourself for the examination after receiving scheduling information via an email. To schedule a testing appointment, log into your assessment account and click on the Schedule Assessment link. If there are no seats available, you may request a seat by clicking on the Request a Seat link. Seat requests usually take a minimum of 3-5 business days to process. Please make sure to allow enough time for your request to be fulfilled. You will be notified via email once a seat is available at a test center near you. The system will not allow you to schedule an appointment within 24 hours of a testing session or request a seat within 48 hours of your expiration date.

What if I need to reschedule (or cancel) my appointment?

You may only cancel or reschedule your appointment up to 24 hours before your scheduled appointment. To cancel and reschedule your appointment, log onto the assessment website and click on the appointment date/time link.

If you are within 24 hours of your scheduled appointment, you are not permitted to reschedule your appointment.

If you fail to attend your scheduled appointment, you will not be allowed to reschedule and will receive an incomplete test result for that job vacancy.

How long will it take to get the assessment results?

A Notice of Result will be available on the Assessment site after you have been checked out from the testing center. You will receive an e-mail message with instructions on how to access your Notice of Result.

How is my score calculated?

Your final exam score is calculated based on your answers to both the non-proctored and the proctored portions of the exam.

What is a passing score?

You must attain a minimum score of 70 (excluding Veterans' Preference points) on the examination to be considered for any of the positions for which you applied. (This answer may change for specific exams, for example for the 714 Data Entry exam, applicants must demonstrate that they can type these items on a computer at the following rate(s) based on the requirements for the position. The lower level passing rate is five correct lines per minute...) Read the specific assessment package you receive, instructions may vary for different exams.

How long are the results of the test valid?

Your examination result is valid through the expiration date shown on your Notice of Result.

If you are an applicant, your results will be maintained in your eCareer Candidate Profile and will be automatically included with your application if you apply for other USPS vacancies requiring this exam.

If you are an employee, your test results may be valid for longer, based on your situation and in accordance with Postal policy.

Postal Police Exam 630E / 630

The 630E exam assesses the level of experience and personality of the applicant to reveal how they will effectively perform duties as a postal service employee. The individual achievement exam is comprised of 50 questions. The applicant has 40 minutes to complete the assessment.

The questions for 630E assesses the personality of the applicant and his/her suitability for the position applied for. There are no right or wrong answers. Your answers reveal whether or not your personality is well suited to the job.

Sample Questions 630E

Overtime and rotating shifts aren't a problem for you.

    A. Strongly Agree
    B. Agree
    C. Disagree
    D. Strongly Disagree

You like to work independently without interruptions.

    A. Strongly Agree
    B. Agree
    C. Disagree
    D. Strongly Disagree

When working within a group, I

    A. take charge and act as a team leader
    B. seldom take a group leader position
    C. never take a group leader position
    D. often step in to act as a group leader
    E. always step in to act as group leader

What type of activities do you like the most?

    A. activities that require planning and attention
    B. activities that require little planning
    C. activities that are physical and challenging
    D. activities that are done while sitting
    E. activities that don't require much thought
    F. outdoor activities
    G. not sure

Answer the questions for Exam 630 E honestly and pick the answer that represents your thoughts. If several answers seem to fit pick the one and **ONLY ONE** reply that best represents how you feel about the question or statement. There are no right or wrong answers on this part of the exam. Use your entire background, including work experience, volunteer work, school work, military service, and anything from your background that will help you relate to the question.

The applicant will be scheduled for the 630 exam if they pass with a grade 70 or better. The 630 exam is comprised of two parts:

- **Part A (Reading)** includes 35 questions with 50 minutes allotted to complete the section. This section tests the applicants reading and comprehension abilities.
- **Part B (Arithmetic Reasoning)** includes 25 questions with 40 minutes to complete the test. Part B tests your verbal and numeric problem solving aptitude.

Part A Reading

The 630 Assessment Guide provides the following information to help you with the reading exam. This is excerpted from the postal service's official guide.

In each of these questions you will be given a paragraph which contains all the information necessary to infer the correct answer. Use only the information provided in the paragraph. Do not speculate or make assumptions that go beyond this information. Also, assume that all information given in the paragraph is true, even if it conflicts with some fact known to you. Only one correct answer can be validly inferred from the information contained in the paragraph.

Pay special attention to negated verbs (for example, "are not") and negative prefixes (for example, "incomplete" or "disorganized"). Also pay special attention to quantifiers, such as "all," "none," and "some." For example, from a paragraph in which it is stated that "it is not true that all contracts are legal," one can validly infer that "some contracts are not legal," or that "some contracts are illegal," or that "some illegal things are contracts," but one cannot validly infer that "no contracts are legal," or that "some contracts are legal." Similarly, from a paragraph that states "all contracts are legal" and "all contracts are two-sided agreements," one can infer that "some two-sided agreements are legal," but one cannot validly infer that "all two-sided agreements are legal."

Bear in mind that in some tests, universal quantifiers such as "all" and "none" often give away incorrect response choices. That is not the case in this test. Some correct answers will refer to "all" or "none" of the members of a group.

Be sure to distinguish between essential information and nonessential, peripheral information. That is to say, in a real test question, the example above ("all contracts are legal" and "all contracts are two-sided agreements") would appear in a longer, full-fledged paragraph. It would be up to you to separate the essential information from its context and then to realize that a response choice that states "some two-sided agreements are legal" represents a valid inference and hence the correct answer.

PART A Sample Questions (Reading)

1) A crime scene requires tight security to protect evidence. If the crime scene isn't immediately secured and access restrictions implemented key evidence could be destroyed or contaminated. The case against anyone charged in the crime could be challenged by the defense with insufficient protections implemented.

The statement supports the conclusion that

A. It is impossible to try a case when a crime scene isn't properly secured
B. The defense will automatically file for a mistrial if the site isn't secured
C. Immediately securing a crime scene protects and prevents evidence contamination
D. Evidence isn't always conclusive at crime scenes even if the area is properly secured

The correct answer is C. This is stated in the second sentence.

Response A is incorrect considering that in the third sentence it only states that "the case against anyone charged in the crime could be challenged by the defense with insufficient protections implemented."

Response B is not correct because all it states is that the crime could be challenged by the defense, not that they will automatically file for a mistrial.

Response D is incorrect because nothing is mentioned about the quality of the evidence or whether or not it is conclusive. Conclusive by definition means putting an end to debate or question especially by reason of irrefutability.

2) A customer at a local store was shot during a robbery and the bullet was recovered during surgery along with several casings at the crime scene. A 9 mm handgun was found several blocks away in a garbage can. Fingerprints were found on the shell casings.

The statement supports the conclusion that

A. The handgun was used during the robbery
B. The bullet recovered during surgery was 9mm
C. The fingerprints on the gun matched the fingerprints on the shell casings
D. Ballistic checks could confirm if the recovered gun was used to shoot the customer if the bullet recovered was 9mm.

The correct answer is D.

Response A is incorrect because there was not a connection made between the gun and robbery in the paragraph. The 9mm gun was found several blocks away however we don't know if the bullet recovered from the patient was a 9mm.

Response B is incorrect. The caliber of the recovered bullet was never mentioned.

Response C was incorrect because no forensics were completed yet.

3) Reports were due on Friday, the day after tomorrow. An internal audit discovered missing equipment on April 2nd and a recent inventory dated March 15th showed all of the missing equipment was accounted for at that time. Three agents had entered the storage facility during the time period in question. The missing equipment included two bullet proof vests and two cases of ammunition.

The statement supports the conclusion that

A. The agency was waiting for the reports to determine who entered the facility and the cost of the missing equipment
B. One of the three agents who entered the storage facility had taken the equipment
C. The equipment probably was removed from the storage facility sometime between March 15th and April 2nd
D. The only missing equipment was two bullet proof vests and two cases of ammunition

The correct answer is C. The second sentence provides the basis for this conclusion.

Response A assumes the reports were related to the incident and that isn't stated in the paragraph, it only states that reports were due on Friday. It doesn't state that a missing equipment or audit response report was due on Friday.

Response B is incorrect because we don't know all of the facts. It could have been the storage facility custodian or a thief may have entered the facility by other routes.

Response D is incorrect because the last sentence states that the missing equipment included two bullet proof vests and two cases of ammunition. There could have been other missing equipment. If the sentence would have stated that the missing equipment was... and not included then D would have also been correct.

> Read each of the 35 questions carefully and don't assume anything. You have 50 minutes, about 1.4 minutes per question. Most of this is common sense however we often read things into a situation typically based on past experience. Focus on the question and only consider what is presented.

Part B Sample Questions (Arithmetic Reasoning)

The 630 Assessment Guide provides the following information to help you with the arithmetic reasoning exam. This is excerpted from the postal service's official guide.

In this part of the test you will have to solve problems formulated in both verbal and numeric form. You will have to analyze a paragraph in order to set up the problem, and then solve it. If the exact answer is not given as one of the response choices, you should select response E, "none of these." Sample questions 3 and 4 are examples of the arithmetic reasoning questions in this test. The use of calculators will NOT be permitted during the test; therefore, they should not be used to solve these sample questions.

1.   A local police department buys bullet proof vests at $700 each for 4 of their new officers. What is the total amount of money the department will spend for bullet proof vests for these officers?

A) $2,100
B) $2,800
C) $1,400
D) $3,500

The correct answer is B. It can be determined by multiplying 4 x $700 = $2,800

2.   An investigator had to use his own car on an official business trip. The agency reimbursed the investigator 40 cents per mile. He traveled round trip to Cleveland and the one way distance was 150 miles. What was the officer reimbursed for his milage?

A) $60
B) $240
C) $120
D) $90

The correct answer is C. Multiply 150 x 2 x .4 = $120

3.   An officer is allocated an annual clothing allowance of $500 and is permitted to submit reimbursement paperwork throughout the year for new purchases. He purchases a new uniform for $175, shoes for $78, and hat for $35. He later buys a second uniform at the same price as the first one he purchased. How much will the officer be reimbursed?

A) $500
B) $288
C) $528
D) $463

The correct answer is D. Multiply 175 x 2 + 78 + 35 = $463

4.   An officer issues a $100 citation for speeding 20 miles over the speed limit in a 25 mile per hour residential zone. Fines are doubled when cited for traveling 10 miles over the limit in residential zones. What fine would a speeder pay if he was traveling 8 miles over the speed limit in a residential zone?

A) $200
B) $100
C) $50
D) None of the above

The correct answer is C. Divide 100/2 = $50

Exam 710/720/725/730 - Clerical Battery Exam

This exam is comprised of 140 questions, divided into seven parts:

- Sequencing
- Comparisons
- Spelling
- Math Computation
- Following Instructions
- Grammar and Punctuation
- Vocabulary and Reading Comprehension

Applicants will receive instructions at the beginning of each test part with each part timed separately. Be aware that after you move on to the next part, you can't return to previous parts. You can't go back to change an answer or to complete an answer after you leave that section.

Test	Description	Number of Items	Time (Min)	Exam 710	Exam 720	Exam 725	Exam 730
Sequencing	Measures ability to put a name or code into the proper sequence.	20	3	✓			✓
Comparisons	Measures ability to compare names, addresses or codes.	30	4	✓			✓
Spelling	Measures spelling ability	20	4	✓	✓		
Math Computation	Measures ability to perform mathematical calculations and reason with numbers.	15	9	✓		✓	✓
Following Instructions	Measures ability to follow instructions	20	18	✓	✓	✓	
Grammar and Punctuation	Measures ability to identify proper grammar and punctuation	20	13	✓	✓		
Vocabulary & Reading Com-prehension	Measures ability to read and understand information.	15	18	✓	✓	✓	

Answer every question if possible. The postal service advises, "It will be to your advantage to select an answer to each question that you can." They further state, " There is no penalty for incorrect answers. If you are unsure of your answer, make the best choice you can. It is important to work quickly and accurately."

The total time allotted the assessment is one hour and 45 minutes. Exam 710/720/725/730 Clerical Battery provides scores for four individual exams.

SAMPLE QUESTIONS (Clerical Test)

The following sample questions show types of questions that you may find in the assessment for the various areas listed above. The questions on the test may be harder or easier than those shown here, but a sample of each kind of question on the test is given.

Read these directions, then look at the sample questions and try to answer them. Each question has several suggested answers lettered A, B, C, etc. Decide which one is the best answer to the question. Your test will be on the computer with the remaining time allotted for each section. All questions are multiple choice. The answers to the sample questions are provided on the following pages. For some questions an explanation of the correct answer is given.

Sequencing (20 items, 3 minutes to complete)

In these sequencing sample questions, there is a name or number at the top and four other names in alphabetical or number order below. Find the correct space for the name or number so that it will be in alphabetical or numeric order with the others, and mark the letter of that space as your answer.

1. Jones, Jane	2. Kessler, Neilson	3. Olsen, C. C.

○ A) →
     Goodyear, G.L.
 ○ B) →
     Haddon, Harry
 ○ C) →
     Jackson, Mary.
 ○ D) →
     Jenkins, Williams
 ○ E) →
	○ A) →
	     Kessel, Carl
	 ○ B) →
	     Kessinger, D. J.
	 ○ C) →
	     Keesler, Karl
	 ○ D) →
	     Kessner, Lewis
	 ○ E) →
		○ A) →
		     Olsen, C. A.
		 ○ B) →
		     Olsen, C. D.
		 ○ C) →
		     Olsen, Charles
		 ○ D) →
		     Olsen, Christopher
		 ○ E) →

4. DeMattia, Jessica	5. 06086011	6. FAC-1975

○ A) →
     DeLong, Jesse
 ○ B) →
     DeMatteo, Jesse
 ○ C) →
     Derbie, Jessie S
 ○ D) →
     DeShazo, L. M.
 ○ E) →
	○ A) →
	     06086002
	 ○ B) →
	     06086010
	 ○ C) →
	     06086017
	 ○ D) →
	     06086020
	 ○ E) →
		○ A) →
		     FAA-1640
		 ○ B) →
		     FAB-1945
		 ○ C) →
		     FAC-0043
		 ○ D) →
		     FAD-1224
		 ○ E) →

> Correct Sequencing Answers to Sample Questions
> 1. E, 2. D, 3. B, 4. C, 5 C, 6 D

Comparisons (30 items 4 minutes to complete)

In this part of the test there are three names, addresses, or codes that are similar and it is your task to compare names, addresses and/or codes. You have to decide which of the selections are exactly identical. Select the ones that are exactly alike, if any.

Compare the data cell information and circle the cells that are exactly identical. You can also circle "All Different" if none are exactly alike. The correct answers are provided below.

7.	David Janson	David Janson	David Jansen	All Different
8.	122497787	122499787	122497887	All Different
9.	DC 37JT-87	DC 37JT-87	DC- 37JT-87	All Different
10.	R. J. Mastersen Jr.	R. J. Masterson Jr.	R. J. Masterson Jr.	All Different
11.	714 Freemont Ave.	714 Freemount Ave.	714 Freemont St.	All Different
12.	999877654	999877754	999877654	All Different
13.	43rd N. Umberlan	43rd N. Umberland	43rd N. Umberlan	All Different
14.	MDJ-BG-8770	MDJ-BG-8790	MDJ-BG-8870	All Different

Comparisons: 7) The first and second should be circled, they are the same. 8) Circle all different. 9) The first and second should be circled, they are the same. 10) The second and third are the same and should be circled. 11) All are different. 12) The first and third should be circled, they are the same. 13) The first and third should be circled, they are the same. 14) Circle all different.

Spelling (20 items 4 minutes)

This part measures your spelling ability. Select the correctly spelled word for each of the following questions. You can also select "none of the above" if you can't find the correctly spelled word in the answers. Answers are provided below.

14.	17.	20.
○ A) athalete ○ B) athelete ○ C) athlete ○ D) none of the above	○ A) elimenate ○ B) eliminate ○ C) elimenat ○ D) none of the above	○ A) predesessor ○ B) predecesar ○ C) predecesser ○ D) none of the above
15.	18.	21.
○ A) occassion ○ B) occasion ○ C) ocassion ○ D) none of the above	○ A) determined ○ B) determend ○ C) determind ○ D) none of the above	○ A) eliminate ○ B) elimenate ○ C) eleminate ○ D) none of the above
16.	19.	22.
○ A) quallifications ○ B) qualefications ○ C) qualifications ○ D) none of the above	○ A) informitive ○ B) informative ○ C) informativi ○ D) none of the above	○ A) presantation ○ B) presentacion ○ C) presentation ○ D) none of the above

Spelling Answers to Sample Questions
14 C, 15 B, 16 C, 17 B, 18 A, 19 B, 20 D, 21 A, 22 C

Math Computation (15 questions 9 minutes)

The math section evaluates your ability to successfully reason with numbers and perform math calculations. Complete the math questions presented and if none of the selections are correct, select "none of the above." Answers follow the examples.

23. 19 + 45 =
 	
    ○ A) 65
    ○ B) 74
    ○ C) 64
    ○ D) 59
    ○ E) none of the above
	26. 200 / 5 =
	
	    ○ A) 45
	    ○ B) 35
	    ○ C) 40
	    ○ D) 50
	    ○ E) none of the above

24. 109 + 27 =
 	
    ○ A) 132
    ○ B) 136
    ○ C) 145
    ○ D) 135
    ○ E) none of the above
	27. 12 x 9 =
	
	    ○ A) 118
	    ○ B) 128
	    ○ C) 98
	    ○ D) 108
	    ○ E) none of the above

25. 64 - 19 =
 	
    ○ A) 40
    ○ B) 37
    ○ C) 32
    ○ D) 34
    ○ E) none of the above
	28. 155 / 10 =
	
	    ○ A) 15.5
	    ○ B) 16
	    ○ C) 14.5
	    ○ D) 14
	    ○ E) none of the above

Math Sample Question Answers
23 C, 24 B, 25 E, 26 C, 27 D, 28 A

Following Instructions (20 questions 18 minutes)

The ability to follow instructions is measured in this section and you must read the question carefully. When you follow the instructions it will direct you to properly identifying a letter-number combination such as D4, F5, G10, or H3.

The next step is to use the "Look-Up Table" to identify the result of the intersection of the two variables you are looking up. For example, to look up the result for "H1" first find the "H" and then the number "1". Look down the "H" column until you come to "1" in the left column. The result is "E". Answers are listed below the practice questions.

LOOK - UP-TABLE

	D	E	F	G	H
1	A	B	C	D	E
2	B	C	D	E	A
3	C	D	E	A	B
4	D	E	A	B	C
5	E	A	B	C	D
6	A	B	C	D	E
7	B	C	D	E	A
8	C	D	E	A	B
9	D	E	A	B	C
10	E	A	B	C	D

Sample Questions	Response Options
29. Use the look-up table using the second letter-number combination from the right D5 F3 G10 H6 E9 G4	○ A ○ B ○ C ○ D ○ E
30. Count each of the F letters in the letters listed below. Now use the count and the letter "G" to obtain your answer. D F G F H E F G	○ A ○ B ○ C ○ D ○ E
31. Look at the letter-number combination below. Locate the second letter-number combination from the left. D2 G4 F6 H5 E10 G3	○ A ○ B ○ C ○ D ○ E
32. Look at the letters listed below. Count each "G" that you find. Use the first letter of the line and your count of the letter "G." F D G H E H F D	○ A ○ B ○ C ○ D ○ E

Following Instructions Sample Question Answers
29 E, 30 A, 31 B, 32 C

Grammar and Punctuation (20 questions 13 minutes)

This part determines your ability to use appropriate grammar and punctuation. Select the sentence that is most appropriate considering proper grammar, punctuation, and usage that would be suitable to use in a formal letter or report. Answers are listed below.

33.

○ A) If properly addressed, the letter will reach my mother and I.
○ B) The letter had been addressed to myself and my mother.
○ C) I believe the letter was addressed to either my mother or I.
○ D) My mother's name, as well as mine, was on the letter.

The answer to question 33 is D). The answer is not A because the word me (reach . . . me) should have been used, not the word I. The answer is not B. The expression, to myself, is sometimes used in spoken English, but it is not acceptable in a formal letter or report. The answer is not C, because the word I has been used incorrectly, just as it was in A.

34.

○ A) Most all these statements have been supported by persons who are reliable and can be depended upon.
○ B) The persons which have guaranteed these statements are reliable.
○ C) Reliable persons guarantee the facts with regards to the truth of these statements.
○ D) These statements can be depended on, for their truth has been guaranteed by reliable persons.

35.

○ A) Brown & Company employees have recently received increases in salary.
○ B) Brown & Company recently increased the salaries of all its employees.
○ C) Recently Brown & Company has increased their employees' salaries.
○ D) Brown & Company have recently increased the salaries of all its employees.

> **Grammar & Punctuation Sample Question Answers**
> **33 D, 34 D, 35 B**

Vocabulary and Reading Comprehension

Your ability to read and comprehend information is measured. For the vocabulary questions, identify the answer that the underlined word most nearly means to you. For reading comprehension questions, read each paragraph and answer the question. Your answer should be based only on what you read in the passage. You answers are listed below.

36. The team was **puzzled** by the news from headquarters. **Puzzled** most nearly means	○ A) surprised ○ B) confused ○ C) happy ○ D) elated

37. Management must be **proactive** when implementing new regulations. **Proactive** most nearly means	○ A) patient ○ B) wait and see ○ C) inflexible ○ D) take the initiative
38. Government regulations often require **comprehensive** review prior to implementation. **Comprehensive** most nearly means	○ A) passive ○ B) quick ○ C) thorough ○ D) inadequate

39. Tracking a supervisors schedule can be difficult if not properly coordinated with all parties. A calendar, spreadsheet or other planning tool must be used to annotate all commitments. One person, normally the secretary, is responsible for this task. The supervisor and staff must keep the secretary apprised of all scheduled events and activities and the secretary must advise the supervisor of any potential conflicts.

Select the statement that best supports this paragraph about a supervisors schedule

    ○ A) only the secretary can be responsible for a supervisor's schedule
    ○ B) the staff must advise the supervisor of all conflicts
    ○ C) must be kept on a wall or desk calendar
    ○ D) is often kept by a secretary

40. Postal clerks have the financial responsibility for selling postage and other supplies offered for sale by the post office. They must also have thorough knowledge of postal mailing regulations such as the acceptability of packages and letters presented to them by customers. Their information and guidance to customers must be accurate.

The paragraph best supports the statement that Postal Clerks

    ○ A) have been extensively trained in other postal jobs
    ○ B) understand postal regulations for mailing letters and packages
    ○ C) Assists with sorting mail for future delivery
    ○ D) must inspect package contents prior to accepting payment

41. It is difficult to distinguish between bookkeeping and accounting. In attempts to do so, bookkeeping is called the art, and accounting the science, of recording business transactions. Bookkeeping gives the history of the business in a systematic manner; and accounting classifies, analyzes, and interprets the facts thus recorded.

The paragraph best supports the statement that

    ○ A) accounting is less systematic than bookkeeping
    ○ B) accounting and bookkeeping are closely related
    ○ C) bookkeeping and accounting cannot be distinguished from one another
    ○ D) bookkeeping has been superseded by accounting.

Vocabulary and Reading Comprehension Sample Question Answers
36 B, 37 D, 38 C, 39 D, 40 B, 41B

Exam 714 - Computer Based Test

This exam is a 30 minute computer administered and scored exam and the time includes all administrative processes. The postal service advises applicants that, "To qualify for the 714 Examination, applicants must demonstrate that they can type these items on the computer at the following rate(s) based on the requirements of the position. The lower level passing rate is five correct lines per minute. The higher level passing rate is seven correct lines per minute. Credit is given only for correctly typed lines."

The exam includes a list of alphanumeric data entry items similar to what is presented in the sample items below. Applicants are required to demonstrate the ability to type. Applicants must type each line as presented on the exercise, begin with the first column. Use either lower-case or capital letters when typing this exercise. At the end of each line, click on "Enter" or "Return" and begin typing the next line. If you make it to the end of the sample first column sample list, continue with the entries from the second column. After finishing both columns, start again with the first column and continue typing until your time is up, five minutes.

Attempt to type the entire sample test once in five minutes. Then count the number of lines that you correctly typed and divide this number by five. This will determine your per minute score. If you correctly type only the column 1 items that is approximately equal to typing 5 correct lines per minute. If you correctly type both columns that approximately equals the typing of 7 correct lines a minute.

You will have five minutes in which to type the test material during the exam. To pass the exam you must type accurately and rapidly.

Exam Results: (Take the test on the next page and enter your results here:

1) _____
2) _____
3) _____

SAMPLE TEST COPY

HAWTHORNE 8Ø162
BRIDGEPORT 35698
06124 4886
BRENTWOOD 76834
49215 222Ø
17523 3453
FIRST ST. 67ØØ-2877
ROSEDALE AVE. 2ØØ-3998
FULLER AVE. 733-889
FRANKLIN AVE. 542Ø-494Ø
212 EAST BLP .LK FL
5489 NINTH AVE
1349 RYE ST
BARDELL, H.K. 11/29/97
GRANGER, K.L. Ø8/21/78
CORN SR. , G.H. 12/22/87
J ON RIBLEY RD.
RETRACE TO COTTAGE
R ON BEECH, R ON BANE
MARRIOTT HOTEL 5687
STATEFARM   INS 13457
AMERICAN   EXPRESS 3278
54.21 DRILL AIR
67.76 SPRING   ARM

16.43 SOLDER TIP
4012 ARMSTRONG DRIVE
1225 ELM BLVD
346 S STATE ST
BROOKHAVEN ST. 6658-879Ø
75986 5583
87345 9146
HAMILTON AVE.   247-29
12498 6875
NEW YORK PL. 7885-1499
COMMERCIAL   ST. 6589-9762

Exam 741/744 - Accounting

This exam tests the applicant's accounting knowledge and skills. If you complete the entire test you will receive a score for two accounting jobs, the 741 junior-level and 744 senior-level positions. Table 4-1 below lists the ten areas of the test and delineates which parts are relevant for each position and the number of items and time allotted for each section.

Read all test instructions carefully the day of the test. Each test is timed. A countdown clock, where appropriate, will show the time remaining on your computer screen. The test will advance automatically to the next section when the previous section time has expired. You can review your answers if the time hasn't expired and make changes. However, you can't return to a part after the time for that part has expired.

The test is comprised of multiple-choice questions. During the test, for most sections, you are required to select your response by clicking on the small circle next to your answer. Some sections require you to highlight answers. Practice items for those sections are provided to familiarize you with the selection process.

You will have approximately 4 hours to complete the assessment, however, you may finish early. The assessment is taken without breaks, take care of any personal needs prior to checking in for the test.

Since this is a four hour test, come prepared and get a good nights sleep the night before. Come early and don't be late. If you are 15 minutes late you won't be allowed to take the exam. Use the sample exam questions provided here and on the official exam assessment package you will receive from the postal service to evaluate your weak areas. If you find any of the 10 tested area questions difficult go back to your course books and study those areas in depth to better prepare for the official exam. The more preparation you have the better.

If you are interested in working for the Post Office or federal civil service in accounting apply early, shortly after you graduate when basic accounting principles are fresh in your mind. Possibly apply for an **internship** while still in school to become familiar with postal and government operations. Interns often are offered full time employment after they graduate. To learn more about available internship programs visit www.federaljobs.net/student.htm. This site provides abundant information for all federal jobs.

Test	Description	Junior 741	Senior 744	Items	Time (Min)
A. Following Instructions	Ability to follow instructions.	✔		17	15
B. Sequencing	Ability to put a name or code in the proper sequence	✔		17	15
C. Detecting Patterns of Trends	Ability to detect patterns or trends	✔	✔	12	15
D. Discovering Errors and Making Comparisons	Ability to compare information and discover errors.	✔	✔	17	15
E. Mathematics and Numerical Reasoning	Ability to perform mathematical calculations and reason with numbers.	✔	✔	17	15
F. Maintaining Records and Using Written Reference Materials	Ability to maintain records and use written reference materials.	✔	✔	17	20
G. Reading Comprehension and Summarizing Information	Ability to read and summarize information.	✔	✔	17	35
H. Accounting and Auditing	Knowledge of accounting and auditing, and ability to apply that knowledge.		✔	22	25
I. Accounts Verification	Ability to verify accounts quickly and accurately.		✔	17	20
J. Bank Account Reconciliation	Ability to reconcile a bank account and checkbook.		✔	12	15

Sample Test Questions

The following test question examples reflect the type of questions that are used on Exam 741/744. Review the questions carefully to determine which areas you need to study more. There are multiple answers for each question, determine which answer is the best. A calculator will be provided by the test center for this exam. Correct answers are provided for the following sample questions.

Part A: Following Instructions

1. Find the sum of the odd numbers below. Subtract three from that number. What is the result?

1 4 6 3 2 8 7 5

- ○ A) 12
- ○ B) 13
- ○ C) 14
- ○ D) 15

2. Add all of the numbers below, divide by 2 and multiply the result by 15. What is the answer?

10 22 44 67 23

- ○ A) 166
- ○ B) 83
- ○ C) 12,245
- ○ D) 1,245

3. Mark the answer that is more than 9,025 but less than 10,793. What is the answer?

- ○ A) 10,793
- ○ B) 9,025
- ○ C) 9,002
- ○ D) 9,026

4. Look at the letters listed below. Identify the middle letter. What is the third letter below that letter in the alphabet? What is the answer?

F J   K L M

- ○ A) K
- ○ B) M
- ○ C) C
- ○ D) H

> Correct Following Instructions Sample Questions
> 1. B, 2. D, 3. D, 4. D

Part B: Sequencing

In these sequencing sample questions, there is a name or number at the top, and four other names in alphabetical or number order below. Find the correct space for the name or number so that it will be in alphabetical or numeric order with the others, and mark the letter of that space as your answer.

5. Jones, Jane	6. B567898	7. Olsen, C. C.
○ A) →	○ A) →	○ A) →
Goodyear, G.L.	A798456	Olsen, C. A.
○ B) →	○ B) →	○ B) →
Haddon, Harry	A980010	Olsen, C. D.
○ C) →	○ C) →	○ C) →
Jackson, Mary.	C176789	Olsen, Charles
○ D) →	○ D) →	○ D) →
Jenkins, Williams	D897654	Olsen, Christopher
○ E) →	○ E) →	○ E) →
8. DeMattia, Jessica	9. 06086011	10. FAC-1975
○ A) →	○ A) →	○ A) →
DeLong, Jesse	06086002	FAA-1640
○ B) →	○ B) →	○ B) →
DeMatteo, Jesse	06086010	FAB-1945
○ C) →	○ C) →	○ C) →
Derbie, Jessie S	06086017	FAC-0043
○ D) →	○ D) →	○ D) →
DeShazo, L. M.	06086020	FAD-1224
○ E) →	○ E) →	○ E) →

> ### Correct Sequencing Answers to Sample Questions
> 5. E, 6. C, 7. B, 8. C, 9 C, 10 D

Part C: Detecting Patterns or Trends

11. Determine the pattern or trend. Select the answer that completes the series.
10, 20, 30, ___ , 50

○ A) 60
○ B) 100
○ C) 40
○ D) none of the above

12. Determine the trend. Sales for associated postal products (holiday cards, shipping supplies, etc.) are shown below. What is the long term trend of these sales over the past 2 years?
Select the answer that completes the series.

Associated Sales Chart

03/31/2013 - $19,453,769
06/30/2013 - $17,987,876
09/30/2013 - $16,356,790
12/31/2013 - $16,323,000
2012 Sales - $67,550,989

○ A) Decreasing
○ B) Increasing
○ C) The same
○ D) Up and down

13. Using the same data from question 12 determine the current year associated sales trend. .
Select the answer that completes the series.

○ A) Decreasing
○ B) Increasing
○ C) The same
○ D) Up and down

Correct Detecting Patterns & Trends Sample Questions
11. C, 12. B, 13. A

Part D: Discovering Errors and Making Comparisons

Compare each set or line of information on the following questions in the **List To Be Verified** to the provided **Correct List**. If you find errors, circle them. If no errors are found, circle **"No Errors."** Online test answers will be either "circled" or highlighted if you click on the cell.

CORRECT LIST			
Steve Jackobs 84-2487 32895-4666 Jackson, MS	Bob Roberts 91-0321 45705-3682 Bangor, ME	Patty Duncon 19-6998 75203-4992 Reno, NV	Robert Katlan 96-6761 19048-3284 Bellevue, WA
Carol Smith 85-8678 37915-2212 Springfield, MO	Terry Brown 34-4205 22261-8854 Ocala, FL	Mark Delucci 59-1506 78993-0023 Erie, PA	Arthur Treacher 27-6176 58742-1192 Lake Dallas, TX
Jackie Sienetta 12-4005 87001-0156 Berkley, CA	Travis Reston 03-4696 92150-4462 North Platte, NE	Arnold Shaw 21-7842 03453-5478 Brookline, OH	Paul Setton 563-8982 60315-7422 Des Moines, IL

LIST TO BE VERIFIED					
	Name	Finance Number	Zip+4	Location	
14.	Arthur Treacher	27-6166	58742-1192	Dallas, TX	No Errors
15.	Jackie Sietta	12-4005	87001-0155	Berkley, CA	No Errors
16.	Travis Reston	03-4696	92150-4462	South Platte, NE	No Errors
17.	Carole Smith	85-8678	37915-2212	Brooklyn, OH	No Errors
18.	Arnold Shawn	21-7842	03453-5478	Brooklyn, NY	No Errors

The correct answers are:

14. Finance Number and Location circled
15. Name and ZIP+4 circled
16. Location circled
17. Name and Location circled
18. Name and Location circled

Part E: Mathematics and Numeric Reasoning

19. 57 x .052

○ A) 2.0
○ B) 1.946
○ C) 2.964
○ D) 109.61

20. 2% of $198,942

○ A) $1,978.48
○ B) $3,481.48
○ C) $3,978.84
○ D) $39,788.4

21. 5690 / 250

○ A) 437.98
○ B) 22.75
○ C) 19.786
○ D) 25.4

Correct Mathematics and Numeric Reasoning Sample Questions
19. C, 20. C, 21. B

Part F: Maintaining Records and Using Written Reference Material

The **Payment Table entries** are based on information provided in the two **Reference Tables**. Use this information from these tables to answer the following questions.

Reference Table One		
Invoice #	Customer #	Customer
6532	3DV45	Dennis P.
5946	5DS42	Jane K.
5990	4FD35	Sam S.
8775	4JY88	Paula C.

Reference Table Two		
Customer ID	Amount Due	Date
3DV45	$75.60	May 21
5DS42	$1,957.85	July 16
4FD35	$124.50	August 30
4JY88	$26,654	June 25

Payment Table		
Invoice	Date	Item #
8775	(A)	1468-3
(B)	July 16	2568-9
5990	(C)	4639-6
(D)	May 21	7756-1

22. What belongs in the pay table space A?

- O A) May 21
- O B) June 25
- O C) August 30
- O D) June 20

23. What belongs in the pay table space B?

- O A) 9775
- O B) 5946
- O C) 5875
- O D) none of the above

24. What belongs in the pay table space C?

- O A) May 21
- O B) June 25
- O C) August 30
- O D) June 20

25. What belongs in the pay table space D?

- O A) 6532
- O B) 5990
- O C) 5946
- O D) 9775

Part G: Reading Comprehension

Answer the question after reading the following carefully. Your answer should only be based on what you read in the paragraph.

26. Tracking a supervisors schedule can be difficult if not properly coordinated with all parties. A calendar, spreadsheet or other planning tool must be used to annotate all commitments. One person, normally the secretary, is responsible for this task. The supervisor and staff must keep the secretary apprised of all scheduled events and activities and the secretary must advise the supervisor of any potential conflicts.

Select the statement that best supports this paragraph about a supervisors schedule

   ○ A) only the secretary can be responsible for a supervisor's schedule
   ○ B) the staff must advise the supervisor of all conflicts
   ○ C) must be kept on a wall or desk calendar
   ○ D) is often kept by a secretary

27. It is difficult to distinguish between bookkeeping and accounting. In attempts to do so, bookkeeping is called the art, and accounting the science, of recording business transactions. Bookkeeping gives the history of the business in a systematic manner; and accounting classifies, analyzes, and interprets the facts thus recorded.

The paragraph best supports the statement that

   ○ A) accounting is less systematic than bookkeeping
   ○ B) accounting and bookkeeping are closely related
   ○ C) bookkeeping and accounting cannot be distinguished from one another
   ○ D) bookkeeping has been superseded by accounting.

Part H: Accounting and Auditing

28. At the end of the fiscal year a company has a $550 debit balance in its office supplies account. A physical inventory of available supplies shows $215 of supplies remaining. The annual income statement will show an office supplies expense of?

○ A) $765
○ B) $335
○ C) $550
○ D) $215

The answer is "B."

Part I: Accounts Verification

The test will present various account verification scenarios for you to evaluate and identify any incorrect entries on the test tables supplied or to provide missing entries. They present typical accounting spreadsheets and data for you to determine the correct answer.

The table listed below shows accounts that have payments that are due today. Using the information available in Columns 1, 2, and 3, determine if the data entries in Columns A and B is correct.

The total of the bill for this account is listed in column one. The terms for the payment are listed in column two. The third column provides the number of the payments that have already been made to date. The amount of the payment due today is listed in column A. Column B shows the balance due after receipt of this payment.

The first three columns are error free. There may be errors in columns A and B. Check the entries. The postal service advises those taking the test that, "If your answer in Column A is different from the one shown, use your figure to calculate Column B. Note that Column B may be correct even if Column A is incorrect. In your calculations, carry numbers to two decimal places and do not round up."

They go on to explain that, "If Column A or B is incorrect, circle the incorrect cell. If both Columns A and B are incorrect, circle both cells. If there are no errors, circle the "No Errors" cell. If there is not enough information to answer the question, circle the Not Enough Information cell. For the online test administration, your answers will be circled or highlighted when you click on the cell with your mouse."

29.

Columns						
1	2	3	A	B		
Total Due	Terms	Payments Made to Date	Payments Due Today	Balance Due		
$600	0-6	3	$100	$200	No Errors	Not Enough Information

The correct answer is "No Errors."

Part J: Bank Account Reconciliation

Reconciliations for the month of June will be performed for this exercise. Account reconciliation is a monthly task and necessary to ensure that bank statement and checking account balances agree. Each of the test questions in the exam explains account reconciliations and transactions that affect checkbook or bank balances.

Analyze the bank statement transactions in the checkbook to determine the appropriate action needed, if any, for reconciliation.

After determining what action or actions to take, select whether that action:

A. Reduces bank balance
B. Increases bank balance
C. Reduces checkbook balance
D. Increases checkbook balance

30. After a review of transactions, four checks that were received for the amount of $75.80 were not deposited at the bank.

O A) REDUCES the bank balance.
O B) INCREASES the bank balance.
O C) REDUCES the checkbook balance.
O D) INCREASES the checkbook balance.

The correct answer is "B." After the checks are deposited the bank account balance would increase.

31. After entering credit card charges into the accounting system, one entry was entered twice in error and this was discovered during the monthly account reconciliations.

O A) REDUCES the bank balance.
O B) INCREASES the bank balance.
O C) REDUCES the checkbook balance.
O D) INCREASES the checkbook balance.

The correct answer is D. After the second incorrect credit card entry was deleted the checking account balance increased by that amount.

Exam 916 - Custodial Maintenance Exam

The custodial exam is made up of 60 multiple choice questions. There are four parts:

1. Vocabulary and reading
2. Safety basics
3. General cleaning
4. Following instructions

All four parts are timed separately and you will be given instructions at the start of each part. The postal service recommends that applicant's, "answer every question. It will be to your advantage to select an answer to each question that you can. If you are unsure of your answer, make the best choice you can. It is important to work quickly and accurately."

You can expect to spend an hour and a half at your scheduled assessment appointment. The areas of Exam 915 are listed on following table.

Test Part	Number of Questions	Time Allowed (Minutes)	Description
Vocabulary & Reading	15	15	Measures ability to read and understand written materials as used in reading product label instructions and warnings, material safety data sheets (MSDS), equipment operating instructions, and cleaning route sheets.
Basic Safety	15	7	Measures knowledge of basic safety principles and practices such as proper lifting techniques, use of personal protective equipment, and awareness of electrical, chemical, and other health hazards in the area of cleaning and building maintenance.
General Cleaning	15	7	Measures knowledge of general cleaning and disinfecting materials, techniques, equipment, and tools commonly used by custodians.
Following Instructions	15	15	Measures ability to understand and carry out instructions similar to those received on the job.

Sample Vocabulary & Reading (15 questions 15 minutes)

The following questions will test your ability to read and understand written information. This information is needed to read label instructions and warnings for cleaning route sheets, various products used such as material safety data sheets (MSDS), and operating instructions for equipment. Carefully read each question and then select the best answer. Answers to the sample questions are listed below each quiz.

1. Avoid breathing caustic product fumes. Caustic most nearly means:
O A) Harmful
O B) Cleaning
O C) Safety
O D) Helpful
O E) Degenerative

2. The contents of a box required special handling and was marked fragile. Fragile most nearly means:

O A) Valuable
O B) Hazardous
O C) Delicate
O D) Tough
O E) Pressurized

3. Safety shoes are mandatory at work especially when carrying heavy loads or working with machinery. Mandatory most nearly means:

O A) Helpful
O B) Optional
O C) Safety
O D) Required
O E) Useful

4. "Walking on elevated surfaces can be hazardous, there are many areas in the work environment where you will have to either work on ladders or on platforms. They will be needed to clean windows, change light bulbs, and to make repairs. Even short step ladders can be dangerous. Whenever working on elevated surfaces be cautious and use all required safety equipment to avoid injury to yourself or to fellow workers."

The quotation best supports the statement that:

○ A) All custodians work on ladders and elevated platforms
○ B) It is unsafe to climb on ladders and elevated surfaces
○ C) Be cautious working on elevated surfaces and use safety equipment
○ D) Short step ladders are dangerous
○ E) Use a ladder when changing light bulbs

```
Vocabulary & Reading Question Answers
           1 A, 2 C, 3D, 4 C
```

Basic Safety (15 questions 7 minutes)

Basic safety principles and practices are presented here to test your knowledge of this subject. Safety areas include use of (PPE) personal protective equipment, proper lifting techniques, and awareness of chemical, electrical and other health hazards encountered while performing building maintenance and cleaning. Select the best answer after reading each question.

Answers are provided below.

5) If a safety climbing belt appears to be damaged what should you do?

○ A) Use it anyway
○ B) Wrap the defective area with duct tape and use it
○ C) Try it on a low rung of the ladder, if it holds use it
○ D) Don't climb & notify your supervisor immediately
○ E) Climb and then notify your supervisor

6. What should be done if you are required to work in a designated high noise area?

○ A) Listen to music using your Ipod
○ B) Focus on the task at hand and ignore the noise
○ C) Wear hearing protection
○ D) Drink plenty of water
○ E) Wear protective eye goggles

7. What does a Material Safety Data Sheet (MSDS) provide to cleaning product users?

○ A) Equipment safety hazards
○ B) Confined space safety precautions
○ C) Climbing safety instructions
○ D) A sheet that needs to be filed in a binder
○ E) Cleaning product health hazards

8. If an electrical cord is frayed or damaged what should be done?

○ A) Use it but be cautious
○ B) Wrap it with electrical tape
○ C) Don't use it near water
○ D) Have the cord replaced at once
○ E) Use duct tape and fasten the damaged area to the floor

9. Safe manual lifting is performed?

○ A) Using your back to handle the full load
○ B) Bending over keeping the knees straight
○ C) Lift while keeping the load close to your body
○ D) Lift alone, no matter how heavy the load
○ E) Twisting from the waist while carrying the weight

10. Standing directly under ladders and other elevated platforms is unsafe because?

○ A) Falling parts, tools, or debris
○ B) Superstition dictates otherwise
○ C) Looking up causes eye irritation
○ D) Ladders are unstable unless supported
○ E) Inadequate ventilation

> Basic Safety Question Answers
> 5 D, 6 C, 7E, 8 D, 9 C, 10 A

General Cleaning (15 questions 7 minutes)

The following questions will test your knowledge of general cleaning and disinfecting substances, equipment, techniques, and tools that custodians often use. Read the question and then select the best answer. Answers are listed after the questions.

11. Which of these items would you use to clean a concrete floor?

O A) Mop
O B) Scraper
O C) Wire Brush
O D) Detergent
O E) All of the above

12. Which of the following is used to clean windows?

O A) Felt duster
O B) Stiff brush
O C) Vacuum
O D) Hand buffer
O E) Cloth and a window cleaner

13. Where would you use a disinfectant?

O A) On windows
O B) On bathroom floors and surfaces
O C) In a deflated tire
O D) To oil a sump pump
O E) To fertilize the lawn

14. Which of the following is used to remove dust from drapes & ledges?

O A) Stiff brush
O B) Power vacuum cleaner
O C) Push broom
O D) Sponge
O E) Dust pan

15. Bleach would be considered a?

O A) Condiment
O B) Disinfectant
O C) Oil
O D) Food
O E) A storage unit

16. What would most commonly be used to change a lightbulb 15 feet off the floor?

○ A) An 6 foot ladder
○ B) A fork lift
○ C) Scaffolding
○ D) The fire department
○ E) A 15 foot extension pole with bulb extractor

17. How would you safely work in an area where high speed machines with moving parts are normally running.

○ A) Clean around the equipment with power on
○ B) Don't clean that area
○ C) Shut the equipment down and clean the area
○ D) Coordinate a shut down and lock out & tag the power source before cleaning
○ E) Carefully work around the equipment as best you can

18. What must you do when working in an area with high dust levels?

○ A) Hold your breath while cleaning the area
○ B) Put a handkerchief over your nose and mouth
○ C) Wait until the dust settles
○ D) Wear an approved protective mask provided by your employer
○ E) Wear gloves to keep dust off your hands

General Cleaning Question Answers
11 E, 12 E, 13 B, 14 B, 15 B, 16 E, 17 D, 18 D

Following Instructions (15 questions 15 minutes)

The ability to follow instructions is measured in this section and you must read the question carefully. When you follow the instructions it will direct you to properly identifying a letter-number combination such as D4, F5, G10, or H3.

The next step is to use the "Look-Up Table" to identify the result of the intersection of the two variables you are looking up. For example, to look up the result for "H1" first find the "H" and then the number "1". Look down the "H" column until you come to "1" in the left column. The result is "E". Answers are listed below the practice questions.

LOOK - UP-TABLE

	D	E	F	G	H
1	A	B	C	D	E
2	B	C	D	E	A
3	C	D	E	A	B
4	D	E	A	B	C
5	E	A	B	C	D
6	A	B	C	D	E
7	B	C	D	E	A
8	C	D	E	A	B
9	D	E	A	B	C
10	E	A	B	C	D

Sample Questions	Response Options
29. Use the look-up table using the third letter-number combination from the right D5 F3 G10 H6 E9 G4	○ A ○ B ○ C ○ D ○ E
30. Count each of the D letters in the letters listed below. Now use the count of the D letters and the letter "F" to obtain your answer. D F G D H E F G	○ A ○ B ○ C ○ D ○ E
31. Look at the letter-number combination below. Locate the second letter-number combination from the left. D2 G4 F6 H5 E10 G3	○ A ○ B ○ C ○ D ○ E
32. Look at the stock items listed below. Use the word with the most letters. Count that word's letters. Use that count with the first letter of that item to obtain your answer. Detergent Light Bulb Brush File	○ A ○ B ○ C ○ D ○ E

Following Instructions Question Answers
29 E, 30 D, 31 B, 32 D

Exam 943 - Auto Mechanic

This exam covers auto mechanic and technician positions. Use the following sample questions to prepare for the exam. Study them carefully. Each question is multiple choice and you must determine the correct answer.

This exam covers two sections:

- Section 1: Automotive Mechanic
- Section 2: Automotive Technician

Automotive Mechanic Questions (60 minutes)

1. A brake pedal that feels spongy usually indicates:

○ A) brakes are out of adjustment
○ B) worn Brake shoes or pads are worn
○ C) air has entered the system
○ D) defective brake caliber

2. Mechanics perform a battery load test to determine if the:

○ A) charging system is defective
○ B) voltage meets a minimum standard
○ C) cold cranking amperes are sufficient
○ D) amperage meets a minimum standard

3. What are two types of Oil pressure gauges:

○ A) magnetic, bimetallic
○ B) thermistor, primary
○ C) secondary, property
○ D) cadmium, electrical

4. Tire wear could be caused by all of the following, if not within the manufacturer's specifications, except:

○ A) caster
○ B) steering axis inclination
○ C) camber
○ D) toe-in

5. Assisted power to the steering is provided by a hydra boost system and what other system?

O A) air-ride suspension
O B) electrical
O C) braking
O D) air conditioner

6. When the ignition key is turned to the START position and there is no cranking or lights the problem could be caused by all of the following answers except a:

O A) burned-out headlight
O B) open circuit
O C) dead battery
O D) open fusible link

> **Automotive Mechanic Question Answers**
> **1 C, 2 B, 3 A, 4 A, 5 C, 6 A**

Automotive Technician Questions (30 minutes)

7. Which one of the following answers represents another way to open an Exhaust Gas Recirculation (EGR) valve other than with vacuum?

O A) spring action
O B) electricity
O C) manually
O D) hydraulic pressure

8. An engine is misfiring only during idle. A four-gas analyzer test by a technician discovers a high hydrocarbon (HC) reading. What is probable cause of the malfunction?

O A) A short in the secondary ignition
O B) The fuel injector is partially clogged
O C) intake manifold leaking
O D) The (EGR) valve that doesn't close all the way

9. With the transmission in the park position the technician notices a high-pitched sound that increases with engine (RPM), what would be the probable cause?

○ A) The torque converter is loose
○ B) The front pump is bad
○ C) The fan belt is broken
○ D) The rear pump is bad

10. Technicians do not have to remove an automatic transmission to perform which of these repairs?

○ A) governor assembly
○ B) stator support assembly
○ C) rear clutch pack
○ D) front pump seal

11. What engine defect will a wet compression test detect?

○ A) head gasket leaking
○ B) valve seals are worn
○ C) worn piston rings
○ D) worn valve seats

Automotive Technician Question Answers
7 B, 8 D, 9 B, 10 A, 11 C

Exam 955 - Mechanical & Electrical Job Skills Exam

This exam is designed to test the applicant's mechanical, electrical, and spatial relations abilities. It also determines how quickly and accurately you are able to work. Read all test instructions carefully the day of the test. Each test is timed. A countdown clock, where appropriate, will show the time remaining on your computer screen. The test will advance automatically to the next section when the previous section time has expired. You can review your answers if the time hasn't expired and make changes. However, you can't return to a part after the time for that part has expired.

The test is comprised of multiple-choice questions. During the test, for most sections, you are required to select your response by clicking on the small circle next to your answer. Some sections require you to highlight answers. Practice items for those sections are provided to familiarize you with the selection process.

You will have approximately 1 hour and 40 minutes to complete the assessment, however, you may finish early. The assessment is taken without breaks, take care of any personal needs prior to checking in for the test.

There are 2 parts to this examination:

- **Multicraft**, - Assesses the applicant's electrical and mechanical job skills, 60 questions, 1 hour
- **Spatial Relations** - Assesses the applicant's visual spatial relations ability

Multicraft Mechanical & Electrical Questions (60 questions, 60 minutes)

1. Which of the following answers is correct concerning the use of a soldering gun?

O A) Tips are not replaceable
O B) Not rated by the number of watts it uses
O C) Has no light
O D) Heats only when trigger is pressed

2. What unit of measure is read on a dial torque wrench?

O A) Pounds
O B) Inches
O C) Centimeters
O D) Foot-pounds

3. What is the purpose of a chuck key?

○ A) Open doors
○ B) Remove drill bits
○ C) Remove set screws
○ D) Unlock chucks

4. Which devise is used to transfer power and rotary mechanical motion from one shaft to another?

○ A) Bearing
○ B) Lever
○ C) Idler roller
○ D) Gear

5. A box wrench is considered safer than an open ended wrench because

○ A) They are larger
○ B) The open end wrench is smaller
○ C) The box wrench is less likely to slip
○ D) The open end wrench has a tighter fit

6. What fastener would you use to join two wires?

○ A) Duct tape
○ B) Wire nut
○ C) Staples
○ D) Paperclip

7. Before working on a piece of powered equipment

○ A) Notify the equipment operator
○ B) Turn off the circuit breaker
○ C) Use lock out / tag out procedures
○ D) Do all of the above

8. An "open electrical circuit" refers to a closed loop being opened. When you connect an ohmmeter to an open circuit, the meter will read?

○ A) Zero
○ B) Infinity
○ C) Read infinity and slowly return to zero
○ D) None of the above

Mechanical & Electrical Sample Question Answers
1 D, 2 D, 3 B, 4 D, 5 C, 6 B, 7 D, 8 B

Spatial Relations (65 questions, 40 minutes)

Visual-spatial skills are used for solving everyday tasks in life. Tasks may include reading maps, merging into traffic, or simply visualizing the area surrounding a new vacation spot to orient yourself to the new environment. Other examples where you would use this skill are loading a truck or stocking your pantry to visualize how best to pack the items inside. If you have difficulty understanding these relationships, after completing the sample questions, there are many study guides available online that can help.

This test part contains two sections. The first section, Matching Parts and Figures, contains questions where you are given two or more flat pieces. You must decide among the four options which one shows how those pieces can fit together without gaps or overlapping. The second section, Spatial Visualization, contains questions where you are given a drawing with top, front and right views. You must decide from the four options which one would have the top, front, and right views as shown in the drawing.

This test part consists of 65 items to be completed in 40 minutes. Your score depends upon how many items you answer correctly. There is no penalty for guessing on this part of the test. It is generally to your advantage to respond to each item, even if you have to guess.

Now, determine your answers to the sample questions provided below. The first two sample questions shown below correspond to the Matching Parts and Figures section.

9. How would the two pieces shown at the top fit together?

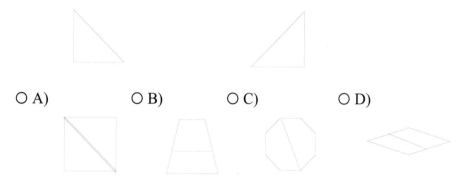

○ A)   ○ B)   ○ C)   ○ D)

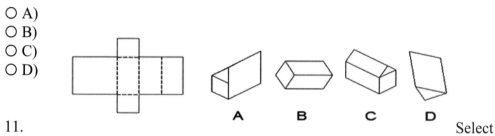

10) Folding the diagram on the left, which picture is the result?

○ A)
○ B)
○ C)
○ D)

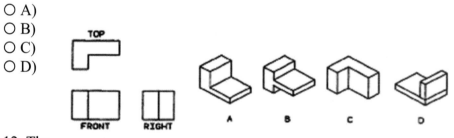

A   B   C   D

11.   Select
The drawing on the right labeled A through D that would have the Top, Front,
and right views as indicted in the drawing at the left.

○ A)
○ B)
○ C)
○ D)

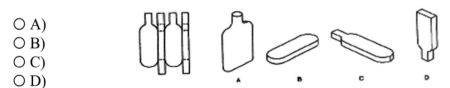

12. The   dra
wing at   the
left is drawn on a flat piece of paper. There are four figures labeled A through D
next to the drawing. After folding the flat piece of paper what form would be
created?

○ A)
○ B)
○ C)
○ D)

```
┌─────────────────────────────────────────────┐
│      Spatial Sample Question Answers          │
│          9 A, 10 A, 11 C, 12 C                │
└─────────────────────────────────────────────┘
```

Chapter Five
The 473 & 473-E Postal Exams

This chapter includes a study guide with sample test questions for the 473 and 473-E Postal Exams. You will also find helpful test taking tips and strategies that you can use for the practice and official exams.

The postal service hires workers for entry-level mail handling jobs from applicants who successfully pass the 473 exam with a score of 70 or higher. Applicants are required to take a 90-minute assessment online (Part D of the 473 exam) when they initially apply. If your results indicate you are suited for the job you will be scheduled to take Parts A, B and C of the 473 exam at a local testing facility.

Parts A, B & C of the exam will be scheduled within fourteen days of applying. Applicants who pass the exam are placed on the hiring register according to score. The highest scoring applicants will be called for an interview, medical screening, and drug test. Disabled veterans who pass the exam are placed at the top of the register by law, ahead of all other applicants who took the exam. The higher your score, the better chance you have of being called for an interview and hired.

In addition to exam results, the postal service will review your employment history, education, military service if applicable, and complete a background check.

CAUTION

You don't have to pay anyone to take a postal exam. Exams are administered at no cost to the job applicant. Job announcements, requiring exams, are posted online or at local, state, and federal buildings. Explore postal service opportunities and occupations on the following web sites:

www.postalwork.net/
www.about.usps.com/careers/welcome.htm

ENTRY LEVEL JOBS COVERED BY THE 473 EXAM

City and Rural Carrier   Mail delivery and collection in the city and suburban areas by foot or vehicle. Must be able to carry 35 pound mail bags and containers or parcels weighing up to 70 pounds. Mail carriers work standing, reaching, and walking most of their workday.

Mail Processing Clerk   Sorts mail manually or by operating and monitoring automated equipment. Clerks transport processed mail in the work area, and bundle and collate mail as necessary. Heavy lifting of mail and containers may be required.

Mail Handler   Responsible for transporting, unloading and loading mail containers and equipment in their facility. They frequently carry equipment and packages that weigh 70 pounds or less and push heavy wheeled containers.

Sales & Services Associate   Responsible for retail sales, customer support and mail distribution. All associates must also complete on-the-job training.

The **473 Major Entry Level Jobs Exam** is also referred to as the 473 Battery Exam. This exam measures an applicant's general aptitude and personal characteristics, not factual knowledge. Previously the 473-C exam was used exclusively for city carriers. Now all of the above listed occupations take the 473 and 473-E exams. Applicants take the 473-E exam, which includes the online assessment, first. If they score 70 or higher they are scheduled for a proctored 473 exam that covers the remainder of the exam.

Review this chapter to improve your test scores and to become familiar with the test taking process and strategies, application forms, answer sheets, and sample questions. The 473 examination and completion of forms will require approximately three hours and thirty minutes, online and proctored sessions combined.

EXAM CONTENT

The five sections of the test are listed in Table 5-1 on page 93. Part D is now completed with the 473-E exam online when you first apply. Parts A through C are proctored exams administered at testing facilities in your area. You will be allowed to work only on one section of the test at a time. If you finish a part early you aren't permitted to proceed to the next part or to return to a part that you previously completed. The computer explains each part in turn and you must follow the instructions.

Table 5-1 Entry-level Battery 473			
Test Unit	**# of Questions**	**Time Allowed**	**Covered Subjects**
Part A Address Checking	60	11 min.	Determine if two addresses are identical.
Part B Forms Completion	30	15 min.	Information identification for completing forms correctly.
Part C Section 1 - Coding	36	6 min.	Using proper code to assign to addresses.
Part C Section 3 - Memory	36	7 min.	Memorize assigned codes for addresses.
Part D Inventory of Personal Experience and Characteristics	150	90 min.	Assess applicant's experience and characteristics related to the job. (Online Assessment)

Address Cross Comparison (Part A)

Part A includes 60 questions and you have 11 minutes to complete this section. You will be tested on how fast and accurately you can compare two address lists. Postal workers must be able to differentiate between two addresses to determine if they are the same or different destinations. Address differences include different spelling or transposed numbers. The questions are multiple choice.

- A is selected if there are no errors.
- B is selected if only the addresses are different.
- C is selected if only the Zip Codes are different.
- D is selected if both the address and Zip Code are different.

Forms Completion (Part B)

Part B includes 30 questions, and you will have 15 minutes to complete this section. You will be provided with various sample forms and asked questions about what is to be entered on the form. For example, you might be given a form with 9 blocks, and block 5 may be the Zip code block. A possible question would be where you would enter the Zip code. The answer would be "block 5." You could also be asked what type of data goes in a specified box such as a number, check mark or name. All 30 questions are multiple choice A, B, C, or D.

Coding (Part C Section 1)

The coding section includes 36 questions and you have six minutes to complete this section. You will be given four delivery routes, A through D, with street addresses. The questions list an address and you have to assign the correct delivery route for the address. The delivery routes will be given to you for the Coding exam and you will have to memorize the routes for the Memory section.

Memory (Part C Section 2)

The memory section includes 36 questions that are similar to the coding section questions. You have to select the correct delivery route, A, B, C, or D, without looking at the chart. You will be given time to memorize the addresses and routes before the exam starts.

Personal Characteristics and Experience (Part D)

This section takes 90 minutes and is completed online when you first apply. The postal service evaluates your personal experience, characteristics and tendencies. For example, you will be asked your likes and dislikes and whether you have experience in certain areas. You really can't prepare for this section; it's your personal profile. If you answer the questions honestly the postal service will be able to identify the job that is best suited to your characteristics. The answers are multiple choice. The question *"Do you like to work in groups?"* would have the answers (A) Strongly Agree, (B) Agree, (C), Disagree, (D) Strongly Disagree. A question similar to *"Are you willing to work rotating shifts?"* would have the answers (A) Very Often, (B) Often, (C) Sometimes, (D) Rarely. We do include some helpful hints on how to prepare for this section later in this chapter.

Exam Process

All exams are multiple choice, and the answers are typically A, B, C or D. However, in Part D there may be up to seven answers, A through G, to choose from. The test is entirely administered and timed by a computer and all the testing instructions are provided by the computer. Prior to starting the exam you will be guided through several practice and instruction screens to familiarize you with the testing process and use of the computer. Several practice exams are provided. The following example shows the typical answer grid that we use throughout this study guide.

Sample Answer Grid			
1	Ⓐ	Ⓑ	Ⓒ Ⓓ
2	Ⓐ	Ⓑ	Ⓒ Ⓓ
3	Ⓐ	Ⓑ	Ⓒ Ⓓ
4	Ⓐ	Ⓑ	Ⓒ Ⓓ

GENERAL INFORMATION

All hiring for the postal service is decentralized. When you apply for a postal job in any city you are applying only for a particular job vacancy. Your exam results can be used to apply for other job applications for a set time period as long as you have your **Exam History Code** that the postal service sends you after passing a test. The applicants with the highest grades are called for an interview. You have to apply for each job opening. If you want to be considered for jobs in other areas you have to apply for jobs in that area.

All postal jobs — just like all federal civil service jobs — are highly competitive and you have to complete a considerable amount of paperwork including writing detailed work experience descriptions back at least 10 years, or to age 16 if you are a recent high school graduate.

EXAM OVERVIEW

The postal service will e-mail you a scheduling notice shortly after registering, applying, and completing your online assessment. The notice will specify the exam locations, various times, and dates available along with a link to the Assessment Introduction Package. Select the location, date and time that best suits your needs. The Assessment Introduction Package provides general test information and several sample test questions for each part of the exam.

The Assessment Introduction Package instructs you to bring the following items with you to the exam:

- Your login ID and Password (Login ID and Password for your assessment account. These are set up when you take the online unproctored Section D assessment)
- A state or federal picture ID (Generally your photo driver's license, passport, U.S. Military ID, etc.)
- Arrive at least 15 minutes early. (If you are more than 15 minutes late you can't take the exam)

> The items listed above are **REQUIRED**. If you neglect to bring a valid photo ID or your user ID and password, or arrive over 15 minutes, late you will not be allowed to take the exam .

The examiner will provide you with disposable ear plugs and assist you with logging in to start the test. The examiner will not have access to any information related to your assessment results or your next step. You will receive an e-mail message with instructions on how to access your test results. You can also check your assessment results as part of your candidate profile in eCareer after your exam is complete. Return to **http://about.usps.com/careers/welcome.htm** to log into eCareer and review your assessment results.[1]

TEST-TAKING STRATEGIES

The following strategies will help you improve your grades and complete more answers on the timed exams. Use these techniques on the practice tests in this book and when you take your actual postal service exam. If you practice these techniques now, when you take the postal exam they will become second nature.

➤ Get plenty of rest the night before the exam.

➤ Eliminate the answers in multiple choice questions that make no sense. You can often eliminate half of the answers through this method. If you have to guess an answer, you improve your chances through the process of elimination.

➤ You will be penalized for guessing on Part A (Address Checking) and Part C (Coding and Memory) due to the methods that the postal service uses to grade these sections. It is also unwise to guess or try to manipulate your answers for Section D (Personal Characteristics). Guessing on Part B (Forms Checking), will not adversely effect your scores.

➤ Don't forget your eyeglasses, hearing aids or anything else that you may need for the exam. Personal items such as cell phones, pagers, and PDAs are not allowed in the testing room.

➤ Review the directions to the testing facility and arrive early. You don't need the additional stress of getting lost on the way to the exam and arriving late. Arriving early will also give you time to get familiar with the testing facility. You can locate directions to the testing site on any of the Internet search engine mapping sites such the one at http://google.com/maps.

➤ The test will take up to 90 minutes including initial introductions and the time it takes to complete the computer familiarization steps. Breaks are not permitted. Take care of personal needs before the test starts and limit your fluid intake.

Excerpted from "Assessment Information Package - Exam 473, U.S. Postal Service"

➤ Be skeptical when an answer includes the words like, "always, never, all, none, generally, or only." These words can be a trap. Only select an answer with these words in it if you are absolutely sure it is the right answer.

➤ If two answers have opposite meanings, take your time and look closer. Many times one of the two is correct.

➤ Make sure when you select your answer to a specific question, that it registered on the screen. Sometimes when I was going between the selected answer and enter keys the answer didn't register and I had to go back and reselect the answer before proceeding.

➤ One word can dramatically change the meaning of a sentence. Read each question word-for-word before answering.

➤ Don't dwell on the exam to the point that it upsets you. Answer the questions that you know first. If you have problems with a question, skip it and go to the next test question. Mentally note the question for review and return to it later, if time permits. After you complete the section, you can return to the unanswered questions you marked for review and give them more thought.

✎ **One word of caution**. Once you finish a section and are directed to go on to the next part, you can't go back to previously completed sections. You can go back only within the current section that you are working on if the time isn't up.

➤ Focus on one question at a time. Don't let your mind wonder back to questions you skipped or to other sections. If you stay focused on each question you will be able to concentrate better on the exam.

If you don't attend your scheduled exam appointment, you are not permitted to reschedule. An incomplete test result will be recorded for the job vacancy. You can reschedule if you contact the assessment center no later than 24 hours before your scheduled exam time.

ADDRESS CHECKING - PART A

Part A includes 60 questions and you have 11 minutes to complete this section. You will be tested on how fast and accurately you can compare two lists. Postal workers must be able to differentiate between two addresses to determine if they are the same or different destinations. Address differences include different spelling or transposed numbers. The questions are multiple choice.

Questions include an address with street or P.O. box, city, and state in the first column of each list and a ZIP code in the second column. The example below shows the address on the left and the Zip code on the right in each list. You will compare the *Correct List* on the left to the *List to be Checked* on the right. You are required to determine if the address to be checked is exactly the same or different as the address and Zip code on the *Correct List*. You must determine if the address and Zip code are exactly the same or different including the numbers, punctuation, capitalization, and spelling. You will make your selections from the list below:

- A is selected if there are no errors, everything is exactly alike.
- B is selected if only the addresses are different.
- C is selected if only the Zip codes are different.
- D is selected if both the address and Zip code are different.

Prior to starting the actual exam you will be given two sample exercises of several questions on each to familiarize you with the process. This introduces you to what is expected on the exam. Complete the four sample questions that follow to better understand the process.

A. No Errors	B. Address Only	C. ZIP Code Only	D. Both

Correct List			List to be Checked		
#	**Address**	**Zip Code**	**Address**	**Zip Code**
S1.	1915 Park Place Fairview, TX	79411	1915 Park Place Fairview, TX	79141
S2.	401 McAuthur Drive Benton, NC	27514-1132	401 McAuther Drive Benton, NC	27514-1132
S3.	6915 Amber Way Pittsburgh, PA	15129-0005	6915 Amber Way Pittsburgh, PA	15129-0005
S4.	19150 First Street Kalamazoo, MI	49007-2334	19105 First Street Kalamizoo, MI	49070-2344

Sample Answer Grid	
S1	Ⓐ Ⓑ Ⓒ Ⓓ
S2	Ⓐ Ⓑ Ⓒ Ⓓ
S3	Ⓐ Ⓑ Ⓒ Ⓓ
S4	Ⓐ Ⓑ Ⓒ Ⓓ

Question S1

You will discover that the street, city and state are identical. However, the ZIP code is different. The third and fourth digits in the Zip code on the *List to be Checked* are reversed. Mark answer **"C"** for Zip Code Only.

Question S2

You will find the addresses have different spellings. McAuthur is spelled McAuther on the *List to be Checked*. The Zip Codes are identical. You will mark **"B"** on the sample answer sheet.

Question S3

The address and Zip Code of both lists are identical. Mark **"A"** on the answer sheet.

Question S4

You will find the street address and Zip Code numbers are different. The *Correct List* street number is 19150 and the list to be corrected street number is 19105. The last two digits of the first five Zip Code numbers are reversed. Also, the Zip Code's last 4 digits are not the same and the name Kalamazoo is misspelled. In this case you would mark **"D"** for both.

Before we start the actual practice exams for address checking there are a number of techniques you can use to improve your score and efficiency so that you will have more time to devote to the exam.

> ***Time is critical***. You will have 11 minutes to complete 60 questions. That's only 11 seconds per question. The more you practice and prepare for the exam the more questions you will be able to answer and the greater chance you have of earning a higher score.

Lets take another look at the four sample questions on the next page. Notice that I underlined the errors. When you start the sample questions and during the test, concentrate on the address first and then move on to the Zip code for each question. You can mark differences on the exam for Part A as stated in the exam instructions. If you find an error in the address, mark it and move on to the Zip code and do the same. Once you find an error in either the address or Zip code, don't look for additional errors. All you need to do is find one and you don't want to waste precious time. You will notice that question S4 on the next page has two errors in the address. Stop after you find the first one, mark it and move on to the Zip code.

Another helpful technique is to memorize the four potential answers now so that you won't waste time searching for the correct answer for each question during the exam. Memorize the answers NOW, before you take the exam.

A. No Errors	B. Address Only	C. ZIP Code Only	D. Both

I try to think of things in what I perceive to be logical order. When I look at the answers it makes sense that **(A)** equals **No Errors**, **(B)** is next and the first column of the *list to be corrected* is the address so I can remember that the answer for "Address Only" **(B)** is the first incorrect answer and it is in the first column of the list to be corrected. Then since the second column in the list to be corrected is the ZIP code, if only the Zip code is incorrect I would mark **(C).** Finally, if both the address and Zip code are incorrect I mark **(D)**. To me this is logical. However we all have our own reality, and you must design a scenario that makes sense to you.

Others use acronyms to remember lists. In this case you can take the first letter of each of the four answers, **NAZB** and memorize this new word.

N = No Errors = **Answer A**
A = Address Only = **Answer B**
Z = Zip Code Only = **Answer C**
B = Both = **Answer D**

	Correct List			List to be Checked	
#	**Address**	**Zip Code**		**Address**	**Zip Code**
S1.	1915 Park Place Fairview, TX	79411		1915 Park Place Fairview, TX	79141
S2.	401 McAuthur Drive Benton, NC	27514-1132		401 McAuther Drive Benton, NC	27514-1132
S3.	6915 Amber Way Pittsburgh, PA	15129-0005		6915 Amber Way Pittsburgh, PA	15129-0005
S4.	19150 First Street Kalamazoo, MI	49007-2334		19105 First Street Kalamizoo, MI	49070-2344

With practice you should be able to complete the 60 questions in the time allotted. If you finish early, go back and review the questions that you found to be alike. You can easily identify them because you won't have any marks on them. Check these first to see if you missed something, then go on to others if time permits.

It is best not to guess on answers in this section due to the way it is scored. The postal service adds the number of questions that you got right and then subtracts one third of the questions you got wrong. Each of the four exam parts is scored differently.

The practice exams for Part A start on the next page. The answer sheet is on the page directly following this practice exam. For your convenience you can copy the answer sheets so that your answer sheet will be next to the exam questions that you are working on. **Be sure to time yourself for this section.** The more you practice the better your score will be. Time this practice exam for 11 minutes.

— Answer Sheet page 133, Answer Key page 137 —

PART A PRACTICE EXAM 1 (Address Checking)

A. No Errors	B. Address Only	C. ZIP Code Only	D. Both

#	Address	ZIP	Address	ZIP
1	P.O. Box 1243 Aikron, OH	44326-3452	P.O. Box 1243 Aikron, OH	44362-2352
2	6000 Buford Dr Houston, TX	77006-0001	6000 Buford Dr Houston, TX	77006-0001
3	505 SE 35th St. Portland, OR	97211-0124	505 SE 53rd St. Portland, OR	92711-0124
4	5990 Lascolinas Circle Lake Worth, FL	33463	5990 Lascolinas Circle Lake Worth, FL	33463
5	P.O. Box 5478 Hollister, FL	32147-7564	P.O. Box 5487 Hollister, FL	32147-7584
6	1767 Timber Road Vista, CA	92080	1766 Timber Road Vista, CA	92080
7	3030 Front Street Raleigh, NC	27610	3030 Front Street Raleigh, NC	27610
8	P.O. Box 10239 Camp Lejeune, NC	28547-0072	P.O. Box 12390 Camp Lejeune, NC	28547-0072
9	102 Madera Drive Eatonville, WA	98328-4461	102 Midera Drive Eatonille, WA	98328-6441
10	81000 Darting Manor Dr. Laurel, MD	29723	81000 Darting Manor Dr. Laurel, MD	29723
11	200 Rock Chain Drive Eagle River, AK	99576	200 Rock Cliff Drive Eagle River, AK	99516
12	206 Chancelor Street Suffolk, VA	23434-9802	206 Chancelor Street Sufolk, VA	24343-9802
13	1015 23rd Street Markham, IL	60427-3772	1015 23rd Street Markham, IL	80427-3772
14	900 School Brook Road Socorro, NM	87801-0212	900 School Brook Ave. Socorro, NM	87801-0121
15	4423 Potter Ave., Apt 23 Fort Wayne, IN	46835	4423 Potter Ave., Apt 23 Fort Wayne, IN	46835
16	1509 Meadow View Drive Dallas, TX	75222	1509 Meadow View Drive Fort Worth, TX	75222
17	P.O. Box 1243 Penn Hills, PA	15255-4432	P.O. Box 12433 Penn Hills, PA	15255-4432
18	3445 Sumpter Avenue Lisbon, IA	52253	3445 Sumpter Avenue Lisbon, IA	52553
19	P.O. Box 666 Ord, NE	68862	P.O. Box 666 Ord, NE	68662
20	1062 Amherst Street Moon Township, PA	15108-2601	1062 Amherst Ave. Moon Township, PA	15108-2601

A. No Errors	B. Address Only	C. ZIP Code Only	D. Both

21	2414 Easton Road Houston, TX	77003-8791	2414 Easton Road Houston, TX	77003-8791
22	4014 E. Belmont Chicago, IL	60614-0201	4014 E. Boumont Chicago, IL	60614-0201
23	5235 Westminster Place Portland, OR	97311-7904	5235 Westminster Place Portland, OR	97113 -7904
24	1001 Highland Avenue Needham, MA	02494	1001 Highland Place Needham, MA	04294
25	P.O. Box 1904 Hempfield, FL	32107-7543	P.O. Box 1904 Hempfield, FL	32107-7543
26	878 N 41 2nd Street Tacoma, WA	98418-2194	878 N 41 2nd Street Tacoma, WA	98418-2004
27	143 North Avenue Outreach, NC	27310	143 South Avenue Outreach, NC	27310
28	P.O. Box 432 Pendalton, SC	29708-1092	P.O. Box 325 Pendalton, SC	29709-1092
29	987 Fifth Avenue Delray, WA	97318-4298	987 Forbes Avenue Delray, WA	97318-4298
30	1208 Elm Street South Park, PA	15244-2787	1208 Elm Street South Park, PA	15244-2787
31	4520 River Road Eagles Nest, AK	99326	4520 River Road Eagles Nest, AK	99326
32	1309 Chambers Lane Wilton, VA	24389-8276	1390 Chambers Lane Wilton, VA	24389-8276
33	P.O. Box 1998 Willshier, IN	70398-0989	P.O. Box 1998 Willshier, IN	70399-0989
34	1902 Stanley Road Saddlebrook, TX	71342-0853	1902 Stanley Road Saddlebrook, TX	71344-0835
35	116 East 9th St. Torrington, CT	06790-2314	116 West 9th St. Torrington, CT	06791-2314
36	142 Midland Drive Dallas, TX	75122-2134	142 Midway Drive Dallas, TX	75122-2134
37	P.O. Box 232 Hershey, PA	18752-2790	P.O. Box 322 Hershey, PA	18752-2790
38	7675 Sharon Street Trusville, AL	35173-8312	7675 Sharon Street Trusville, AL	53573-8312
39	P.O. Box 1546 Erie, PA	16842-1978	P.O. Box 1546 Erie, PA	16842-1978
40	150 Mission Avenue Godfrey, VA	22689	160 Mission Avenue Godfrey, VA	22589

| A. No Errors | | B. Address Only | | C. ZIP Code Only | | D. Both | |

#	Address	ZIP	Address	ZIP
41	52 Saratoga Street Gloversville, NY	12078	52 Saratoga Street Gloversville, NY	12068-2310
42	244 North Adams Ave Eldridge, IL	61534-2101	244 South Adams Ave Eldridge, IL	61534-2101
43	6543 Marcie St. Labrook, LA	70013-2345	6543 Marty St. Labrook, LA	70113-2345
44	P.O. Box 1567 Falstaff, AZ	85287-9436	P.O. Box 1567 Falstaff, AZ	85287-9436
45	348 Park Place Harlenton, NY	12044-2107	348 Park Place Harlenton, NY	12045-2107
46	1414 16th St., Apt. 345 Tacoma, WA	98433-2224	1414 17th St., Apt. 345 Tacoma, WA	98433-2224
47	78 Lake Rd. Woodbury, NY	11779-0124	78 Lakefront Rd. Woodbury, NY	11799-0124
48	P.O. Box 1990 Randolph, NC	28649-9089	P.O. Box 1990 Randolph, NC	28649-9089
49	987 Atlantic Ave. Ocean City, NY	07200-0989	987 Atlantic Ave. Ocean City, NY	07201-0989
50	229 Westover Terrace Oklahoma, City, OK	74022-1524	229 Westover Place Oklahoma, City, OK	74022-1524
51	5120 Trenton Blvd. Wilkinsburg, PA	15219-0236	5120 Trenton Blvd. Wilkinsburg, PA	15219-0236
52	145 River Rd. Pittsburgh, PA	15222-3245	144 River Rd. Pittsburgh, PA	15221-3245
53	Manor Hall East, #456 York, PA	17404-5645	Manor Hall East, #456 York, PA	17440-5645
54	4545 S. Beacon Chicago, IL	60676-4253	4545 N. Beacon Chicago, IL	60676-4253
55	1990 Westend Dr. Boston, MA	10846-9056	1990 Westward Dr. Boston, MA	10845-9056
56	124 South Park Ave. Sandford, FL	33354-0967	124 South Park Ave. Sandford, FL	33354-0967
57	P.O. Box 1987 Seaward, LA	70124	P.O. Box 1987 Seaward, LA	70224
58	653 Northwood St. Trenton, MI	46798-2354	653 Northview St. Trenton, MI	46798-2354
59	P.O. Box 516 Chicago, IL	60654-9176	P.O. Box 515 Chicago, IL	60654-9176
60	1911 Macie St. Bradbury, NY	11687-7658	1911 Macie St. Bradbury, NY	11687-7658

FORMS CHECKING - PART B

This section includes 30 questions that have to be completed in 15 minutes. There will be six questions for each of five different forms on the exam. Before starting the actual test, the examiners will give you a two-minute exercise with several questions that you will answer. These questions are not graded. After the introductory exercise you will start the actual exam.

Refer to the Domestic Return Receipt form on the next page to answer the first two sample questions for practice and use the same for the first six questions of the timed exam.

Sample Questions

S1. Where do you enter the sender's address on this form?
A. Box 3 (Front)
B. Box 10 (Back)
C. Box 3 and 10
C. None of the above

ANSWER: The sender's address is entered in Box 10 and the correct answer is B.

S2. The letter will be sent certified. Each certified letter has an article number. What two blocks must be filled out to designate a certified mailing?
A. Box 1 and 2
B. Box 10 and 1
C. Box 4 and 5
D. Box 3 only

ANSWER: The correct answer is C. Questions can be tricky if you read more into the question than what is presented. In this example, all certified mailings are assigned an article number that is listed in block 4 and you would check the certified box in block 5. Even though the remainder of the form must be filled out before it can be processed, the question is only asking about what must be filled out to designate a certified mailing. Focus on what they give you in the question, the known facts.

PRACTICE EXAM PART B

Use the **Domestic Return Receipt** form on the next page for the first 6 questions of the exam. You have 15 minutes for the 30 questions or 30 seconds per question. Set your timer for three minutes for each six question segment. The questions are on the opposite page so that you can easily refer to the forms as needed. Take a few seconds after you set the timer to familiarize yourself with the form. Copy the answer sheet in the back of this section and have the answer sheet next to the questions so you can easily mark your answers and not lose time.

— **Answer Sheet page 133, Answer Key page 137** —

DOMESTIC RETURN RECEIPT (Back)

SENDER INSTRUCTIONS
Print your name, address, and ZIP Code in the space provided.
- Complete items 1,2,3, and 4 on the reverse.
- Attach to front of article if space permits, otherwise affix to back of article.
- Endorse article "Return Receipt Requested" adjacent to number.

RETURN

TO ➡

Print Sender's name, address, and ZIP Code in the space below.

10. _____

_____

_____

DOMESTIC RETURN RECEIPT (Front)

● **SENDER:** Compare items 1 and 2 when additional services are desired, and complete 3 and 4. Put your address in the "RETURN TO" Space on the reverse side. Failure to do this will prevent this card from being returned to you. <u>The return receipt fee will provide you the name of the person delivered to and the date of delivery</u>. For additional fees the following services are available. Consult postmaster for fees and check box(es) for additional service(s) requested.

1. ☐ Show to whom delivered, date, and addresses's address.   **2.** ☐ Restricted Delivery
↑ *(Extra charge)* ↑   ↑ *(Extra charge)* ↑

3. Article Addressed to:	**4.** Article Number:
	5. Type of Service: ☐ Registered ☐ Insured ☐ Certified ☐ COD ☐ Express Mail
	Always obtain signature of addresses or agent and <u>DATE DELIVERED</u>.
6. Signature - Addressee	9. Addressee's Address *(ONLY if requested and fee paid)*
7. Signature - Agent	
8. Date of Delivery	

Start section 1 of your timed exercise, set your timer for 3 minutes. There are five sections with 6 questions each.

1. Where would you enter the article number for a certified mailing on this form?

   A. Box 10
   B. Box 4
   C. Box 3 and 9
   D. Box 3 only

2. The person sending a certified letter wants to receive the return receipt at his home address. Where does he put his return address?

   A. Box 3
   B. Box 9
   C. Box 10
   D. The article number in Box 4 and signs in Box 7

3. Which of these would indicate restricted delivery?

   A. Box 5
   B. Box 2
   C. A signature in Box 7 and Box check mark in Box 1
   D. Box 1, 3, and 7

4. Which of these could be a correct answer for Box 8?

   A. A check mark
   B. Article number
   C. Signature
   D. March 15, 2005

5. Which one of the following could be the correct entry for Box 5?

   A. Your initials
   B. 4/19/2005
   C. A check mark
   D. None of the above

6. Which of the following should have a name entered?

   A. Box 1
   B. Box 4
   C. Box 6
   D. Box 2

Practice Exam - Section 2 of Part B

Authorization to Hold Mail
Postmaster - Please hold mail for:

1. Name(s)

2. Address

3a. Begin Holding Mail (Date)	**3b.** Resume Delivery (Date)

4. ☐ **Option A**
I will pick up all accumulated mail when I return and understand that mail delivery will not resume until I do. (This is suggested if your return date may change or if no one will be at home to receive mail)

5. ☐ **Option B**
Please deliver all accumulated mail and resume normal delivery on the ending date shown above.

6. Customer Signature

For Post Office Use Only

7. Date Received

8a. Clerk	**8b.** Bin Number
9a. Carrier	**9b.** Route Number

Customer Option A Only

Carrier: Accumulated mail has been picked up:

10a. Resume delivery on (date) _____

10b. By: _____

Start section 2 of your timed exercise, questions 7 through 12. Set your timer for 3 minutes. There are five sections with 6 questions each.

7. Joe Smith and Bob Barker live at the same address. Bob is going on an extended vacation and will be away for two months. Joe is not leaving and wants his mail to continue. What name(s) should you enter in Box 1?

    A. Joe Smith
    B. Joe Smith and Bob Barker
    C. Bob Barker
    D. The postmaster's name

8. If you check Option B, which of the following statements is correct?

    A. The person will pick up his accumulated mail when he returns.
    B. Your mail carrier will deliver your mail when you return after you contact the Post Office.
    C. Your mail carrier will restart delivery on a predetermined date.
    D. None of the above

9. What fields would the customer complete on this form?

    A. Blocks 1, 2, 3a, and 6 only
    B. Blocks 1 through 6 only
    C. Blocks 7 through 10b
    D. All of the above

10. Which of the selections specify the date to start holding mail?

    A. Box 3b
    B. Box 7
    C. Box 3a
    D. Line 10a

11. What would be a correct entry for line 10a?

    A. Jay W. Brook
    B. A check mark
    C. June 1, 2005
    D. 13547

12. Postal Clerk Jim McKee accepted Jeff Brown's Authorization to Hold Mail. Jeff's carrier is Janet Ward. What box is Jim McKee's name entered in?

    A. Box 1
    B. Box 9a
    C. Box 1 and 6
    D. None of the above

Practice Exam - Section 3 of Part B

Certificate of Bulk Mailing

MAILER: Prepare this statement in ink. Affix meter stamp or uncanceled postage stamps covering the fee in the block to the right. Present for certification.				7. Meter stamp or postage (uncanceled) stamps in payment of fee to be affixed here and canceled by postmarking, including date.			

Fee for Certification		USE CURRENT RATE CHART					
1. Up to 1,000 pieces (1 certificate for total number)							
2. For each additional 1,000 pieces, or fraction							
3. Duplicate Copy							

4a. Number of identical Pieces	4.b Class of Mail	4c. Postage on Each	4d. Number of Pieces to the Pound	4e. Total Number of Pounds	4f. Total Postage Paid	4g. Fee Paid

5a. Mailed For	5b. Mailed By

Postmaster's Certificate

6. It is hereby certified that the above-described mailing has been received and number of pieces and postage verified.

(Postmaster or Designee)

Start section 3 of your timed exercise, questions 13 through 18. Set your timer for three minutes. There are five sections with six questions each.

13. ACME Int'l is mailing its annual catalog under the bulk mail rates program. The company hired Abbott Services to pick up the bulk mailing of 1,000 pounds that included 5,000 individual pieces of first class mail. What figure would be placed in block 4d?

    A. 1000
    B. 5
    C. 5000
    D. ZERO

14. Using the same example as question 13, what would be entered on Line 5a and 5b?

    A. 5a "Postmaster" and 5b "Abbott Services"
    B. 5a "Cost Reduction" and 5a "ACME Int'l"
    C. 5a "ACME Int'l" and 5b "Abbott Services"
    D. None of the above

15. Can a Designee sign this form for the Postmaster?

    A. Yes
    B. No
    C. Never
    D. Only in block 5b

16. What could be the class of mail entered in block 4b?

    A. First
    B. 15th
    C. No Class
    D. None of the above

17. The mailer has 15 identical pieces for this mailing. Where would you enter this information?

    A. Box 4e
    B. No identical pieces can be added
    C. Box 4a
    D. In the remarks in Box 6

18. Where do you attach the meter stamp or postage on this form?

    A. You affix postage to each piece of mail, not to the Certificate of Bulk Mailing.
    B. To the back of the certificate
    C. In Box 7
    D. In Box 6

Practice Exam - Section 4 of Part B

<table>
<tr><td colspan="3">Bar Code</td><td colspan="4">EXPRESS MAIL</td><td>Mailing Label</td></tr>
<tr><td colspan="4">ORIGIN (POSTAL USE ONLY)</td><td colspan="5">DELIVERY (POSTAL USE ONLY)</td></tr>
<tr>
<td>PO ZIP Code

1a.</td>
<td>Day of Delivery

1b. □ Next □ Second</td>
<td colspan="2">Flat Rate Envelope

1c. □</td>
<td>Delivery Attempt

1d. Mo.   Day</td>
<td>Time

1e. □ AM □ PM</td>
<td colspan="3">Employee Signature

1f.</td>
</tr>
<tr>
<td>Date In

2d.</td>
<td>2b. □ 12 noon □ 3 PM</td>
<td colspan="2">Postage

2c. $</td>
<td>Delivery Attempt

2d. Mo.   Day</td>
<td>Time

2e. □ AM □ PM</td>
<td colspan="3">Employee Signature

2f.</td>
</tr>
<tr>
<td>Time In

3a. □ AM □ PM</td>
<td>Military

3b. □ 2nd Day □ 3rd Day</td>
<td colspan="2">Return Receipt Fee

3c.</td>
<td>Delivery Attempt

3d. Mo.   Day</td>
<td>Time

3e. □ AM □ PM</td>
<td colspan="3">Employee Signature

3f.</td>
</tr>
<tr>
<td>Weight

4a. Lbs. Ozs.</td>
<td>Int'l Alpha Country Code

4b.</td>
<td>COD Fee

4c.</td>
<td>Insurance Fee</td>
<td colspan="2">CUSTOMER USE ONLY
6. □ WAIVER OF SIGNATURE</td>
<td colspan="3"></td>
</tr>
<tr>
<td>No Delivery

5a. □ Wknd □ Holiday</td>
<td>Acceptance Clerk Initials

5b.</td>
<td colspan="2">Total Postage & Fees

5c. $</td>
<td colspan="2">Customer Signature
NO DELIVERY □ Weekend □ Holiday</td>
<td colspan="3"></td>
</tr>
<tr>
<td colspan="4">CUSTOMER USE ONLY</td>
<td colspan="5"></td>
</tr>
<tr>
<td colspan="4">Method of Payment

7a. Express Mail Corp Acct. No.</td>
<td colspan="5">Federal Agency Acct. No.

7b. Or Postal Service Acct. No.</td>
</tr>
<tr>
<td colspan="4">8a. from: (PLEASE PRINT)   PHONE :</td>
<td colspan="5">8b. TO: (PLEASE PRINT)   PHONE:

□ □ □ □ □ + □ □ □ □
zip + 4</td>
</tr>
</table>

Start section 4 of your timed exercise, questions 19 through 24. Set your timer for three minutes. There are five sections with six questions each.

19. Which of the following answers could be a correct entry for Box 1d?

    A. $18.65
    B. 12 Noon
    C. 6/15
    D. 6/15/05

20. Joe Smith dropped a Flat Rate Express Mail package at the Post Office at 11:00 AM on 8/11/05. The postal clerk informed Joe that his package would be delivered by noon the next day. How would the clerk note this on the form?

    A. Write the date 8/12/05 in Box 1d and the time in 1e.
    B. Check "Noon" in Box 2b and "Next" in Box 1b
    C. Write the date 8/12/05 in 3c
    D. None of the above

21. The customer requests no weekend delivery and "Waiver of Signature." How does the customer select these options?

    A. Signs Box 6
    B. Customer signs his name and checks "Waiver of Signature" and "Weekend" in Box 6.
    C. Checks "Waiver of Signature in Box 6
    D. None of the above

22. The mail carrier was unable to make delivery on his first attempt on 8/12/05 because the customer was not home. The carrier (employee) did not leave the package. Where does the carrier sign this form?

    A. Box 6
    B. Box 1f
    C. Box 2f and 3f
    D. None of the above

23. The clerk weighed the Express Mail package and advised the customer that the package would cost $17.95 to mail overnight. Where does the clerk initial the mailing label and enter the package weight?

    A. Initial in Box1f and weight in Box 2c
    B. Initial in Box 5b and weight in Box 4a
    C. Enter $17.95 in Box 2c and Initial in Box 6
    D. No initials or weight is required on this form

24. Where would you enter the recipient's ZIP code on this form?

    A. Box 8a
    B. Box 4c
    C. Box 8b
    D. Zip code not required

Practice Exam - Section 5 of Part B

Application for Post Office Box or Caller Service		
Customers: Complete white boxes	Post Office: Complete shaded boxes	
1a. Name(s) to which box number(s) is (are) assigned		1b. Box or Caller Number _____ through _____
2a. Name of person applying, Title (if representing an organization), and name of organization *(if different from name in Box 1a above)*		2b. Will this box be used for: ☐ Personal use ☐ Business use
3a. Address *(number, street, apt. no., city, state, Zip Code)*. When address changes, cross out address here and put new address on back.		3b. Telephone number *(Include area code)*

4a. Data application received	4b. Box size needed	4c. ID and physical address verified by *(initials)*	4d. Dates of service _____ through _____
5a. Two types of identification are required. One must contain a photograph of the addressee(s). Social security cards, credit cards, and birth certificates are unacceptable as identification. Write in identifying information. Subject to verification.		5b. Eligibility for Carrier Delivery ☐ City ☐ Rural ☐ HCR ☐ None	5c. Service Assigned ☐ Box ☐ Caller ☐ Reserve #
		6. List name(s) of minors or names of others **receiving mail** in individual box. Other persons must present two forms of valid ID. If applicant is a firm, name each member **receiving mail**. Each member must have verifiable ID upon request. *(Continue on reverse side)*	
WARNING: *The furnishing of false or misleading information on this form or omission of information may result in criminal sanctions (including fines and imprisonment) and/or civil sanctions (including multiple damages and civil penalties) (18U.S.C. 1001)*		7. Signature of applicant (Same as item 3). I agree to comply with all Postal rules regarding Post Office box or caller services.	

Start section 5 of your timed exercises, questions 25 through 30. Set your timer for three minutes. This is the last set of six questions.

25. David Jones is applying to open a post office box in Canton, Ohio. He has his driver's license photo ID and his Social Security card for identification. Will the postal service process his request?

   A. The clerk will accept his application and attach photocopies of his photo ID and Social Security Card to the application.
   B. Yes; however, the customer must also supply a certified copy of his birth certificate within 15 business days.
   C. No
   D. None of the above

26. What boxes on this form must the customer fill out?

   A. Box 1a, 1b, 2a, 2b, 3a, 6, and 7
   B. All but 1b, 4a, 4b, 4c, 4d, 5a, 5b, and 5c
   C. Box 1a, 3a, 2b, 6 and 7
   D. All of the above

27. What is required to be verified by the postal clerk prior to accepting your application?

   A. That you are a U.S. citizen
   B. You are eligible for carrier delivery
   C. Two forms of ID, one being a photo ID
   D. Your age

28. What would a correct entry be for Box 3a?

   A. Your name
   B. Names of all using the Post Office Box
   C. 324 Main St., Oil City, PA 15434
   D. (123) 456-7890

29. What would a correct entry be for Box 6?

   A. 1878 Forbes Ave., Fargo, ID 25678
   B. Bob Evans and Elizabeth Tyler
   C. Your signature
   D. None of the above

30. Jane Mansfield has two small children and an invalid parent that lives with her. Where does Jane list the names of others in her household who will use this box?

   A. Box 5a
   B. Nowhere; only the primary box holder's name goes on this form.
   C. All must sign box 7
   D. Box 6

CODING AND MEMORY - PART C
Coding Section

The coding and memory sections both use the same "Coding Guide." You have to assign a given address to the proper delivery route for 36 questions in six minutes for the coding section. The coding section is open book and you will refer to the Coding Guide while answering your questions. The Memory Section of Part C requires you to remember the coding guide you used in the Coding Section and assign delivery routes without looking at the guide.

CODING GUIDE	
Address Range	**Delivery Route**
400 – 499 Amherst Ave 101 – 190 Canton St. 1 – 29 Sutton Way	A
500 – 799 Amherst Ave 30 – 199 Sutton Way	B
2500 – 2699 University Blvd. 191 – 299 Canton St. 5 – 25 Rural Route 5	C
All mail that does not fall in one of the address ranges listed above.	D

Address Range - The Coding Guide is divided into two columns. The first column are the Address Ranges for each route. If you look at the first address range of Route A notice that all addresses from 400 through 499 Amherst Avenue are included in route A. Route B picks up the remaining Amherst Avenue addresses from 500 to 799.

Delivery Route - Each delivery route has multiple addresses assigned to that carrier. Route B includes the addresses from 500 to 799 Amherst Avenue and from 30 to 199 Sutton Way. For example, if a letter was addressed 101 Sutton Way you would select Route B for the answer.

Delivery Route D includes all addresses not assigned to a specific route. If you are given the address 332 Canton St. or 1905 Fifth Avenue you would select Delivery Route D as your answer. These addresses are not included in routes A, B, or C.

Sample Questions

	Address	Delivery Route			
1.	425 Amherst Ave.	A	B	C	D
2.	202 Sutton Way	A	B	C	D
3.	277 Canton St.	A	B	C	D
4.	10 Rural Route 6	A	B	C	D
5.	67 Sutton Way	A	B	C	D
6.	2601 University Blvd.	A	B	C	D

You are permitted to look at the Coding Guide while answering the Coding questions in this section. Use the sample answer sheet for the practice exams. Note that the Delivery Routes are listed A through D to the right of the questions in the exam booklet. Mark your answers as prompted by the computer on the actual tests.

Sample Question Answers

Question 1 – The address 425 Amherst Ave. Is in the address range as noted on the coding guide for delivery route A. You would darken answer A on the answer sheet. Remember to NOT put your answers in the exam booklet. Place your answer sheet next to the questions and darken the answer **"A"** on the answer sheet.

CAUTION: When you get to the memory section this will be even more critical. Note the spelling for the street address in this question. It is spelled "Amherst Ave." You will run into answers that are very similar to the street address. For example, Amherst can also be spelled "Amhurst." Look at the entire address. If the street address in question 1 would have been spelled "Amhurst" the answer would have been D, not A.

Question 2 – Sutton Way is located in range A and B for street numbers from 1-199. The address in question two is 202 Sutton Way which is beyond the range of either route A or B. The answer is **"D"** (all mail that does not fall in one of the address ranges listed in A, B or C)

Question 3 – The answer for this question would be **"C."** You will find the address range from 191 - 299 Canton St. In Route C.

Question 4 – You will find a Rural Route in Route C. However, it is Rural Route 5, not Route 6. The correct answer is **"D"** (all mail that does not fall in one of the address ranges listed in A, B or C).

Question 5 – The correct answer is **"B."** 67 Sutton Way is in the address range of 30 - 199 Sutton Way in Route B.

Question 6 – 2601 University Blvd is listed in Route C and the address range is 2500 - 2699. Therefore, the correct answer is **"C."**

The Coding practice exam follows. You will have six minutes to complete this section. Copy the answer sheet in the back of this section and place it next to your book. Time the exam to see how many questions you can answer in the time allotted. The Coding Guide was repeated on this page and on page 120 so that the questions would be next to the Coding Guide. You are permitted to use the Coding Guide for this section.

PART C
Coding Section Practice Exam
36 Questions

CODING GUIDE	
Address Range	**Delivery Route**
400 – 499 Amherst Ave 101 – 190 Canton St. 1 – 29 Sutton Way	A
500 – 799 Amherst Ave 30 – 199 Sutton Way	B
2500 – 2699 University Blvd. 191 – 299 Canton St. 5 – 25 Rural Route 5	C
All mail that does not fall in one of the address ranges listed above.	D

— Answer Sheet page 133, Answer Key page 137 —

CODING EXAM PRACTICE QUESTIONS

START TIME: _____

	Address	Delivery Route			
1.	20 Rural Route 5	A	B	C	D
2.	104 Sutton Way	A	B	C	D
3.	401 Amhurst Ave.	A	B	C	D
4.	1901 University Blvd.	A	B	C	D
5.	587 Amherst Ave.	A	B	C	D
6.	4 Sutton Way	A	B	C	D
7.	2601 Universal Blvd.	A	B	C	D
8.	197 Canton St.	A	B	C	D
9.	145 Sutton Way	A	B	C	D
10.	188 Canton St.	A	B	C	D
11.	401 Amherst Ave.	A	B	C	D
12.	2599 University Blvd.	A	B	C	D
13.	199 Sutton Way	A	B	C	D
14.	399 Canton St.	A	B	C	D
15.	634 Amherst Ave.	A	B	C	D
16.	189 Canton St.	A	B	C	D
17.	2499 University Blvd.	A	B	C	D
18.	2589 University Blvd.	A	B	C	D

TURN PAGE
TO CONTINUE

CONTINUE EXAM

CODING GUIDE	
Address Range	**Delivery Route**
400 – 499 Amherst Ave 101 – 190 Canton St. 1 – 29 Sutton Way	A
500 – 799 Amherst Ave 30 – 199 Sutton Way	B
2500 – 2699 University Blvd. 191 – 299 Canton St. 5 – 25 Rural Route 5	C
All mail that does not fall in one of the address ranges listed above.	D

CONTINUE EXAM

	Address	Delivery Route			
19.	3 Sutton way	A	B	C	D
20.	118 Sutton Way	A	B	C	D
21.	301 Canton St.	A	B	C	D
22.	24 Rural Route 5	A	B	C	D
23.	489 Amherst Ave.	A	B	C	D
24.	2601 Universal Blvd.	A	B	C	D
25.	597 Amherst Ave.	A	B	C	D
26.	19 Rural Route 5	A	B	C	D
27.	264 Canton St.	A	B	C	D
28.	127 Canton St.	A	B	C	D
29.	29 Sutton Way	A	B	C	D
30.	125 Rural Route 5	A	B	C	D
31.	616 Amherst Ave.	A	B	C	D
32.	2695 University Blvd.	A	B	C	D
33.	114 Sutton Way	A	B	C	D
34.	3 Sutton Way	A	B	C	D
35.	29 Rural Route 5	A	B	C	D
36.	201 Canton St.	A	B	C	D

STOP

Record Time Here: _____ Minutes
(You are limited to 6 minutes)

CODING AND MEMORY - PART C
Memory Section

Now that you completed the initial coding section, it's time to work on Part C (Section 2) memorization. You will use the same coding guide that was used in the previous section, and during the actual exam you will be given a short practice section as noted below:

Exam Schedule

- For the first section the examiners will give you three minutes to memorize the Coding Guide. Following this session you will be given 90 seconds to answer eight practice questions without the aide of the Coding Guide. You have to answer the questions from memory.
- Immediately following the practice session the examiners will allow you to study the same Coding Guide for another five minutes before taking the actual 36-question test. You will be allowed seven minutes after the study period to complete the 36 questions without the aide of the Coding Guide. You must answer the questions from memory. The questions for this section are numbered 37 to 72 because the exam for part C includes the first 36 questions that you answered in Section 1 of Part C.

The questions for the memory section are similar to the questions from the previous section. The only difference between the two sections is that in Section One you are allowed to view the Coding Guide while taking the exam. In Section Two you must answer questions 37 - 72 from memory. This is considered by many to be the hardest part of the exam. However, there are techniques that you can use to help you through this section and improve your scores.

Memorization Techniques

Efficient Utilization of Time

You have several study and practice sessions prior to the memory exam. You have an initial two-minute study period in the previous Coding Section along with a 90-second practice exam. **Remember that the same coding guide is used for both the coding and memory sections.** In the memory section you have a three minute study period and then a five-minute study period prior to the 36-question exam. All these pre-exam exercises are to familiarize you with the memorization section. This study guide provides sufficient familiarization so that you can put these sessions to much better use.

I suggest that you use the entire time to study and memorize the Coding Guide. This will give you over 11 minutes to memorize the guide.

If you decide to use the time as suggested above, be sure to at least mark the sample questions associated with the two pre-exam exercises so that test monitors won't stop you to explain the process. Just mark them randomly when told to and then continue studying the Coding Guide.

Number Sequence and Address Ranges

Several memory techniques were discussed earlier in Part A for address checking. The techniques listed here will help you memorize the address ranges and delivery routes in any coding guide.

CODING GUIDE	
Address Range	**Delivery Route**
400 – 499 Amherst Ave 101 – 190 Canton St. 1 – 29 Sutton Way	A
500 – 799 Amherst Ave 30 – 199 Sutton Way	B
2500 – 2699 University Blvd. 191 – 299 Canton St. 5 – 25 Rural Route 5	C
All mail that does not fall in one of the address ranges listed above.	D

The goal is to simplify the Coding Guide to manageable bits that you can recall easily. To do this you have to rearrange the information into a condensed and logical order that you can recall during the exam. To master this technique you need to practice on this Coding Guide and then go on to take the memory test.

Look at the Coding Guide. You will notice that street addresses repeat in the various routes. For example, Amherst Ave. is listed in Route A and B, Sutton Way repeats in A and B, and Canton St. repeats in A and C. Rural Route 5 and University Blvd. are only in route C. The goal is to put these streets into an order and number sequence that you can remember and do it within the allotted time.

Notice that most of the address ranges run sequentially. Amherst Ave. runs from 400 - 499 in Route A and from 500 - 799 in Route B. Canton St., runs from 101 - 190 in Route A and from 191 - 299 in Route C. Two addresses, University Blvd., and Rural Route 5, are only in Delivery Route C. Rewrite the addresses and routes as follows:

- Amherst Ave. 400 - 499A - 799B
- Canton St. 101 - 190A - 299C
- Sutton Way 1 - 29A - 199B
- University Blvd. 2500 - 2699C
- Rural Route 5 - 25C

Remember one key fact. **The second sequential range is actually one count higher than the highest count for that street**. For example, Amherst is listed as "Amherst Ave. 400 - 499A - 799B." Route A runs from 400 - 499, add (1) to 499 and that equals 500. Therefore, Route B Amherst Ave. addresses run from 500 to 799. You only have to remember three numbers with this technique as long as you remember that the second range starts at the very next number in the first range –500 in this example.

Most exams have sequential routes. If you run into a Coding Guide that has non-sequential street addresses, you will have to add the complete second address range to the quick reference memory chart. If the B Route for Amherst Ave. was 601 - 799, you would write the line as "Amherst Ave. 400 - 499A - 601 -799B."

Here are several other techniques that will help you remember the revised lists. You may also have your own memory methods that you use to recall key information. Find out what works best for you and use them to your benefit.

- Reorder the list and use an acronym to recall the list. An acronym is an abbreviation that you can easily recall to start the process. An acronym example would be "IRS," which stands for "Internal Revenue Service." look at the list to see what abbreviation you can devise to help you remember the list. I reorganized the original list to the following:

- Canton St. 101 - 190A - 299C
- Amherst Ave. 400 - 499A - 799B
- Rural Route 5 - 25C
- University Blvd. 2500 - 2699C
- Sutton Way 1 - 29A - 199B

The acronym that I came up with is **CARUS**. Write it out in a horizontal line on your test guide just as a memory jogger. You may not have time to write your entire list down, but this can help.

C = **C**anton St. 101 - 190A - 299C
A = **A**mherst Ave. 400 - 499A - 799B
R = **R**ural Route 5 - 25C
U = **U**niversity Blvd. 2500 - 2699C
S = **S**utton Way 1 - 29A - 199B

Now let's go a little further and use other memory joggers to help you memorize the list. Now that you have the list rewritten and reordered, how do you remember the address ranges?

1. Use associations to remember what is on the list. First, write down the acronym on your test booklet. You have to remember that C = Canton St. Now the routes associated with Canton St. are A and C. C is the first letter of the CARUS in your mind. Let it also equal A for Route A and now the second route will be C for the C in Canton, whatever makes sense to you. Now you know that C = Canton St., and that Canton St. is in Routes A and C. If words don't come to you, just take the first letter of each street in whatever order makes sense to you.

2. Look at the numbers 101-299 for Canton St. next. Where does the route separate? For C = Canton St. subtract 109 and that is where the split is. You can also just remember the three numbers. Coincidentally, 109 is the first two digits of 101 and the last digit of 299. Say it over several times in your head C = Canton St. = 101 - 190A - 299C. You already know that the second route starts at 191, one count up from 190.

3. I believe the easiest way to remember the address ranges and routes is to remember the entire string. Use the acronym to jog your memory and then say C = Canton St. = 101 - 190A - 299C. Close your eyes for a second and visualize the street, numbers and routes. With the acronym **CARUS** and visualization, you should be able to remember this short list in the time offered especially if you use all of the study periods, as recommended, to your advantage.

4. Many who take the exam try to streamline the amount of information to memorize even further by abbreviating the street names. Recall our discussion earlier when you had several street names with different spellings such as "Amherst" and "Amhurst." The actual exam will also include different designators and instead of using "Sutton Way" on a question it may read "Sutton Terrace." Therefore, if you only remembered "Sut" or "Sutton" you would not know what the correct answer was for that question.

5. You may be allowed to take notes during the memory test. If allowed, you can write the acronym that you devise on the note paper they provide and quickly note the street names and ranges. However, you need to practice before attempting this, otherwise you may take too much time and not finish the exam.

PART C
Coding Memory Section Practice Exam

You will be given five minutes to study the Coding Guide. Turn to page 123 and study the Coding Guide for <u>five minutes</u>. (Time this exercise.) We will use the same Coding Guide as the one used in the previous section that they do in the actual exam. A second practice exam follows this one using a different Coding Guide to give you more practice with this section.

If you don't have someone to time you, enter your start time below, and when you finish write down the stop time. Determine the total time used for the exam. Place a copy of the answer sheet next to your book for this section.

— **Answer Sheet page 133, Answer Key page 137** —

START TIME _____

	Address	Delivery Route			
37.	22 Sutton Way	A	B	C	D
38.	27 Rural Route 5	A	B	C	D
39.	534 Amherst Ave.	A	B	C	D
40.	2601 University Blvd.	A	B	C	D
41.	189 Canton St.	A	B	C	D
42.	34 Sutton Way	A	B	C	D
43.	2701 Universal Blvd.	A	B	C	D
44.	1924 Rural Route 5	A	B	C	D
45.	299 Canyon St.	A	B	C	D
46.	168 Canton St.	A	B	C	D
47.	521 Amherst Ave.	A	B	C	D
48.	189 Sutton Way.	A	B	C	D
49.	199 Sutton Place	A	B	C	D
50.	2599 University Blvd.	A	B	C	D
51.	2501 University Blvd.	A	B	C	D
52.	29 Sutton Way	A	B	C	D
53.	45 Sutton Way.	A	B	C	D
54.	35 Rural Route 5	A	B	C	D

CONTINUE EXAM

	Address	Delivery Route			
55.	19 Sutton Way	A	B	C	D
56.	31 Sutton Way	A	B	C	D
57.	205 Canton St.	A	B	C	D
58.	2691 University Blvd.	A	B	C	D
59.	432 Amherst Ave.	A	B	C	D
60.	801 Amherst Ave.	A	B	C	D
61.	151 Canton St.	A	B	C	D
62.	45 Sexton Way	A	B	C	D
63.	19 Rural Route 5	A	B	C	D
64.	619 Amherst Ave.	A	B	C	D
65.	107 Sutton Way	A	B	C	D
66.	140 Canton St.	A	B	C	D
67.	435 Fifth Ave.	A	B	C	D
68.	1500 University Blvd.	A	B	C	D
69.	122 Sutton Way	A	B	C	D
70.	35 Smithton Place	A	B	C	D
71.	578 Amherst Ave.	A	B	C	D
72.	149 Canton St.	A	B	C	D

STOP

Record Time Here: _____ Minutes

(You are limited to 7 minutes)

The memory section is considered by many to be the most difficult. Therefore, we included several practice exams. Before going on to the next memory practice exam, review pages 122 to 125. Experiment with the memory techniques offered in this study guide or use your own unique methods to memorize the following new Coding Guide.

PART C
Coding Memory Section Practice Exam 2

You will be given five minutes to study this new Coding Guide. (Time this exercise.) If you don't have someone to time you, enter your start time below and when you finish write down the stop time. Determine the total time used for the exam. Remember, in the actual exam you only have seven minutes to complete this section. Place a copy of the answer sheet next to your book for this section.

START TIME _____

CODING GUIDE	
Address Range	**Delivery Route**
1891 – 3100 Eagle LN 25 – 40 Amberwood Hwy 200 – 499 Lemington CT	A
3101 – 3800 Eagle LN 500 – 799 Lemington CT	B
620 - 800 Trent Pkwy 6000 – 10000 Bedford Ave. 41 – 100 Amberwood Hwy	C
All mail that does not fall in one of the address ranges listed above.	D

STOP TIME _____

You are given 5 minutes to memorize
this Coding Guide before starting the next practice exam.

START TIME _____

7 Minutes to Complete Practice Memory Exam 2

— Answer Sheet page 133, Answer Key page 137 —

	Address	Delivery Route			
37.	50 Amberwood Hwy	A	B	C	D
38.	3199 Eagle LN	A	B	C	D
39.	199 Lemington CT	A	B	C	D
40.	621 Trent Pkwy	A	B	C	D
41.	7067 Bedford Ave.	A	B	C	D
42.	1955 Eagle LN	A	B	C	D
43.	99 Amberwood Hwy	A	B	C	D
44.	501 Lemington CT	A	B	C	D
45.	899 Trent Pkwy	A	B	C	D
46.	3788 Eagle LN	A	B	C	D
47.	25 Amberwood Hwy	A	B	C	D
48.	800 Lexington CT	A	B	C	D
49.	2205 Eagle LN	A	B	C	D
50.	719 Trent Pkwy	A	B	C	D
51.	125 Amberwood Hwy	A	B	C	D
52.	6099 Bedford Ave.	A	B	C	D
53.	700 Lemington CT	A	B	C	D
54.	1898 Eagle LN	A	B	C	D

Continued on next page

CONTINUE EXAM

	Address	Delivery Route			
55.	9989 Bedford Ave.	A	B	C	D
56.	701 Lemington CT	A	B	C	D
57.	43 Amberwood Hwy	A	B	C	D
58.	2901 Eagle LN	A	B	C	D
59.	799 Trent Pkwy	A	B	C	D
60.	7001 Bedford Ave.	A	B	C	D
61.	29 Amberwood Hwy	A	B	C	D
62.	278 Lemington CT	A	B	C	D
63.	3201 Eagle LN	A	B	C	D
64.	619 Amherst Ave	A	B	C	D
65.	654 Trent Pkwy	A	B	C	D
66.	30 Amberwood Hwy	A	B	C	D
67.	775 Lemington CT	A	B	C	D
68.	2677 Eagle LN	A	B	C	D
69.	8888 Bedford Ave.	A	B	C	D
70.	700 Trent Pkwy	A	B	C	D
71.	199 Amberwood Hwy	A	B	C	D
72.	4102 Eagle LN	A	B	C	D

STOP

Record Time Here: _____ Minutes
(You are limited to 7 minutes)

PERSONAL EXPERIENCE AND CHARACTERISTICS INVENTORY
PART D

Part D is administered online when you first apply. If your results indicated you are well suited for postal employment you will be scheduled to take Parts A, B and C at a local testing facility. This section takes 90 minutes to complete and has 150 questions. The postal service evaluates your personal experience, characteristics and tendencies. You will be asked your likes and dislikes, whether you have experience in certain areas. You really can't prepare for this section; it's your personal profile. if you answer the questions honestly the postal service will be able to identify the job that is best suited to your characteristics.

The answers are multiple choice. The question *"Do you like to work in groups?"* would have the answers (A) Strongly Agree, (B) Agree, (C), Disagree, (D) Strongly Disagree. A question similar to *"Are you willing to work rotating shifts?"* would have the answers (A) Very Often, (B) Often, (C) Sometimes, (D) Rarely.

Content and Structure

Part D is divided into two groups. The first group of questions includes multiple choice questions or statements with the following possible answers:

A. Strongly Agree	OR	A. Very Often
B. Agree		B. Often
C. Disagree		C. Sometimes
D. Strongly Disagree		D. Rarely

The second group of questions can have as few as four to as many as nine answer choices. You choose the answer that best describes your personal feelings and concerns.

Several typical question/statements are listed below so that you will know what to expect:

S1.   You like to work independently without interruptions.

A. Strongly Agree
B. Agree
C. Disagree
D. Strongly Disagree

S2.   You like to carefully prepare for events or activities in advance.

A. Very Often
B. Often
C. Sometimes
D. Rarely

S3.   What type of activities do you like the most?

    A. activities that require planning and attention
    B. activities that require little planning
    C. activities that are physical and challenging
    D. activities that are done while sitting
    E. activities that don't require much thought
    F. outdoor activities
    G. not sure

Answer the questions honestly and pick the answer that represents your thoughts. If several answers seem to fit pick the one and **ONLY ONE** reply that best represents how you feel about the question or statement. There are no right or wrong answers on this part of the exam. You can select only one answer for each question. Use your entire background, including work experience, volunteer work, school work, military service, anything from your background that will help you relate to the question.

> If you complete this section early you can turn
> in your booklet and leave the exam room.

You need to be careful with this section. The design of the questions can reveal whether you are trying to manipulate the exam. Questions are reworded or come from a different perspective, and it is impossible to remember all your answers and then evaluate what each question may mean to the examiners. The questions were designed by professionals, and the postal service has not released any information on how this section is evaluated and scored. These types of tests are typically used to evaluate work ethics, attitudes, teamwork, customer service, skills, performance, and productivity.

SAMPLE ANSWER SHEETS

The next four pages have two complete sets of answer sheets that you can use for the practice exams. You can also make up additional practice exam questions and make copies of the answer sheets for additional practice. If you don't have a copy machine handy you can remove the next two pages and use the answer sheet for the practice exams. You will still have another set of answer sheets on pages 135 and 136.

The answer sheet layout is not identical to what you will find in the exam. Both sides of the actual exam answer sheet are used. Your personal information will be placed at the top of the front and answer sheet and Part A and B answers are placed at the bottom. The back of the actual sheet is used to mark your answers for Part C and D. Our layout is different to accommodate the practice tests.

SAMPLE ANSWER SHEET (1)

Part A- Address Checking

1 Ⓐ Ⓑ Ⓒ Ⓓ	16 Ⓐ Ⓑ Ⓒ Ⓓ	31 Ⓐ Ⓑ Ⓒ Ⓓ	46 Ⓐ Ⓑ Ⓒ Ⓓ
2 Ⓐ Ⓑ Ⓒ Ⓓ	17 Ⓐ Ⓑ Ⓒ Ⓓ	32 Ⓐ Ⓑ Ⓒ Ⓓ	47 Ⓐ Ⓑ Ⓒ Ⓓ
3 Ⓐ Ⓑ Ⓒ Ⓓ	18 Ⓐ Ⓑ Ⓒ Ⓓ	33 Ⓐ Ⓑ Ⓒ Ⓓ	48 Ⓐ Ⓑ Ⓒ Ⓓ
4 Ⓐ Ⓑ Ⓒ Ⓓ	19 Ⓐ Ⓑ Ⓒ Ⓓ	34 Ⓐ Ⓑ Ⓒ Ⓓ	49 Ⓐ Ⓑ Ⓒ Ⓓ
5 Ⓐ Ⓑ Ⓒ Ⓓ	20 Ⓐ Ⓑ Ⓒ Ⓓ	35 Ⓐ Ⓑ Ⓒ Ⓓ	50 Ⓐ Ⓑ Ⓒ Ⓓ
6 Ⓐ Ⓑ Ⓒ Ⓓ	21 Ⓐ Ⓑ Ⓒ Ⓓ	36 Ⓐ Ⓑ Ⓒ Ⓓ	51 Ⓐ Ⓑ Ⓒ Ⓓ
7 Ⓐ Ⓑ Ⓒ Ⓓ	22 Ⓐ Ⓑ Ⓒ Ⓓ	37 Ⓐ Ⓑ Ⓒ Ⓓ	52 Ⓐ Ⓑ Ⓒ Ⓓ
8 Ⓐ Ⓑ Ⓒ Ⓓ	23 Ⓐ Ⓑ Ⓒ Ⓓ	38 Ⓐ Ⓑ Ⓒ Ⓓ	53 Ⓐ Ⓑ Ⓒ Ⓓ
9 Ⓐ Ⓑ Ⓒ Ⓓ	24 Ⓐ Ⓑ Ⓒ Ⓓ	39 Ⓐ Ⓑ Ⓒ Ⓓ	54 Ⓐ Ⓑ Ⓒ Ⓓ
10 Ⓐ Ⓑ Ⓒ Ⓓ	25 Ⓐ Ⓑ Ⓒ Ⓓ	40 Ⓐ Ⓑ Ⓒ Ⓓ	55 Ⓐ Ⓑ Ⓒ Ⓓ
11 Ⓐ Ⓑ Ⓒ Ⓓ	26 Ⓐ Ⓑ Ⓒ Ⓓ	41 Ⓐ Ⓑ Ⓒ Ⓓ	56 Ⓐ Ⓑ Ⓒ Ⓓ
12 Ⓐ Ⓑ Ⓒ Ⓓ	27 Ⓐ Ⓑ Ⓒ Ⓓ	42 Ⓐ Ⓑ Ⓒ Ⓓ	57 Ⓐ Ⓑ Ⓒ Ⓓ
13 Ⓐ Ⓑ Ⓒ Ⓓ	28 Ⓐ Ⓑ Ⓒ Ⓓ	43 Ⓐ Ⓑ Ⓒ Ⓓ	58 Ⓐ Ⓑ Ⓒ Ⓓ
14 Ⓐ Ⓑ Ⓒ Ⓓ	29 Ⓐ Ⓑ Ⓒ Ⓓ	44 Ⓐ Ⓑ Ⓒ Ⓓ	59 Ⓐ Ⓑ Ⓒ Ⓓ
15 Ⓐ Ⓑ Ⓒ Ⓓ	30 Ⓐ Ⓑ Ⓒ Ⓓ	45 Ⓐ Ⓑ Ⓒ Ⓓ	60 Ⓐ Ⓑ Ⓒ Ⓓ

Part B – Forms Completion

1 Ⓐ Ⓑ Ⓒ Ⓓ	16 Ⓐ Ⓑ Ⓒ Ⓓ
2 Ⓐ Ⓑ Ⓒ Ⓓ	17 Ⓐ Ⓑ Ⓒ Ⓓ
3 Ⓐ Ⓑ Ⓒ Ⓓ	18 Ⓐ Ⓑ Ⓒ Ⓓ
4 Ⓐ Ⓑ Ⓒ Ⓓ	19 Ⓐ Ⓑ Ⓒ Ⓓ
5 Ⓐ Ⓑ Ⓒ Ⓓ	20 Ⓐ Ⓑ Ⓒ Ⓓ
6 Ⓐ Ⓑ Ⓒ Ⓓ	21 Ⓐ Ⓑ Ⓒ Ⓓ
7 Ⓐ Ⓑ Ⓒ Ⓓ	22 Ⓐ Ⓑ Ⓒ Ⓓ
8 Ⓐ Ⓑ Ⓒ Ⓓ	23 Ⓐ Ⓑ Ⓒ Ⓓ
9 Ⓐ Ⓑ Ⓒ Ⓓ	24 Ⓐ Ⓑ Ⓒ Ⓓ
10 Ⓐ Ⓑ Ⓒ Ⓓ	25 Ⓐ Ⓑ Ⓒ Ⓓ
11 Ⓐ Ⓑ Ⓒ Ⓓ	26 Ⓐ Ⓑ Ⓒ Ⓓ
12 Ⓐ Ⓑ Ⓒ Ⓓ	27 Ⓐ Ⓑ Ⓒ Ⓓ
13 Ⓐ Ⓑ Ⓒ Ⓓ	28 Ⓐ Ⓑ Ⓒ Ⓓ
14 Ⓐ Ⓑ Ⓒ Ⓓ	29 Ⓐ Ⓑ Ⓒ Ⓓ
15 Ⓐ Ⓑ Ⓒ Ⓓ	30 Ⓐ Ⓑ Ⓒ Ⓓ

Part C - Coding

1	Ⓐ Ⓑ Ⓒ Ⓓ	13 Ⓐ Ⓑ Ⓒ Ⓓ	25 Ⓐ Ⓑ Ⓒ Ⓓ
2	Ⓐ Ⓑ Ⓒ Ⓓ	14 Ⓐ Ⓑ Ⓒ Ⓓ	26 Ⓐ Ⓑ Ⓒ Ⓓ
3	Ⓐ Ⓑ Ⓒ Ⓓ	15 Ⓐ Ⓑ Ⓒ Ⓓ	27 Ⓐ Ⓑ Ⓒ Ⓓ
4	Ⓐ Ⓑ Ⓒ Ⓓ	16 Ⓐ Ⓑ Ⓒ Ⓓ	28 Ⓐ Ⓑ Ⓒ Ⓓ
5	Ⓐ Ⓑ Ⓒ Ⓓ	17 Ⓐ Ⓑ Ⓒ Ⓓ	29 Ⓐ Ⓑ Ⓒ Ⓓ
6	Ⓐ Ⓑ Ⓒ Ⓓ	18 Ⓐ Ⓑ Ⓒ Ⓓ	30 Ⓐ Ⓑ Ⓒ Ⓓ
7	Ⓐ Ⓑ Ⓒ Ⓓ	19 Ⓐ Ⓑ Ⓒ Ⓓ	31 Ⓐ Ⓑ Ⓒ Ⓓ
8	Ⓐ Ⓑ Ⓒ Ⓓ	20 Ⓐ Ⓑ Ⓒ Ⓓ	32 Ⓐ Ⓑ Ⓒ Ⓓ
9	Ⓐ Ⓑ Ⓒ Ⓓ	21 Ⓐ Ⓑ Ⓒ Ⓓ	33 Ⓐ Ⓑ Ⓒ Ⓓ
10	Ⓐ Ⓑ Ⓒ Ⓓ	22 Ⓐ Ⓑ Ⓒ Ⓓ	34 Ⓐ Ⓑ Ⓒ Ⓓ
11	Ⓐ Ⓑ Ⓒ Ⓓ	23 Ⓐ Ⓑ Ⓒ Ⓓ	35 Ⓐ Ⓑ Ⓒ Ⓓ
12	Ⓐ Ⓑ Ⓒ Ⓓ	24 Ⓐ Ⓑ Ⓒ Ⓓ	36 Ⓐ Ⓑ Ⓒ Ⓓ

Part C - Memory

37	Ⓐ Ⓑ Ⓒ Ⓓ	49 Ⓐ Ⓑ Ⓒ Ⓓ	61 Ⓐ Ⓑ Ⓒ Ⓓ
38	Ⓐ Ⓑ Ⓒ Ⓓ	50 Ⓐ Ⓑ Ⓒ Ⓓ	62 Ⓐ Ⓑ Ⓒ Ⓓ
39	Ⓐ Ⓑ Ⓒ Ⓓ	51 Ⓐ Ⓑ Ⓒ Ⓓ	63 Ⓐ Ⓑ Ⓒ Ⓓ
40	Ⓐ Ⓑ Ⓒ Ⓓ	52 Ⓐ Ⓑ Ⓒ Ⓓ	64 Ⓐ Ⓑ Ⓒ Ⓓ
41	Ⓐ Ⓑ Ⓒ Ⓓ	53 Ⓐ Ⓑ Ⓒ Ⓓ	65 Ⓐ Ⓑ Ⓒ Ⓓ
42	Ⓐ Ⓑ Ⓒ Ⓓ	54 Ⓐ Ⓑ Ⓒ Ⓓ	66 Ⓐ Ⓑ Ⓒ Ⓓ
43	Ⓐ Ⓑ Ⓒ Ⓓ	55 Ⓐ Ⓑ Ⓒ Ⓓ	67 Ⓐ Ⓑ Ⓒ Ⓓ
44	Ⓐ Ⓑ Ⓒ Ⓓ	56 Ⓐ Ⓑ Ⓒ Ⓓ	68 Ⓐ Ⓑ Ⓒ Ⓓ
45	Ⓐ Ⓑ Ⓒ Ⓓ	57 Ⓐ Ⓑ Ⓒ Ⓓ	69 Ⓐ Ⓑ Ⓒ Ⓓ
46	Ⓐ Ⓑ Ⓒ Ⓓ	58 Ⓐ Ⓑ Ⓒ Ⓓ	70 Ⓐ Ⓑ Ⓒ Ⓓ
47	Ⓐ Ⓑ Ⓒ Ⓓ	59 Ⓐ Ⓑ Ⓒ Ⓓ	71 Ⓐ Ⓑ Ⓒ Ⓓ
48	Ⓐ Ⓑ Ⓒ Ⓓ	60 Ⓐ Ⓑ Ⓒ Ⓓ	72 Ⓐ Ⓑ Ⓒ Ⓓ

SAMPLE ANSWER SHEET (21)

Part A- Address Checking

1 Ⓐ Ⓑ Ⓒ Ⓓ	16 Ⓐ Ⓑ Ⓒ Ⓓ	31 Ⓐ Ⓑ Ⓒ Ⓓ	46 Ⓐ Ⓑ Ⓒ Ⓓ
2 Ⓐ Ⓑ Ⓒ Ⓓ	17 Ⓐ Ⓑ Ⓒ Ⓓ	32 Ⓐ Ⓑ Ⓒ Ⓓ	47 Ⓐ Ⓑ Ⓒ Ⓓ
3 Ⓐ Ⓑ Ⓒ Ⓓ	18 Ⓐ Ⓑ Ⓒ Ⓓ	33 Ⓐ Ⓑ Ⓒ Ⓓ	48 Ⓐ Ⓑ Ⓒ Ⓓ
4 Ⓐ Ⓑ Ⓒ Ⓓ	19 Ⓐ Ⓑ Ⓒ Ⓓ	34 Ⓐ Ⓑ Ⓒ Ⓓ	49 Ⓐ Ⓑ Ⓒ Ⓓ
5 Ⓐ Ⓑ Ⓒ Ⓓ	20 Ⓐ Ⓑ Ⓒ Ⓓ	35 Ⓐ Ⓑ Ⓒ Ⓓ	50 Ⓐ Ⓑ Ⓒ Ⓓ
6 Ⓐ Ⓑ Ⓒ Ⓓ	21 Ⓐ Ⓑ Ⓒ Ⓓ	36 Ⓐ Ⓑ Ⓒ Ⓓ	51 Ⓐ Ⓑ Ⓒ Ⓓ
7 Ⓐ Ⓑ Ⓒ Ⓓ	22 Ⓐ Ⓑ Ⓒ Ⓓ	37 Ⓐ Ⓑ Ⓒ Ⓓ	52 Ⓐ Ⓑ Ⓒ Ⓓ
8 Ⓐ Ⓑ Ⓒ Ⓓ	23 Ⓐ Ⓑ Ⓒ Ⓓ	38 Ⓐ Ⓑ Ⓒ Ⓓ	53 Ⓐ Ⓑ Ⓒ Ⓓ
9 Ⓐ Ⓑ Ⓒ Ⓓ	24 Ⓐ Ⓑ Ⓒ Ⓓ	39 Ⓐ Ⓑ Ⓒ Ⓓ	54 Ⓐ Ⓑ Ⓒ Ⓓ
10 Ⓐ Ⓑ Ⓒ Ⓓ	25 Ⓐ Ⓑ Ⓒ Ⓓ	40 Ⓐ Ⓑ Ⓒ Ⓓ	55 Ⓐ Ⓑ Ⓒ Ⓓ
11 Ⓐ Ⓑ Ⓒ Ⓓ	26 Ⓐ Ⓑ Ⓒ Ⓓ	41 Ⓐ Ⓑ Ⓒ Ⓓ	56 Ⓐ Ⓑ Ⓒ Ⓓ
12 Ⓐ Ⓑ Ⓒ Ⓓ	27 Ⓐ Ⓑ Ⓒ Ⓓ	42 Ⓐ Ⓑ Ⓒ Ⓓ	57 Ⓐ Ⓑ Ⓒ Ⓓ
13 Ⓐ Ⓑ Ⓒ Ⓓ	28 Ⓐ Ⓑ Ⓒ Ⓓ	43 Ⓐ Ⓑ Ⓒ Ⓓ	58 Ⓐ Ⓑ Ⓒ Ⓓ
14 Ⓐ Ⓑ Ⓒ Ⓓ	29 Ⓐ Ⓑ Ⓒ Ⓓ	44 Ⓐ Ⓑ Ⓒ Ⓓ	59 Ⓐ Ⓑ Ⓒ Ⓓ
15 Ⓐ Ⓑ Ⓒ Ⓓ	30 Ⓐ Ⓑ Ⓒ Ⓓ	45 Ⓐ Ⓑ Ⓒ Ⓓ	60 Ⓐ Ⓑ Ⓒ Ⓓ

Part B – Forms Completion

1 Ⓐ Ⓑ Ⓒ Ⓓ	16 Ⓐ Ⓑ Ⓒ Ⓓ
2 Ⓐ Ⓑ Ⓒ Ⓓ	17 Ⓐ Ⓑ Ⓒ Ⓓ
3 Ⓐ Ⓑ Ⓒ Ⓓ	18 Ⓐ Ⓑ Ⓒ Ⓓ
4 Ⓐ Ⓑ Ⓒ Ⓓ	19 Ⓐ Ⓑ Ⓒ Ⓓ
5 Ⓐ Ⓑ Ⓒ Ⓓ	20 Ⓐ Ⓑ Ⓒ Ⓓ
6 Ⓐ Ⓑ Ⓒ Ⓓ	21 Ⓐ Ⓑ Ⓒ Ⓓ
7 Ⓐ Ⓑ Ⓒ Ⓓ	22 Ⓐ Ⓑ Ⓒ Ⓓ
8 Ⓐ Ⓑ Ⓒ Ⓓ	23 Ⓐ Ⓑ Ⓒ Ⓓ
9 Ⓐ Ⓑ Ⓒ Ⓓ	24 Ⓐ Ⓑ Ⓒ Ⓓ
10 Ⓐ Ⓑ Ⓒ Ⓓ	25 Ⓐ Ⓑ Ⓒ Ⓓ
11 Ⓐ Ⓑ Ⓒ Ⓓ	26 Ⓐ Ⓑ Ⓒ Ⓓ
12 Ⓐ Ⓑ Ⓒ Ⓓ	27 Ⓐ Ⓑ Ⓒ Ⓓ
13 Ⓐ Ⓑ Ⓒ Ⓓ	28 Ⓐ Ⓑ Ⓒ Ⓓ
14 Ⓐ Ⓑ Ⓒ Ⓓ	29 Ⓐ Ⓑ Ⓒ Ⓓ
15 Ⓐ Ⓑ Ⓒ Ⓓ	30 Ⓐ Ⓑ Ⓒ Ⓓ

Part C - Coding

1	Ⓐ Ⓑ Ⓒ Ⓓ	13	Ⓐ Ⓑ Ⓒ Ⓓ	25	Ⓐ Ⓑ Ⓒ Ⓓ
2	Ⓐ Ⓑ Ⓒ Ⓓ	14	Ⓐ Ⓑ Ⓒ Ⓓ	26	Ⓐ Ⓑ Ⓒ Ⓓ
3	Ⓐ Ⓑ Ⓒ Ⓓ	15	Ⓐ Ⓑ Ⓒ Ⓓ	27	Ⓐ Ⓑ Ⓒ Ⓓ
4	Ⓐ Ⓑ Ⓒ Ⓓ	16	Ⓐ Ⓑ Ⓒ Ⓓ	28	Ⓐ Ⓑ Ⓒ Ⓓ
5	Ⓐ Ⓑ Ⓒ Ⓓ	17	Ⓐ Ⓑ Ⓒ Ⓓ	29	Ⓐ Ⓑ Ⓒ Ⓓ
6	Ⓐ Ⓑ Ⓒ Ⓓ	18	Ⓐ Ⓑ Ⓒ Ⓓ	30	Ⓐ Ⓑ Ⓒ Ⓓ
7	Ⓐ Ⓑ Ⓒ Ⓓ	19	Ⓐ Ⓑ Ⓒ Ⓓ	31	Ⓐ Ⓑ Ⓒ Ⓓ
8	Ⓐ Ⓑ Ⓒ Ⓓ	20	Ⓐ Ⓑ Ⓒ Ⓓ	32	Ⓐ Ⓑ Ⓒ Ⓓ
9	Ⓐ Ⓑ Ⓒ Ⓓ	21	Ⓐ Ⓑ Ⓒ Ⓓ	33	Ⓐ Ⓑ Ⓒ Ⓓ
10	Ⓐ Ⓑ Ⓒ Ⓓ	22	Ⓐ Ⓑ Ⓒ Ⓓ	34	Ⓐ Ⓑ Ⓒ Ⓓ
11	Ⓐ Ⓑ Ⓒ Ⓓ	23	Ⓐ Ⓑ Ⓒ Ⓓ	35	Ⓐ Ⓑ Ⓒ Ⓓ
12	Ⓐ Ⓑ Ⓒ Ⓓ	24	Ⓐ Ⓑ Ⓒ Ⓓ	36	Ⓐ Ⓑ Ⓒ Ⓓ

Part C - Memory

37	Ⓐ Ⓑ Ⓒ Ⓓ	49	Ⓐ Ⓑ Ⓒ Ⓓ	61	Ⓐ Ⓑ Ⓒ Ⓓ
38	Ⓐ Ⓑ Ⓒ Ⓓ	50	Ⓐ Ⓑ Ⓒ Ⓓ	62	Ⓐ Ⓑ Ⓒ Ⓓ
39	Ⓐ Ⓑ Ⓒ Ⓓ	51	Ⓐ Ⓑ Ⓒ Ⓓ	63	Ⓐ Ⓑ Ⓒ Ⓓ
40	Ⓐ Ⓑ Ⓒ Ⓓ	52	Ⓐ Ⓑ Ⓒ Ⓓ	64	Ⓐ Ⓑ Ⓒ Ⓓ
41	Ⓐ Ⓑ Ⓒ Ⓓ	53	Ⓐ Ⓑ Ⓒ Ⓓ	65	Ⓐ Ⓑ Ⓒ Ⓓ
42	Ⓐ Ⓑ Ⓒ Ⓓ	54	Ⓐ Ⓑ Ⓒ Ⓓ	66	Ⓐ Ⓑ Ⓒ Ⓓ
43	Ⓐ Ⓑ Ⓒ Ⓓ	55	Ⓐ Ⓑ Ⓒ Ⓓ	67	Ⓐ Ⓑ Ⓒ Ⓓ
44	Ⓐ Ⓑ Ⓒ Ⓓ	56	Ⓐ Ⓑ Ⓒ Ⓓ	68	Ⓐ Ⓑ Ⓒ Ⓓ
45	Ⓐ Ⓑ Ⓒ Ⓓ	57	Ⓐ Ⓑ Ⓒ Ⓓ	69	Ⓐ Ⓑ Ⓒ Ⓓ
46	Ⓐ Ⓑ Ⓒ Ⓓ	58	Ⓐ Ⓑ Ⓒ Ⓓ	70	Ⓐ Ⓑ Ⓒ Ⓓ
47	Ⓐ Ⓑ Ⓒ Ⓓ	59	Ⓐ Ⓑ Ⓒ Ⓓ	71	Ⓐ Ⓑ Ⓒ Ⓓ
48	Ⓐ Ⓑ Ⓒ Ⓓ	60	Ⓐ Ⓑ Ⓒ Ⓓ	72	Ⓐ Ⓑ Ⓒ Ⓓ

Answer Key
Practice Exams

Address Checking Page 102 - 104		**Forms Completion** Pages 107 - 115

#	Ans	#	Ans	#	Ans
1.	C	31.	A	1.	B
2.	A	32.	B	2.	C
3.	D	33.	C	3.	B
4.	A	34.	C	4.	D
5.	D	35.	D	5.	C
6.	B	36.	B	6.	C
7.	A	37.	B	7.	C
8.	B	38.	C	8.	C
9.	D	39.	A	9.	B
10.	A	40.	D	10.	C
11.	D	41.	C	11.	C
12.	D	42.	B	12.	D
13.	C	43.	D	13.	B
14.	D	44.	A	14.	C
15.	A	45.	C	15.	A
16.	B	46.	B	16.	A
17.	B	47.	D	17.	C
18.	C	48.	A	18.	C
19.	C	49.	C	19.	C
20.	B	50.	B	20.	B
21.	A	51.	A	21.	B
22.	B	52.	D	22.	B
23.	C	53.	C	23.	B
24.	D	54.	B	24.	C
25.	A	55.	D	25.	C
26.	C	56.	A	26.	B
27.	B	57.	C	27.	C
28.	D	58.	B	28.	C
29.	B	59.	B	29.	B
30.	A	60.	A	30.	D

Answer Key
Practice Exams
Coding & Memory Pages 119 - 130

Coding	Memory (1)	Memory (2)
1. C	37. A	37. C
2. B	38. D	38. B
3. D	39. B	39. D
4. D	40. C	40. C
5. B	41. A	41. C
6. A	42. B	42. A
7. D	43. D	43. C
8. C	44. D	44. B
9. B	45. D	45. D
10. A	46. A	46. B
11. A	47. B	47. A
12. C	48. B	48. D
13. B	49. D	49. A
14. D	50. C	50. C
15. B	51. C	51. D
16. A	52. A	52. C
17. D	53. B	53. B
18. C	54. D	54. A
19. A	55. A	55. C
20. B	56. B	56. B
21. D	57. C	57. C
22. C	58. C	58. A
23. A	59. A	59. C
24. D	60. D	60. C
25. B	61. A	61. A
26. C	62. D	62. A
27. C	63. C	63. B
28. A	64. B	64. D
29. A	65. B	65. C
30. D	66. A	66. A
31. B	67. D	67. B
32. C	68. D	68. A
33. B	69. B	69. C
34. A	70. D	70. C
35. D	71. B	71. D
36. C	72. A	72. D

Chapter Six
The Interview Process

There are several types of interviews you may encounter. The most common interview is called a *Structured Interview*. Most traditional interviews are based on this format. Below are descriptions of several interview types that you may encounter and what you can expect in each of them.[1]

TYPES OF INTERVIEWS

■ *Screening Interview*. A preliminary interview either in person or by phone, in which an agency or company representative determines whether you have the basic qualifications to warrant a subsequent interview.

■ *Structured Interview*. In a structured interview, the interviewer explores certain predetermined areas using questions which have been written in advance. The interviewer has a written description of the experience, skills and personality traits of an "ideal" candidate. Your experience and skills are compared to specific job tasks. This type of interview is very common.

■ *Targeted Interview*. Although similar to the structured interview, the areas covered are much more limited. Key qualifications for success on the job are identified and relevant questions are prepared in advance.

■ *Situational Interview*. Situations are set up which simulate common problems you may encounter on the job. Your responses to these situations are measured against pre-determined standards. This approach is often used as one part of a traditional interview rather than as an entire interview format.

---

[1] The Job Search Guide, U.S. Department of Labor.

INTERVIEW NOTIFICATION

The following email interview notification was received by an applicant on April 23, 2018. You can expect a similar email message if you are selected for an interview. We changed the name of the applicant and position type.

Sample Notification Letter

April 23, 2018

Dear Ms. Sara Smith

This letter is in reference to your application for job posting POSTMASTER RELIEF (RMPO) - 20 HR - LANESVILLE NY 12450 NC10173672

We would like to interview you so you can learn more about this employment opportunity and we can learn more about you. Please open the document(s) attached to this correspondence and follow the instructions and guidance contained in the attachments.

If you need to change the time and/or date schedule for this appointment. You MUST notify the official as mentioned in the attached notification.

Sincerely,

Human Resources

THIS IS AN AUTOMATIC SYSTEM GENERATED EMAIL. PLEASE DO NOT RESPOND TO THIS MESSAGE.

Attached to this email will be an instructional document with the date, time, and location of the interview with contact information. You must bring the following items to the interview:

- 1 or 2 BLACK PENS
- A copy of your Social Security Card
- A copy of your drivers license or US Passport
- SELECTIVE SERVICE CARD (if card is unavailable, go to www.ssa.gov to obtain & print the verification, applies to all males 18 yrs,' - 26 years old.
- (Note: ALL MALES BORN AFTER 12/31/1959 MUST BE REGISTERED WITH SELECTIVE SERVICE.

General Information:
- **This is not an offer of employment. Do not resign from your present position at this time."**

- Your application may not have gaps between periods of employment /unemployment going back 7 years or to your 16th birthday, whichever is more recent. Please be prepared with dates, complete addresses, and phone numbers etc. to complete this information; if not previously provided.
- Failure to report to this interview as scheduled will result in you no longer being considered for this position. Late arrivals will not be interviewed. There is no alternate date. If you cannot attend or are no longer interested, withdraw your application through eCareer.

The interview strategies discussed below can be used effectively in any type of interview you may encounter.

BEFORE THE INTERVIEW

Prepare in advance. The better prepared you are, the less anxious you will be and the greater your chances for success.

- *Role Play.* Find someone to role play the interview with you. This person should be someone with whom you feel comfortable and with whom you can discuss your weaknesses freely. The person should be objective and knowledgeable, perhaps a business associate.

- Use a mirror or video camera when you role play to see what kind of image you project.

Assess your interviewing skills.

- What are your strengths and weaknesses? Work on correcting your weaknesses, such as speaking rapidly, talking too loudly or softly, and nervous habits such as shaking hands or inappropriate facial expressions.

- Learn the questions that are commonly asked and prepare answers to them. Examples of commonly asked interview questions are provided later in this chapter. Practice giving answers which are brief but thorough.

- Decide what questions you would like to ask and practice politely interjecting them at different points in the interview.

Evaluate your strengths

- Evaluate your skills, abilities and education as they relate to the type of job you are seeking.

■   Review the job announcement and/or job description and match your skills, education, and background to the targeted position. Summarize your strengths during the interview in relevant questions.

Assess your overall appearance.

■   Find out what clothing is appropriate for your job occupation. Acceptable attire for most professional positions is conservative.

■   Your clothes should be clean and pressed and your shoes polished.

■   Your hair must be neat, nails clean, and generally well groomed.

Research the postal service. The more you know about the postal service and the job you are applying for, the better you will do on the interview.

Professional applicants and applicants for positions that do not require entrance exams should have extra copies of their résumé or application available to take on the interview. The interviewer may ask you for extra copies. Make sure you bring along the same version of your résumé or application that you originally provided. You can also refer to your résumé to complete applications that ask for job history information (i.e., dates of employment, names of former employers and their telephone numbers, job responsibilities and accomplishments.)

Arrive early to the interview. Plan to arrive 10 to 15 minutes early. Give yourself time to find a restroom so you can check your appearance.

It's important to make a good impression from the moment you enter the reception area. Greet the receptionist cordially and try to appear confident. If you are asked to fill out an application while you're waiting, be sure to fill it out completely and print the information neatly.

Don't make negative comments about anyone or anything, including former employers.

DURING THE INTERVIEW

The job interview is usually a two-way discussion between you and a prospective employer. The interviewer is attempting to determine whether you have what the postal service needs, and you are attempting to determine whether you would accept the job if offered. Both of you will be trying to get as much information as possible in order to make those decisions.[2]

The interview that you are most likely to face is a structured interview with a traditional format. It usually consists of three phases. The introductory phase covers the greeting, small talk and an overview of which areas will be discussed during the interview. The middle phase is a question-and-answer period. The interviewer asks most of the questions, but you are given an opportunity to ask

---

[2] Postal Service Handbook EL-312

questions as well. The closing phase gives you an opportunity to ask any final questions you might have, cover any important points that haven't been discussed and get information about the next step in the process.

Introductory Phase. This phase is very important. You want to make a good first impression and, if possible, get additional information you need about the job and the company.

- Make a good impression. You have only a few seconds to create a positive first impression which can influence the rest of the interview and even determine whether you get the job.

  The interviewers first impression of you is based mainly on non-verbal clues. The interviewer is assessing your overall appearance and demeanor. When greeting the interviewer, be certain your handshake is firm and that you make eye contact. Wait for the interviewer to signal you before you sit down.

  Once seated, your body language is very important in conveying a positive impression. Find a comfortable position so that you don't appear tense. Lean forward slightly and maintain eye contact with the interviewer. This posture shows that you are interested in what is being said. Smile naturally at appropriate times. Show that you are open and receptive by keeping your arms and legs uncrossed. Avoid keeping your handbag on your lap. Pace your movements so that they are not too fast or too slow. Appear relaxed and confident.

- Prepare questions in advance to get needed information. If you weren't able to get complete information about the job in advance, you should try to get it as early as possible in the interview. Knowing the following things will allow you to present those strengths and abilities that the employer wants.

  - Why does the postal service need someone in this position?

  - Exactly what would they expect of you?

  - Are they looking for traditional or innovative solutions to problems?

- When should you ask questions? The problem with a traditional interview structure is that your chance to ask questions occurs late in the interview. How can you get the information you need early in the process without making the interviewer feel that you are taking control?

  Deciding exactly when to ask your questions is the tricky part. Timing is everything. You may have to make a decision based on intuition and your first impressions of the interviewer. Does the interviewer seem comfortable or nervous, soft-spoken or forceful, formal or casual? These signals will help you to judge the best time to ask your questions.

The sooner you ask the questions, the less likely you are to disrupt the interviewer's agenda. However, if you ask questions too early, the interviewer may feel you are trying to control the interview.

Try asking questions right after the greeting and small talk. Since most interviewers like to set the tone of the interview and maintain initial control, always phrase your questions in a way that leaves control with the interviewer. Perhaps you can say, "Would you mind telling me a little more about the job so that I can focus on the information that would be most important to the postal service?"

You may want to wait until the interviewer has given an overview of what will be discussed. This overview may answer some of your questions or may provide some details that you can use to ask additional questions. Once the middle phase of the interview has begun, you may find it more difficult to ask questions.

Middle Phase. During this phase of the interview, the interviewer will ask questions about your work experience, skills, education, and interests. You are being assessed on how you'll perform the job in relation to the agency's objectives.

All responses should be concise. Use examples to illustrate your point whenever possible. Your responses should be prepared in advance so they are well phrased and effective. Be sure they do not sound rehearsed. Remember that your responses must always be adapted to the present interview. Incorporate any information you obtained earlier in the interview with the responses you had prepared in advance, and then answer in a way that is appropriate to the question.

FREQUENTLY ASKED QUESTIONS

Question: "Tell me about yourself."

Reply: Briefly describe your experience and background. If you are unsure what information the interviewer is seeking, say, "Are there any areas in particular you'd like to know about?"

Question: "What is your weakest point?" (A stress question)

Reply: Mention something that is actually a strength. Some examples are:

"I'm something of a perfectionist."

"I'm a stickler for punctuality."

"I'm tenacious."

Give a specific situation from your previous job to illustrate your point.

Question: "What is your strongest point?"

Reply: "I work well under pressure." or

"I am a team player."

If you have just graduated from college you might say,

"I am eager to learn, and I don't have to unlearn old techniques."

Give a specific example to illustrate your point.

Question: "What do you hope to be doing five years from now?"

Reply: "I hope I will still be working here and will have increased my level of responsibility based on my performance and abilities."

Question: "Why have you been out of work for so long?" (A stress question)

Reply: "I spent some time re-evaluating my past experience and the current job market to see what direction I wanted to take." or

"I had offers, but I'm not just looking for another job; I'm looking for a career."

Question: "What do you know about the postal service? Why do you want to work here?"

Reply: This is where your research will come in handy.

"The postal service is a leader in mail delivery, and three of the postal service's six product lines would qualify as Fortune 500 companies:" (Mention one or two of the following.)

- Correspondence and transactions
- Business Advertising
- Expedited Delivery
- Publications Delivery
- Standard Package Delivery
- International Mail

"The postal service has a superior reputation, with operating revenue exceeding $70 billion a year."[3]

Try to get the interviewer to give you additional information about the postal service by saying that you are interested in learning more about the agency's objectives. This will help you to focus your response on relevant areas.

Question: "What is your greatest accomplishment?"

Reply: Give a specific illustration from your previous or current job where you saved the company money or helped increase its profits. If you have just graduated from college, try to find some accomplishment from your school work, part-time jobs or extra-curricular activities.

Question: "Why should we hire you?" (A stress question)
Reply: Highlight your background based on the postal service's current needs. Recap your qualifications, keeping the interviewer's job description in mind. If you don't have much experience, talk about how your education and training prepared you for this job.

Question: "Why do you want to make a change now?"

Reply: "I want to develop my potential." or

"The opportunities in my present company are limited."

Question: "Tell me about a problem in your last job and how you resolved it."

Reply: The employer wants to assess your analytical skills and see if you are a team player. Select a problem from your last job and explain how you solved it.

Some Questions You Should Ask.

✎ "What are the postal service's current challenges?"

✎ "Could you give me a more detailed job description?"

✎ "Why is this position open?"

✎ "Are there opportunities for advancement?"

✎ "To whom would I report?"

---

[3] USPS Financial Highlights, Annual Performance Plan 2018.

Closing Phase. During the closing phase of an interview, you will be asked whether you have any other questions. Ask any relevant question that has not yet been answered. Highlight any of your strengths that have not been discussed. If another interview is to be scheduled, get the necessary information. If this is the final interview, find out when the decision is to be made and when you can call. Thank the interviewer by name and say goodbye.

ILLEGAL QUESTIONS

During an interview, you may be asked some questions that are considered illegal. It is illegal for an interviewer to ask you questions related to sex, age, race, religion, national origin, marital status, or to delve into your personal life for information that is not job-related. What can you do if you are asked an illegal question? Take a moment to evaluate the situation. Ask yourself questions like:

✎ How uncomfortable has this question made you feel?

✎ Does the interviewer seem unaware that the question is illegal?

✎ Is this interviewer going to be your boss?

Then respond in a way that is comfortable for you.

If you decide to answer the question, be succinct and try to move the conversation back to an examination of your skills and abilities as quickly as possible. For example, if asked about your age, you might reply, "I'm in my forties, and I have a wealth of experience that would be an asset to your agency." If you are not sure whether you want to answer the question, first ask for a clarification of how this question relates to your qualifications for the job. You may decide to answer if there is a reasonable explanation. If you feel there is no justification for the question, you might say that you do not see the relationship between the question and your qualifications for the job and you prefer not to answer it.

AFTER THE INTERVIEW

You are not finished yet. It is important to assess the interview shortly after it is concluded. Following your interview you should:

■ Write down the name, phone number, e-mail address, and title (be sure the spelling is correct) of the interviewer.

■ Review what the job entails and record what the next step will be.

■ Note your reactions to the interview; include what went well and what went poorly.

- Assess what you learned from the experience and how you can improve your performance in future interviews.

PHONE FOLLOW-UP

If you were not told during the interview when a hiring decision will be made, call after one week.

At that time, if you learn that the decision has not been made, find out whether you are still under consideration for the job. Ask if there are any other questions the interviewer might have about your qualifications and offer to come in for another interview if necessary. Reiterate that you are very interested in the job.

- If you learn that you did not get the job, try to find out why. You might also inquire whether the interviewer can think of anyone else who might be able to use someone with your abilities, either in another department or at another agency.

- If you are offered the job, you have to decide whether you want it. If you are not sure, thank the employer and ask for several days to think about it. Ask any other questions you might need answered to help you with the decision.

- If you know you want the job and have all the information you need, accept the job with thanks and get the details on when you start. Ask when the postal service will be sending a letter of confirmation, as it is best to have the offer in writing.

Who Gets Hired?

In the final analysis, the postal service will hire someone who has the abilities and talents which fulfill its needs. It is up to you to demonstrate at the interview that you are the person the agency wants to hire.

Chapter Seven
Veterans Preference

The federal government and postal service have a long and outstanding record of employing veterans. Veterans hold a higher percentage of jobs in the government than they do in private industry.

Over 24% of all federal employees are veterans.

The federal civil service and the postal service are guided by the Veterans' Preference Act of 1944 and the program is administered by the Office of Personnel Management (OPM). The postal service's Employment and Placement Handbook, EL-312, provides detailed guidance on this program. You will find both OPM and postal service guidance referenced in this chapter. [1]

In certain circumstances the spouse, widow/widower, or mother of a veteran may be eligible to claim veterans' preference when the veteran is unable to use it.

SPECIAL HIRING INITIATIVES FOR VETERANS

Executive Order 13518 established a Council on Veterans Employment to enhance recruitment of and promote employment opportunities for veterans in the government. The goal was to make the federal government a leader in promoting employment for veterans.

VETERANS PREFERENCE

Veterans' Preference gives eligible veterans preference in appointment over many other applicants. Veterans' Preference applies to virtually all new appointments in the competitive service, postal service, and many in the excepted service. Veterans' Preference does not guarantee veterans a job and it doesn't apply to internal agency actions such as promotions, transfers, reassignments, and reinstatements.

---

[1] Titles 5 and 39 U.S.C. Code of Federal Regulations

Not all veterans receive preference for federal civilian employment, and not all active duty service qualifies for Veterans' Preference. Only veterans discharged or released from active duty in the Armed Forces under honorable conditions are eligible for Veterans' Preference. This means preference eligibles must have been discharged under an honorable or general discharge. If you are a "retired member of the Armed Forces," you are not included in the definition of preference eligible unless you are a disabled veteran, or you retired below the rank of major or its equivalent.

There are two types of preference eligibles: those with a service-connected disability (formerly titled 10 point preference) and those without (formerly titled 5 point preference). Under hiring reform the point system is being replaced with a category rating system. Until hiring reform is fully implemented you may encounter the old terminology of 5 and 10 point preference. Preference eligibles are divided into four basic groups as follows:

- CPS – Disability rating of 30% or more (10 points)

- CP – Disability rating of at least 10% but less than 30% (10 points)

- XP – Disability rating less than 10% (10 points)

- TP – Preference eligibles with no disability rating (5 points)

When agencies used a numerical rating and ranking system to determine the best qualified applicants for a position, an additional 5 or 10 points was added to the numerical score of qualified preference eligible veterans.

The category rating system places preference eligibles who have a compensable service-connected disability of 10 percent or more (CPS, CP) at the top of the highest category on the referral list (except for scientific or professional positions in the competitive service at the GS-9 level or higher). XP and TP preference eligibles are placed above non-preference eligibles within their assigned category. [2]

The Veterans Preference Advisor system allows veterans to examine the preferences for which they might be entitled with regard to federal jobs. This system was developed by the Veterans Employment and Training Service.

To explore the Veterans Preference program, visit OPM's Web site at http://www.fedshirevets.gov/Index.aspx.

Vets Without a Service Connected Disability — *(Five Point Preference)*

If your active duty service meets any of the following, and you do not have a disability rating from the Department of Veterans Affairs (VA) of 10% or more, you have preference. This preference entitles you to be hired before a non-veteran

---

[2] Postal Handbook EL-312-441.1 Group 1, and 441.2 Group 2, Applicants Claiming Preference

whose application is rated in your same category. To meet this criterion, your service must meet one of the following conditions:

- 180 or more consecutive days, any part of which occurred during the period beginning September 11, 2001 and ending on a future date prescribed by Presidential proclamation or law as the last date of Operation Iraqi Freedom, OR

- Between August 2, 1990 and January 2, 1992, OR

- 180 or more consecutive days, any part of which occurred after January 31, 1955 and before October 15, 1976.

- In a war, campaign or expedition for which a campaign badge has been authorized or between April 28, 1952 and July 1, 1955.

Vets with a Service Connected Disability — *(Ten-Point Preference)*

You are a 10 point preference eligible if you served at any time, and you:

- have a service connected disability

- received a Purple Heart

- are the spouse, widow, widower, or mother of a deceased or disabled veteran (derived preference)[3]

> ### PURPLE HEART RECIPIENTS ARE CONSIDERED TO HAVE A SERVICE-CONNECTED DISABILITY

When applying for federal jobs, eligible veterans should claim preference on their application or résumé. Applicants claiming disability, 10-point preference, must complete form SF-15, Application for 10-Point Veteran Preference or an equivalent form for the postal service. Veterans who are still in the service may be granted five points tentative preference on the basis of information contained in their applications, but they must produce a DD Form 214 prior to appointment to document their entitlement to preference.

Note: Reservists who are separated from the reserves but don't currently receive retired pay aren't considered "retired military" for purposes of veterans' preference.

---

[3] Derived preference, www.fedshirevets.gov/job/familypref/index.aspx

If you are not sure of your preference eligibility, visit the OPM's website, Feds Hire Vets at www.fedshirevets.gov/Index.aspx and/or the Veterans Guide at www.fedshirevets.gov/hire/hrp/vetguide/index.aspx. You can also contact an agency designated veterans' hiring program coordinator.

A preference eligible who is passed over on a list of eligibles is entitled, upon request, to a copy of the agency's reasons for the pass-over and the examining office's response.

If the preference eligible is a 30 percent or more disabled veteran, the agency must notify the veteran and OPM or the postal service's HR office of the proposed pass-over. The veteran has 15 days from the date of notification to respond to OPM. OPM then decides whether to approve the pass-over based on all the facts available and notifies the agency and the veteran.

> Entitlement to veterans' preference does not guarantee a job. There are many ways an agency can fill a vacancy other than by appointment from a list of eligibles.

Filing Applications After Examinations Close

A 10-point preference eligible may file an application at any time for any position for which a nontemporary appointment has been made in the preceding three years; for which a list of eligibles currently exists that is closed to new applications; or for which a list is about to be established. Veterans wishing to file after the closing date should contact the agency or postal service facility that announced the position for further information. [4]

SPECIAL APPOINTING AUTHORITIES

The following special authorities permit the noncompetitive appointment of eligible veterans in the federal Civil Service. Use of these special authorities is entirely discretionary with the agency; no one is **entitled** to one of these special appointments:

VETERANS' RECRUITMENT APPOINTMENT (VRA)

The VRA is a special authority that agencies and the postal service can use to appoint an eligible veteran without competition. In the civil service VRA applicants can be hired at any grade level through General Schedule (GS) 11 or

---

[4] Postal Handbook EL-312-322.7 (Delayed and Reopened Examinations)

equivalent. The postal service may hire career and noncareer entry-level positions under this program. [5]

The VRA is an excepted appointment to a position that is otherwise in the competitive service. After two years of satisfactory service, the veteran is converted to a career-conditional appointment in the competitive service.

A VRA eligible who is currently working as a casual or temporary postal employee may be considered for noncompetitive conversion to a career vacancy. The authority may not be used to fill career rural carrier vacancies, positions filled through the Maintenance Selection System, or career data conversion operator positions in remote encoding centers. The VRA eligible must have worked in the temporary appointment for at least 60 days and must meet the qualification requirements of the position, including any currently required examination.[6]

When two or more VRA applicants are preference eligibles, the agency must apply veterans preference as required by law. (While all VRA eligibles have served in the armed forces, they do not necessarily meet the eligibility requirements for veterans preference under section 2108 of title 5, United States Code.)

Veterans' Recruitment Appointment (VRA) is an excepted authority that allows agencies, to appoint eligible veterans without competition. If you:

■   are in receipt of a campaign badge for service during a war or in a campaign or expedition; OR

■   are a disabled veteran, OR

■   are in receipt of an Armed forces Service Medal for participation in a military operation, OR

■   are a recently separated veteran (within the last 3 years), AND

■   separated under honorable conditions (this means an honorable or general discharge), you are VRA eligible.

You can be appointed under this authority at any grade level up to and including a GS-11 or equivalent. This is an excepted service appointment. After successfully completing 2 years, you will be converted to the competitive service. Veterans' preference applies when using the VRA authority.

Agencies can also use VRA to fill temporary (not to exceed 1 year) or term (more than 1 year but not to exceed 4 years) positions. If you are employed in a temporary or term position under VRA, you will not be converted to the competitive service after 2 years. There is no limit to the number of times you can apply under VRA.

---

[5] Postal Handbook EL-312-233.36 (Noncompetitive Appointment of VRA Eligibles)

[6] Postal Handbook EL-312-233.361 (Use of VRA Authority to Fill Career Positions)

Eligibility Requirements

In addition to meeting the criteria above, eligible veterans must have been separated under honorable conditions (i.e., the individual must have received either an honorable or general discharge under honorable conditions).

Clarifications

Under the eligibility criteria, not all five-point preference eligible veterans may be eligible for a VRA appointment. For example, a veteran who served during the Vietnam era (i.e., for more than 180 consecutive days, after January 31, 1955, and before October 15, 1976) but did not receive a service-connected disability or an Armed Forces Service Medal or campaign or expeditionary medal would be entitled to five-point veterans' preference. This veteran, however, would not be eligible for a VRA appointment under the above criteria.

As another example, a veteran who served during the Gulf War from August 2, 1990, through January 2, 1992, would be eligible for veterans' preference solely on the basis of that service. However, service during that time period, in and of itself, does not confer VRA eligibility on the veteran unless one of the above VRA eligibility criteria is met.

Lastly, if an agency has two or more VRA candidates and one or more is a preference eligible, the agency must apply veterans' preference. For example, one applicant is VRA eligible on the basis of receiving an Armed Forces Service Medal (this medal does not confer veterans' preference eligibility). The second applicant is VRA eligible on the basis of being a disabled veteran (which does confer veterans' preference eligibility). In this example, both individuals are VRA eligible but only one of them is eligible for veterans' preference. As a result, agencies must apply the procedures of 5 CFR 302 when considering VRA candidates for appointment.

How to Apply

Veterans should contact the agency or postal service human resource office where they are interested in working to find out about VRA opportunities. Complete a federal style résumé and/or currently required application and forward it with a cover letter to selected offices. Refer to the District Office contact information in Appendix C and contact your local postmaster. Also, visit www.federaljobs.net for direct links to more than 140 federal agency recruiting sites.

Send a cover letter with your application explaining that you are a VRA candidate and would like to be considered for an appointment. Send a copy of your DD-214 form, number 4 copy, with your cover letter and application.

Follow up each submission with a phone call. It helps to call an agency or postal facility first to obtain a name and address to which you can send an application. Send applications to every office and department that interests you.

Agencies do not have to hire through the VRA program. Only if your education and work experience meets their requirements, they have openings, and like what they see will they make you an offer. Be tactful and don't be demanding.

THIRTY PERCENT OR MORE DISABLED VETERANS

These veterans may be given a temporary or term appointment (not limited to 60 days or less) to any position for which qualified (there is no grade limitation). After demonstrating satisfactory performance, the veteran may be converted at any time to a career-conditional appointment.

Eligibility

■   retired from active military service with a service-connected disability rating of 30% or more; or

■   you have a rating by the Department of VA showing a compensable service-connected disability of 30% or more.

How to Apply

Veterans should contact the federal agency or postal service personnel office where they are interested in working to find out about opportunities. Veterans must submit a copy of a letter dated within the last 12 months from the Department of Veterans Affairs or the Department of Defense certifying receipt of compensation for a service-connected disability of 30 percent or more.

Disabled Veterans Enrolled in VA Training Programs

Disabled veterans eligible for training under the Department of Veterans Affairs' (VA) vocational rehabilitation program may enroll for training or work experience at an agency under the terms of an agreement between the agency and VA. The veteran is not a federal employee for most purposes while enrolled in the program, but is a beneficiary of the VA.

The training is tailored to individual needs and goals, so there is no set length. If the training is intended to prepare the individual for eventual appointment in the agency (rather than just work experience), OPM must approve the training plan. Upon successful completion, the veteran will be given a Certificate of Training showing the occupational series and grade level of the position for which trained. This allows any agency to appoint the veteran noncompetitively for a period of one year. Upon appointment, the veteran is given a Special Tenure Appointment which is then converted to career-conditional with OPM approval.

In all cases, you must provide acceptable documentation of your preference or appointment eligibility. The number 4 copy of your DD-214, "Certificate of Release or Discharge from Active Duty," is necessary to document the character of service. If claiming 10-point preference, you will need to submit a Standard Form 15, "Application for 10-point Veterans' Preference."

VETERANS EMPLOYMENT OPPORTUNITIES ACT (VEOA)

The Veterans Employment Opportunities Act (VEOA) was passed in 1998 and it gives veterans access to federal job opportunities that might otherwise be closed to them. The law requires that:

- Agencies allow eligible veterans to compete for vacancies advertised under the agency's merit promotion procedures when the agency is seeking applications from individuals outside its own workforce.

- All merit promotion announcements open to applicants outside an agency's workforce include a statement that these eligible veterans may apply.

The law also establishes a new redress system for preference eligibles and makes it a prohibited personnel practice for an agency to knowingly take or fail to take a personnel action if that action or failure to act would violate a statutory or regulatory veterans preference requirement.

This authority permits an agency to appoint an eligible veteran who has applied under an agency merit promotion announcement that is open to candidates outside the agency.

To be eligible a candidate must be a preference eligible or a veteran separated after three years or more of continuous active service performed under honorable conditions.

Those with derived preference are also eligible for VEOA. There is not a requirement to select a VEOA applicant over another applicant as in a VRA appointment to an external announcement. Another difference is that there is no requirement for the positions applied for to be lower than a GS-11 as there is under VRA criteria.

Terms and Conditions of Employment

Veterans receiving a VEOA appointment will be given a career or career conditional appointment in the competitive service. Veterans interested in applying under this authority should seek out agency merit promotion announcements open to candidates outside the agency. There is no advantage for veterans with career status or reinstatement eligibility to apply under VEOA, because they already have the eligibility to apply to merit promotion announcements, and there is no preferential treatment for those applying under VEOA.

Positions Restricted to Preference Eligibles

Certain positions; including custodian, laborer custodian, elevator operator, and window cleaner, whether career or noncareer, are restricted to applicants eligible for veterans' preference. This rule applies only to appointments from external recruitment sources (whether competitive or noncompetitive). [7]

---

[7] Postal Handbook EL-312-232.52, Positions restricted to applicants eligible for veterans' preference.

Chapter Eight
Job Descriptions

There are over 2,000 occupational codes identified in the Postal Service's Position Directory.[1] This chapter features 24 job descriptions — a cross-section of postal service occupations, from accountants and engineers to welders and custodians.

Mail carrier and clerk occupations are presented in Chapter Three. These job descriptions represent a cross-section of available postal service jobs. Many of these jobs are first offered to qualified postal employees. If they can't fill these positions in-house, they advertise jobs to the general public.

POSITION DESCRIPTIONS

Accounting Technician
Architect/engineer
Area Maintenance Technician
Automotive Mechanic
Budget and Financial Analyst
Building Equipment Mechanic
Carrier (City)
Casual
Computer Systems Analyst
Custodian
Data Collection Technician
Distribution Clerk

Electronics Technician
Financial Services Coordinator
Flat Sorting Machine Operator
Human Resource Specialist
Maintenance Mechanic
Mechanical Engineer
Nurse, Occupational Health
Police Officer, Postal
Rural Carrier
Secretary
Telecommunications Specialist
Window Clerk

---

[1] Employee Master File /RDL/OCCLIST

ACCOUNTING TECHNICIAN, PS-06 Occupation Code: 0525-31XX

Ensures the proper completion of a designated major segment of accounting work in a district office; or serves as assistant to the postmaster in performing accounting and clerical duties involved in the preparation, maintenance, and consolidation of accounts and related reports in a post office.

DUTIES AND RESPONSIBILITIES

1. Performs, with assistance of accounting clerks if needed, either duty 2 or 3, in combination with duty 3. In a smaller post office having characteristics like those in the basic function, and subject to the provisions of postal service directives concerning internal control and separation of duties, performs any combination of duties 5 through 8.

2. In the accounting area, receives daily cash reports from all reporting units of the post office, verifies and balances reports with supporting documents, consolidates the data in one cash report, and posts the daily financial report. Items which are questionable are taken up with the reporting unit or individual in order to determine the correct entries. Reporting units are debited or credited as necessary.

3. In the budget and cost control area, receives reports and data relating to mail volume, workload, and cost ascertainment from the various reporting units, examines reports for completeness and tabulates and posts data in accordance with daily and periodic reporting requirements. Discusses with supervisor data submitted by their units in order that further necessary information and explanation may be obtained. Documents explanatory information for subsequent analysis and inclusion in management reports.

4. In addition, works closely with the supervisor in preparing weekly, biweekly, accounting period, or other periodic reports. Gives guidance and instruction to and acts as group leader for any assigned clerical assistance. May maintain accounts, reflecting trust funds, suspense items and inventories of accountable paper, stamp stock, and fixed credits. Participates with the supervisor interpreting instructions and regulations in implementing procedures pertaining to accounting. May be required to research, compile and record data for special studies and reports on various phases of postal activities as desired by the postmaster or higher authority.

5. Receives daily cash reports from all reporting units of the post office, verifies and balances reports with supporting documents, consolidates into one cash report, and posts the cashbook. Items which are questionable are taken up with the reporting unit or individual to determine the correct entries.

6. Receives reports and data relating to mail volume, workload, and cost ascertainment from the various reporting units, examines reports for completeness and accuracy, makes the necessary computations, consolidates the information in accordance with daily and periodic reporting requirements. Discusses with supervisors figures submitted by them to obtain further information and explanation as required. Prepares explanatory comments for inclusion in the reports.

7. Works closely with the postmaster in preparing required accounting period reports including operating report, financial statement, workload and mail volume reports.

8. May maintain stamp stock and fill requisitions for window clerks, stations and branches.

ARCHITECT/ENGINEER, EAS-20 Occupation Code: 0808-3020

Performs design work and assists in administering design and construction contracts within a district office.

DUTIES AND RESPONSIBILITIES

1. Provides architect/engineering consulting services, evaluates technical problems, and surveys technical alternatives for construction projects within a district office.

2. Participates in the analysis, evaluation, and determination of feasibility, costs, and technical problems related to the planning, design, installation, testings, and operation of advanced engineered systems and equipment in support of construction projects.

3. Oversees construction term contracts to ensure compliance with contract requirements and adherence to established policies and procedures.

4. Participates in the activities related to the design, construction, testing, start-up, and operation of facilities, systems, and/or equipment.

5. Participates in the preparation of requests for proposal, including specifications and drawings; participates in the evaluation of contractor bids.

6. Reviews contractor specifications and drawings for technical accuracy and compliance with contract requirements.

7. Attends preconstruction and final acceptance meetings for progress review; makes on-site inspections during installation and test, and reports discrepancies in contract work.

8. Works with architects, engineers, contractors, construction representatives, and others involved in the design and construction of postal facilities.

9. Provides technical assistance to employees and others in the development of facility projects.

AREA MAINTENANCE TECHNICIAN, PS-08 Occupation Code: 4801-20XX

Installs, maintains, repairs, removes, and disposes of postal equipment as appropriate at post offices (offices not having maintenance capability) within the geographic area served by the area maintenance office to which assigned. Installs, moves, or repairs post office screen-line equipment, lock boxes, furniture, and mechanical equipment, supervising such additional help as projects may require.

DUTIES AND RESPONSIBILITIES

1. At regional direction, moves and sets up offices in new or remodeled postal quarters; assembles, installs screen-lines, workroom, lobby, and operating equipment. Supervises carpenters and/or helpers as projects may require. Classifies or assists postmasters in

classification of postal equipment for disposal or refurbishing. Under postmaster's authority, purchases materials and employs helpers as warranted.

2. Makes major and minor repairs to postal operating equipment in offices without maintenance capabilities; conducts maintenance inspections and provides operating, minor repair, and maintenance instruction to postal employees in the offices served. Whenever possible, conducts maintenance inspection and the instruction of postal employees in conjunction with emergency service trips to installations.

3. Troubleshoots, repairs, overhauls, and installs postal operating equipment such as, but not limited to, stamp vending machines, canceling machines, scales, print punch money order machines, tying machines, conveyors, safe and vault locks and other components, protective systems and devices, time clocks, and money changers. Keeps abreast of current maintenance criteria and affects service accordingly.

4. Maintains inventory of all postal operating equipment in the offices served by the area maintenance office. Makes recommendations to supervisors and/or obtains stock of operating equipment repair parts, maintaining inventories at levels prescribed by the region or the department. Maintains record of parts in stock; ships parts to territory offices as required to meet respective office needs. Keeps records of parts used, frequency of replacements, and submits reports to the regional office at prescribed intervals.

5. Installs and maintains protective systems and devices on safes and vaults in post offices. Opens safes and vaults, changes and repairs combinations, and disarms systems and devices.

6. Provides emergency service and makes minor repairs to air conditioning systems at government owned buildings not under service contracts. Prepares report of needs for the postmaster if the lessor has maintenance responsibility or the manufacturer if the system is under warranty.

7. Initiates reports to the regional office on major work assignments, shortages of equipment, and completed screen line installations. Makes reports of unsatisfactory conditions relating to equipment damage, classification, and deficiencies. Makes written recommendations for equipment improvements, operations, and fabrication changes.

8. Drives motor vehicle to respective offices to effect on-the-scene repairs and screen-line installation or modifications. Communicates with postmasters by phone, correspondence, and personal visits to investigate reports of malfunctions, disorders, or other needs within the area maintenance office territory.

9. Performs other maintenance duties as instructed by the postmaster at the area maintenance office when not engaged in area maintenance duties.

10. Uses various hand and power tools and testing devices incident to the mechanical, electrical and electronic, and carpentry trades.

11. Observes established safety practices and procedures and instructs helpers accordingly.

AUTOMOTIVE MECHANIC, PS-06 Occupation Code: 5823-03XX

Repairs vehicles, including the removal and installation of complete motors, clutches, transmissions, and other major component parts.

DUTIES AND RESPONSIBILITIES

1. Diagnoses mechanical and operating difficulties of vehicles, repairing defects, replacing worn or broken parts.

2. Adjusts and tunes up engines, cleaning fuel pumps, carburetors, and radiators; regulates timing, and makes other necessary adjustments to maintain in proper operating condition trucks that are in service.

3. Repairs or replaces automotive electrical equipment such as generators, starters, ignition systems, distributors, and wiring; installs and sets new spark plugs.

4. Conducts road tests of vehicles after repairs, noting performance of engine, clutch, transmission, brakes, and other parts.

5. Operates standard types of garage testing equipment.

6. Performs other duties as assigned, such as removing, disassembling, reassembling, and installing entire engines; overhauling transmission, rear end assemblies, and braking systems; straightening frames and axles, welding broken parts where required; making road calls to make emergency repairs; and making required truck inspections.

BUDGET AND FINANCIAL ANALYST (DISTRICT), EAS-19 Occupation Code: 0504-5022

Performs all activities for the development and control of district operating and capital budgets; performs research and analysis of district financial operations.

DUTIES AND RESPONSIBILITIES

1. Develops, prepares, allocates, implements, monitors, and controls the district operating and capital budgets; includes current estimates of future financial performance; and integrates planning assumptions into operating budget plans.

2. Integrates all district functions into the planning process and validates budget and financial forecasts developed by managers.

3. Provides ongoing analyses to support operations management and improve overall financial and work hour performance, including the analysis and validation of major capital, facility, and program expenditures and packages.

4. Develops and implements business planning and forecasting techniques and monitors effectiveness; analyzes operating results to identify improvement opportunities and evaluate the effectiveness of cost reduction program implementation.

5. Develops and presents training for operating managers to increase their understanding of the budget process and the financial analysis techniques used for performance measurement.

6. Provides technical guidance to financial and operating employees in the development of capital investment strategies and operating expense budgets; maintains an effective financial planning and forecasting process for all district organizations.

BUILDING EQUIPMENT MECHANIC, PS-07 Occupation Code: 5306-07XX

Performs involved trouble shooting and complex maintenance work on building and building equipment systems, preventative maintenance and preventative maintenance inspections of buildings, building equipment and building systems, and maintains and operates a large automated air conditioning system and a large heating system.

DUTIES AND RESPONSIBILITIES

1. Performs, on building and building equipment, the more difficult testing, diagnosis, maintenance, adjustment and revision work, requiring a thorough knowledge of the mechanical, electrical, and electronic, pneumatic, or hydraulic control and operating mechanisms of the equipment. Performs trouble shooting and repair of complex supervisory group control panels, readout and feedback circuits and associated mechanical and electrical components throughout the installation; locates and corrects malfunctions in triggering and other electro mechanical and electronic circuits.

2. Observes the various components of the building systems in operation and applies appropriate testing methods and procedures to insure continued proper operation.

3. Locates the source of, and rectifies trouble in, involved or questionable cases, or in emergency situations where expert attention is required to locate and correct the defect quickly to avoid or minimize interruptions.

4. Installs or alters building equipment and circuits as directed.

5. Reports the circumstances surrounding equipment and failures, and recommends measures for their correction.

6. Performs preventive maintenance inspections of building equipment to locate incipient mechanical malfunctions and the standard of maintenance. Initiates work orders requesting corrective actions for conditions below standard; assists in the estimating of time and materials required. Recommends changes in preventative maintenance procedures and practices to provide the proper level of maintenance; assists in the revision of preventive maintenance checklists and the frequency of performing preventive maintenance routes. In instances of serious equipment failures, conducts investigation to determine the cause of the breakdown and to recommend remedial action to prevent recurrence.

7. Uses necessary hand and power tools, specialized equipment, gauging devices, and both electrical and electronic test equipment.

8. Reads and interprets schematics, blue prints, wiring diagrams and specifications in locating and correcting potential or existing malfunctions and failures.

9. Repairs electromechanically operated equipment related to the building or building systems. Repairs, installs, modifies, and maintains building safety systems, support systems and equipment.

10. Works off ladders, scaffolds, and rigging within heights common to the facility. Works under various weather conditions outdoors.

11. Completes duties and tasks related to building equipment maintenance as required.

12. Observes established safety practices and requirements pertaining to the type of work involved; recommends additional safety measures as required.

13. In addition, may oversee the work of lower-level maintenance employees, advising and instructing them in proper and safe work methods and checking for adherence to instructions; make in-process and final operational checks and tests of work completed by lower level maintenance employees.

14. Performs other job-related tasks in support of primary duties.

CARRIER (CITY), PS-05 Occupation Code: 2310-01XX

Delivers and collects mail on foot or by vehicle under varying conditions in a prescribed area within a city. Maintains pleasant and effective public relations with route customers and others, requiring a general familiarity with postal laws, regulations, and procedures commonly used within the geography of the city. (Refer to Chapter Three for a complete description of Clerk and Mail Carrier occupations.)

CASUAL, EAS-07 Occupation Code: 5201-1001

Performs mail handling, mail processing, mail delivery, mail collection, mail transportation, and custodial functions, or a combination of such duties on a supplemental basis. (Refer to Chapter Three for a complete description of Clerk and Mail Carrier occupations.)

COMPUTER SYSTEMS ANALYST/PROGRAMMER (PDC), DCS-20 Occupation Code: 0334-3056

Analyzes and evaluates existing and proposed systems and develops computer programs, systems, and procedures to process data.

DUTIES AND RESPONSIBILITIES

1. Translates user requirements to automate problem analysis and record keeping activities into detailed program flowcharts.

2. Prepares programming specifications and diagrams and develops coding logic flowcharts.

3. Codes, tests, debugs, and installs computer programs and procedures.

4. Reviews and updates computer programs and provides the necessary documentation for the computer operations function.

5. Prepares charts and diagrams to assist in problem analysis.

6. Prepares detailed program specifications and flowcharts and coordinates the system's installation with the user.

7. Provides technical advice and guidance to programmers assigned on a project basis; provides advice and assistance to managers involved in installing an automated system.

8. Has regular contact with contract employees and computer equipment vendors

CUSTODIAN, PS-02 Occupation Code: 3566-04XX

Performs manual laboring duties in connection with custody of an office or building.

DUTIES AND RESPONSIBILITIES

1. Performs any one or a combination of the duties listed below.

2. Moves furniture and equipment.

3. Uncrates and assembles furniture and fixtures, using bolts and screws for assembly.

4. Loads and unloads supplies and equipment.

5. Removes trash from work areas, lobbies, and washrooms.

6. Tends to lawns, shrubbery, and premises of the post office and cleans ice and snow from the sidewalks and driveways.

7. Stacks supplies in storage rooms and on shelves, and completes forms or records as required.

8. May perform cleaning duties as assigned.

DATA COLLECTION TECHNICIAN, PS-06 Occupation Code: 0301-69XX

Collects, records, and analyzes a variety of statistical data on selected operating and financial activities. Performs relief assignments for PSDS Technicians.

DUTIES AND RESPONSIBILITIES

1. Collects, records, and analyzes statistical data under any number of national data collection systems.

2. Operates computer equipment to enter data; recognizes diagnostic messages and takes appropriate actions; and performs data transfer functions through telecommunications systems.

3. Reviews input and output data to determine accuracy and compliance with national programs. Analyzes and edits data to detect and correct errors.

4. Updates national databases; maintains and updates records and files.

5. Participates in data collection activities in support of special studies or national programs.

6. Reads and interprets reference manuals and other written materials.

7. May drive a vehicle to other facilities when work assignments require.

8. Performs other job-related tasks in support of primary duties.

DISTRIBUTION CLERK, PS-05 Occupation Code: 2315-04XX

Separates mail in a post office, terminal, airport mail facility or other postal facility in accordance with established schemes, including incoming or outgoing mail or both. (Refer to Chapter Three for a complete description of Clerk and Mail Carrier occupations.)

ELECTRONICS TECHNICIAN, PS-10 Occupation Code: 0856-01XX

Carries out all phases of maintenance, troubleshooting, and testing of electronic circuitry used in equipment and systems requiring a knowledge of solid state electronics. Instructs and provides technical support on complex systems and on combinational (hardware/software) or intermittent problems.

DUTIES AND RESPONSIBILITIES

1. Performs the testing, diagnosis, maintenance, and revision work requiring a knowledge of solid state electronics.

2. Observes the various equipment and systems in operation and applies appropriate testing and diagnostic methods and procedures to ensure proper operation.

3. Locates source of equipment and system failures, rectifies trouble in involved cases, or provides instructions to be used by maintenance employees performing repair work.

4. Makes or participates with contractor representative or electronic technician installing or altering equipment and systems as required.

5. Creates reports on equipment and system failures which require corrective action by contractor and follows up to see that appropriate action is taken.

6. Makes preventive maintenance inspections to discover incipient malfunctions and to review the standards of maintenance. Recommends changes in preventive maintenance procedures and practices as found to be necessary.

7. Programs scheme and/or scheme changes into memory units as requested by management.

8. Furnishes pertinent data to superiors and contract employees on operation and testing problems.

9. Participates in training programs: classroom, on-the-job, and correspondence, at postal facilities, trade schools, and manufacturer's plants as required. May assist in developing and implementing training programs. Instructs equal or lower level employees as required.

10. Observes established safety regulations pertaining to the type of work involved.

11. May drive vehicle or utilize other available mode of transportation to work site when necessary.

12. Provides technical support to other electronic technicians to resolve complex, combinational (hardware/software), and/or intermittent failures.

13. Performs such other duties as may be assigned.

FINANCIAL SERVICES COORDINATOR, EAS-18 Occupation Code: 0510-5050

Coordinates, analyzes, and monitors district wide financial accounting programs and processes; coordinates the implementation of new accounting and timekeeping policies and procedures; provides technical guidance to post offices and field units in the resolution of daily accounting problems.

DUTIES AND RESPONSIBILITIES

1. Analyzes, evaluates, and determines the need for changes to district financial accounting programs and processes; identifies deficiencies and problems; and recommends and implements corrective actions to improve quality and reduce errors.

2. Provides guidance and training to post office and field unit employees concerning financial accounting procedures, including the proper recording of statements of accounts and adjustments of daily unit financial statements.

3. Resolves accounting problems, including those associated with banking, payables, and payroll adjustments.

4. Monitors revenue reporting and performs audits of financial activities to ensure financial integrity.

5. Coordinates district accounting programs and processes with the Postal Data Center and other functional areas.

6. Implements national, area, and district accounting and timekeeping policies and procedures.

7. Provides technical advice, guidance, assistance, and training to post offices and field units throughout the district area on the full range of accounting and timekeeping programs and processes.

FLAT SORTING MACHINE OPERATOR, PS-05 Occupation Code: 2315-20XX

Operates a single or multi-position, electromechanical operator-paced flat sorting machine in the distribution of flats requiring knowledge and application of approved machine distribution of directs, alphabetical or geographic groupings, by reading the ZIP code on each flat. (Refer to Chapter Three for a complete description of Clerk and Mail Carrier occupations.)

HUMAN RESOURCES SPECIALIST, EAS-16 Occupation Code: 0201-5117

Performs technical staff work in support of the implementation and administration of one or more human resources programs.

OPERATIONAL REQUIREMENTS

In addition to the following program responsibilities, oversees and coordinates the activities of a small size group of lower level employees, including making assignments, monitoring and reviewing work, providing continuing technical guidance, approving leave, and taking disciplinary action.

DUTIES AND RESPONSIBILITIES

1. PERSONNEL SERVICES: Implements and administers employee compensation and benefits programs (including wage and salaries), pay procedures and rules, performance evaluations, merits, suggestions, incentive and superior accomplishment awards, quality step increases, retirements, and insurance.

2. Provides information to and processes requests from state unemployment compensation agencies for separated employees; testifies in unemployment compensation hearings.

3. Administers employment and selection policies, procedures, and processes for bargaining, initial level supervisor, non-bargaining, and postmaster positions.

4. Coordinates entrance and in-service examination programs; oversees all procedures and processes related to examination scheduling, conducting, processing, grading, notification, and forwarding of test data.

5. SAFETY AND HEALTH: Monitors compliance with safety and health standards and regulations; conducts periodic inspections; ensures accurate accident reporting; analyzes accident rates and trends; and provides for improvement of safety awareness and accident prevention through training and promotional activities.

6. Implements Wellness Program by coordinating programs, services, and activities that promote employee health efforts.

7. Administers procedures under which employees with substance abuse and other personal problems are referred to external providers contracted under the Employee Assistance Program.

8. INJURY COMPENSATION: Provides comprehensive case management in the review and processing of injury compensation claims, including authorization and control of continuation of pay; controversion of claims; identification of possible fraud and abuse; third party claims and recovery; assignment to limited duty; and referral to the rehabilitation program, or for second opinions or fitness for duty exams.

9. TRAINING: Plans, schedules, implements, administers, coordinates, evaluates, and performs employee training, career planning and development, diagnostic testing, and counseling services; conducts workshops, orientations, and demonstrations; coordinates managerial and supervisory training; and provides guidance to employees, job trainers, and management regarding training and instructional processes.

MAINTENANCE MECHANIC, PS-05

Independently performs semi-skilled preventive, corrective, and predictive maintenance tasks associated with the upkeep and operation of various types of mail processing, buildings and building equipment, customer service and delivery equipment.

DUTIES AND RESPONSIBILITIES

1. Independently performs preventive maintenance and minor repairs on plumbing, heating, refrigeration, air-conditioning, low-voltage electrical systems, and other building systems and equipment.

2. Performs preventive maintenance and routine repairs on simple control circuitry, bearings, chains, sprockets, motors, belts and belting, and other moving parts or wearing surfaces of equipment.

3. Assembles, installs, replaces, repairs, modifies and adjusts all types of small operating equipment such as letter boxes, mechanical scales, stamp vending equipment, building service equipment, manhandling equipment and related equipment.

4. Under the direction of skilled maintenance employees, or clearly written instructions from either hard copy or electronic format, performs specific tasks related to disassembling equipment, replacing parts, relocating and reassembling equipment; assists higher level workers in locating and repairing equipment malfunctions.

5. Maintains an awareness of equipment operation, especially excessive heat, vibration, and noise, reporting malfunctions, hazards or wear to supervisor.

6. Uses a variety of hand and power tools, gauging devices and test equipment required, or as directed, to perform the above tasks.

7. May drive a vehicle to transport tools, equipment, employees, materials or in the normal performance of assigned duties.

8. Completes or initiates work record sheets, as required. Takes readings from meters, gauges, counters and other monitoring and measuring devices. Maintains logs and other required records; reports on breakdowns and equipment being tested.

9. Follows established safety practices and requirements while performing all duties.

10. May serve as a working leader over a group of lower-level employees assigned to a specific task.

11. Performs other duties as assigned.

MECHANICAL ENGINEER, EAS-24 Occupation Code: 0830-4012

Plans, organizes, and executes the design, construction, installation, and implementation of new systems, equipment, or controls of major magnitude and scope, in support of the mail processing objectives of the postal service.

DUTIES AND RESPONSIBILITIES

1. Translates operating objectives for mail processing into functional requirements for facilities, or equipment; oversees the reporting, analysis, and evaluation of data from field operating units related to mail volume, productivity, or costs; integrates this information with technical data to determine functional specifications.

2. Oversees the preparation and justification of engineering proposals and alternatives for complex mechanized systems equipment; evaluates engineered systems and related costs to determine alternatives to support mail processing objectives; provides program cost estimates; develops and recommends plans for program implementation.

3. Oversees engineering activities related to the design, construction, installation, test, and start-up of mechanized systems and equipment; provides technical management of contracts; evaluates contractor bids; makes recommendations affecting the selection of contractors; determines criteria for performance evaluation of prototype equipment; controls program costs; certifies contractor requests for payment.

4. Coordinates planning and implementation of mechanization systems and equipment programs with headquarters and field employees.

5. Provides mechanical engineering consulting services, as required.

6. Has frequent contact with contractors, professional consultants, officials of government agencies, and equipment manufacturers.

NURSE, OCCUPATIONAL HEALTH, PNS-01 Occupation Code: 0610-4001

Provides professional nursing services to employees under the general direction of a medical officer. Implements and participates in programs to provide preventative medical care and health maintenance services in support of postal service safety and health goals and objectives.

DUTIES AND RESPONSIBILITIES

1. Implements, monitors, and participates in occupational health programs and services within a postal facility.

2. Provides professional nursing care to employees; administers medications at the direction of a physician; and makes arrangements for physicians' care.

3. Provides continuous health or injury care, under physicians' instructions, to employees with prolonged illnesses or injuries.

4. Assists medical officer in conducting re-employment or fitness-for-duty physical examinations; performs routine examinations for items such as vision, hearing, and blood

pressure; and makes recommendations regarding suitability for employment and/or referral for additional testing and evaluation.

5. Advises or counsels employees regarding general and/or mental health care; assists employees with doctor and/or community service referrals, when necessary.

6. Prepares, updates, and maintains confidential health records for employees using the health and medical unit; compiles and analyzes various medical data and reports; and prepares regular summary reports.

7. Requisitions appropriate quantities and types of medical supplies and maintains security of supplies and equipment.

8. Regularly checks first aid boxes to ensure an adequate supply of necessary items.

9. Maintains the health/medical unit in a sanitary and orderly condition.

10. Provides continuous medical monitoring of workers exposed to potentially harmful substances.

11. Reports on-the-job injuries and other safety and health matters to appropriate postal officials.

12. Maintains familiarity with Workers Compensation and safety and personnel practices and procedures relative to occupational health programs.

13. Serves as liaison with employees, supervisors, physicians, PAR and safety employees; refers employees for participation in the PAR and other health related programs.

14. Performs related clerical duties.

15. Makes frequent contact with private physicians and representatives of hospitals and health clinics. Has occasional contact with customers, contractors' employees, and representatives of emergency services and social agencies.

16. Provides professional advice and guidance to supervisors regarding administrative procedures; provides health care advice and counseling to employees.

17. Exercises a normal regard for the safety of self and others.

POLICE OFFICER, POSTAL (B), PPO-06

Performs a variety of duties pertaining to the security of postal buildings, personnel, property, mail, and mail-in-transit in support of the postal security program.

DUTIES AND RESPONSIBILITIES

1. Performs a variety of duties pertaining to the security of postal buildings, personnel, property, mail, and mail-in-transit.

2. Carries a firearm and exercises standard care required by the Postal Inspection Service on firearms and use of reasonable force. Maintains assigned firearms in good condition.

3. Maintains incidents reported and daily logs of orders and basic information for the security force.

4. Answers the office telephone and responds to reports and inquiries.

5. Performs patrol duty, as assigned, on foot or by motor vehicle to maintain order and safeguard the facility, property, and personnel; ensures the application of security measures in mail handling areas.

6. Maintains contact with other security force personnel; responds to emergencies and other conditions, including burglaries and hold-ups, requiring immediate attention.

7. Controls access to building at an assigned post; enforces the regulations requiring identification.

8. Makes arrests and testifies in court on law violations within assigned authority.

9. Performs other job-related tasks in support of the primary duties.

RURAL CARRIER, RCS-00

Cases, delivers, and collects mail along a prescribed rural route using a vehicle; provides customers on the route with a variety of services. (Refer to Chapter Three for a complete description of clerk and mail carrier occupations.)

SECRETARY, EAS-11 Occupation Code: 0318-2041

Provides secretarial support for a manager and his/her staff. Processes information in accordance with established organizational and functional area administrative practices and procedures.

DUTIES AND RESPONSIBILITIES

1. Produces reports, letters and other documentation using word processing equipment, and monitors peripheral equipment.

2. Accesses, retrieves, and/or updates files and other data maintained on computers.

3. Sends and receives electronic messages, files and other documentation via the local area network.

4. Produces charts, tables and other documentation using various graphics packages.

5. Compiles information on a variety of subjects; reviews periodicals, publications, and industry related documents, bringing those of interest to the managers attention.

6. Reviews materials prepared for accuracy and proper format; ensures compliance with established collective bargaining policies.

7. Performs routine clerical duties such as, answering telephones, operating office equipment, requisitioning supplies, and coordinating printing, maintenance, and other service requests.

8. Screens, logs, and routes office mail.

9. Performs other administrative duties, such as maintaining a variety of reports, such as: time and attendance records, correspondence control, training plans, etc., and maintains office files.

TELECOMMUNICATIONS SPECIALIST, EAS-17 Occupation Code: 0393-5001

Provides analysis, coordination, and technical support for the voice and data telecommunications activities in a district.

DUTIES AND RESPONSIBILITIES

1. Analyzes voice and data telecommunications requirements, including networks and hardware; recommends new and improved services, and coordinates acquisition and implementation.

2. Prepares recommendations for system changes to improve effectiveness and reduce telecommunications costs; coordinates with national telecommunications network program specialists, and implements approved changes.

3. Coordinates the acquisition and installation of new telecommunications hardware; performs preacceptance tests to verify proper operations; makes changes to telecommunications control systems to activate or restrict specific services to designated lines, and oversees equipment repair projects.

4. Monitors all aspects of the telecommunications system, including line traffic and overall system usage; oversees the verification and certification of monthly billings; prepares analyses and reports for management review.

5. Prepares and implements training for telecommunications system users throughout the district.

6. Troubleshoots network and equipment problems and resolves or coordinates resolution with vendors.

7. Has regular contact with representatives of local telecommunication service vendors.

8. Provides technical guidance to employees on telecommunications system operations.

WINDOW CLERK, PS-05

Performs a variety of services at a public window of a post office or post office branch or station. Maintains pleasant and effective public relations with customers and others, requiring a general familiarity with postal laws, regulations, and procedures commonly used. (Refer to Chapter Three for a complete description of clerk and mail carrier occupations.)

Chapter Nine
Postal Inspectors

Postal inspectors investigate criminal activities involving the security and integrity of the United States postal system. Approximately 4,000 postal inspectors, evidence technicians, support staff, and uniformed postal police ensure the safety of postal employees, the postal system, and the public. The Postal Inspection Service investigates and enforces over 200 laws covering crimes that may adversely affect the mail, and provide considerable protection against identity theft and consumer fraud. The chief postal inspector and the head of the Postal Inspection Service report directly to the postmaster general.[1]

Inspectors carry firearms, make arrests, testify in court, serve subpoenas, and write comprehensive reports. It is a demanding position, often requiring frequent and extended travel and absences from home. Postal inspectors may work under hazardous conditions, have irregular work hours, and be assigned anywhere in the country.

The Postal Inspection Service is able to recruit college graduates with no previous work experience. This program began about 10 years ago. If you do not meet one of the special requirements in the *Application for U.S. Postal Inspector,* but have a conferred, four-year college degree with a minimum GPA of 3.0, or an advanced degree, you may apply to become a postal inspector. To apply, submit Form 168, *Application for U.S. Postal Inspector,* along with a copy of your college transcript.

Federal law enforcement agents in the GS-1811, Criminal Investigating Series, may apply through an expedited recruitment process by submitting a copy of a current SF 50, *Notification of Personnel Action,* with their application. If the

---

[1]USPS O.C. List and http://postalinspectors.uspis.gov/aboutus/mission.aspx

applicant has Top Secret clearance, the process may be further expedited by including a letter from their agency's security control officer certifying the clearance, the date it was originally issued and any updates, as well as copies of SF 86, *Questionnaire for National Security Positions,* for the original clearance and any updates.[2]

Overview

The United States Postal Service was founded by Benjamin Franklin and it is one of the oldest federal law enforcement agencies. The Postal Inspection Service has a long, proud and successful history of fighting criminals who attack our nation's postal system and misuse it to defraud, endanger or otherwise threaten the American public. As the primary law enforcement arm of the postal service, the Postal Inspection Service is a highly specialized, professional organization performing investigative and security functions essential to a stable and sound postal system.

Congress empowered the postal service "to investigate postal offenses and civil matters relating to the postal service." Through its security and enforcement functions, the Postal Inspection Service provides assurance to American businesses and customers for the safe exchange of their correspondence, funds, and securities through the U.S. mail and that postal employees are afforded the opportunity to work in a safe environment.

As fact-finding and investigative agents, postal inspectors are federal law enforcement officers who carry firearms, make arrests, and serve federal search warrants and subpoenas. Inspectors work closely with U.S. Attorneys, other law enforcement agencies, and local prosecutors to investigate postal cases and prepare them for court. There are approximately 1,750 postal inspectors stationed throughout the United States, covering investigations of crimes that adversely affect or fraudulently use the postal system.

To assist in carrying out its responsibilities, the Postal Inspection Service maintains a security force staffed by 830 uniformed postal police officers who are assigned to critical postal facilities throughout the country. The officers provide perimeter security, escort high-value mail shipments, and perform other essential protective functions.

The Postal Inspection Service operates five forensic crime laboratories strategically located in cities across the country. The labs are staffed with forensic scientists and technical specialists, who assist inspectors in analyzing evidentiary material needed for identifying and tracing criminal suspects and in providing expert testimony for cases brought to trial.

---

[2] Postal Inspection web page, http://postalinspectors.uspis.gov/

The Postal Inspection Service recruits for the following positions:

- ➤ Postal inspectors
- ➤ Postal police officers
- ➤ Forensic scientists
- ➤ Information technology specialists
- ➤ Security electronic technicians
- ➤ Administrative support specialists

Requirements for U.S. Postal Inspectors[3]

U.S. postal inspectors are federal law enforcement officers. Postal inspectors have investigative jurisdiction in all criminal matters involving the integrity and security of the postal service.

Postal inspectors investigate criminal, civil, and administrative violations of postal laws and are responsible for protecting the revenue and assets of the postal service. Inspectors are required to carry firearms, make arrests, testify in court, serve subpoenas, and write comprehensive reports. They must operate motor vehicles and may undergo moderate to arduous physical exertion under unusual environmental conditions. It is essential that inspectors be in sound physical condition and be capable of performing vigorous physical activities on a sustained basis. The activities may require inspectors to perform the following: climb ladders; work long and irregular hours; occupy cramped or crowded spaces for extended periods of time; exert physical force in the arrest, search, pursuit, and restraint of another person; and protect themselves and others from imminent danger.

The duties of the position require the ability to communicate with people from all walks of life, be proficient with firearms, have skills in self-defense, and have the ability to exercise good judgment. Inspectors may be relocated according to the needs of the service.

The recruitment process is extremely thorough, and there is intense competition for relatively few positions. The recruitment and selection process must be completed prior to the applicant's 37th birthday.

This position is exempt from the Fair Labor Standards Act (FLSA) and does not qualify for overtime compensation. Postal inspector salaries are based on the Inspection Service Law Enforcement (ISLE) pay system. The ISLE pay grades and steps correspond to the General Schedule (GS) pay scale for law enforcement officers.

Candidates must:

- ✓ Applicants must be U.S. citizens and at least 21 years of age and less than 37 years of age at the time of appointment, except for preference eligible veterans for whom there is currently no maximum age limit.

---

[3] Excerpted from http://postalinspectors.uspis.gov/employment/eligibility.aspx

✓ Possess a conferred four-year degree from an accredited college or university.

✓ Pass a comprehensive visual exam.

✓ Pass a hearing acuity test.

✓ Be in good physical condition, with weight in proportion to height, and possess emotional and mental stability. See Postal Inspector Height/Weight Chart.

✓ Have no felony convictions (felony charges may render candidates ineligible).

✓ Have no misdemeanor conviction of domestic violence (other misdemeanor charges or convictions may render candidates ineligible).

✓ Have a current, valid state driver's license, held for at least two years.

✓ Have the ability to demonstrate the following attributes, as measured by the Assessment Center evaluation:

- Write and speak English clearly.
- Schedule and complete activities in a logical, timely sequence.
- Comprehend and execute instructions written and spoken in English.
- Think clearly and comprehend verbal and nonverbal information.
- Interact with others to obtain or exchange information or services.
- Perceive or identify relevant details and associate them with other facts.

Special Knowledge

There are four special knowledge tracks that make applicants more competitive for the position of postal inspector: language skills, postal experience, specialized nonpostal skills, and academic achievement. Candidates without special knowledge will be only minimally qualified.

Language Skills

Applicants seeking to enter the recruitment process under the language skills track must have advanced competency in a foreign language deemed as needed by the Postal Inspection Service to meet its investigative mission.

Applicants must pass a formal proficiency test administered by a contractor of the Postal Inspection Service. In addition to the language requirement, applicants in this track must have one year of full-time work experience with the same company or firm within two years of the date of their application.

The current list is as follows:

Arabic	Armenian	Cambodian	Cantonese
Czech	Dutch	Egyptian	Farsi (Persian)
French	German	Greek (modern)	Haitian-Creole
Hebrew	Hindi	Hmong	Indonesian
Italian	Japanese	Korean	Lao
Mandarin	Norwegian	Polish	Portuguese
Punjabi	Russian	Serbo-Croatian	Slovak
Spanish	Swahili	Swedish	Tagalog
Thai	Turkish	Ukrainian	Urdu
Vietnamese			

Postal Experience

Candidates seeking consideration under the specialized postal experience track must within the last two years have been a U.S. Postal Service employee, contractor, or intern.

Specialized Nonpostal Experience

Applicants seeking consideration under the specialized nonpostal skill track must have experience in one of the areas of expertise designated as critical to the needs of the Postal Inspection Service. Candidates must also have one year of full-time work experience with the same company or firm within two years of the date of their application. Critical areas of expertise follow:

✓ **Military experience.** Candidates must have served at least two years in the military and received an honorable discharge. Candidates with international or bioterrorism experience preferred.

✓ **Law degree.** Candidates must have a Juris Doctor degree and one year of full-time work experience with the same company or firm within two years of the date of their application.

✓ **Certifications in auditing or investigations.** Candidates with certifications in auditing, such as Certified Public Accountant (CPA), Certified Management Accountant (CMA), Certified Internal Auditor (CIA), and Certified Information Systems Auditor (CISA), or investigative certifications in protection, security, or fraud examination, such as Certified Protection Professional (CPP) and Certified Fraud Examiner

(CFE), are eligible under this skill track. Candidates must provide proof of certification and one year of full-time work experience in this field.

✓ **Specialized Computer Education**. Candidates with a four-year degree in computer science, computer engineering, telecommunications, management information systems, electronic commerce, decision and information science, or computer information systems and one year of full-time work experience in this field are eligible under this skill track.

✓ **Specialized Computer Expertise.** Candidates who are currently employed, and have been employed for at least one year in a position specializing in computer forensics, Internet investigations, Internet security, network security, or information systems security and one year of full-time work experience in this field are eligible under this skill track.

✓ **Certifications in Computer Systems.** Candidates with a certification as a Microsoft Certified Systems Engineer (MCSE), Microsoft Certified Professional + Internet (MCP+I), Cisco Certified Network Professional (CCNP), Certified Novell Engineer (CNE), A+ Certified Computer Technician, Certified Information Systems Security Professional (CISSP), Linux certification, or Sun Systems Certified Administrator and one year of full-time work experience in this field are eligible under this skill track.

✓ **Law Enforcement.** Candidates with at least one full year of law enforcement experience as detectives, criminalists, and polygraph examiners or as patrol, probation, correction, and parole officers are eligible under this skill track, but must provide examples of the type of work conducted. (This track excludes clerical or technical support personnel.)

✓ **Bioterrorism Investigations.** Candidates with at least one full year of bioterrorism investigation experience are eligible under this skill track. Specific examples of the type of work conducted will be required.

Academic Achievement

To increase competitiveness and acquire a more diversified candidate pool, candidates may enter the recruitment process along a fourth track, academic achievement with or without work experience.

- Academic achievement with work experience. Candidates with at least one year of full-time work experience with the same company, within two years of the date of their application, are eligible under this skill track.

- Candidates with a bachelor's degree (B.A. or B.S. in any field) must have two years of full-time work experience.

- Candidates with an advanced degree (M.A., M.S., or Ph.D. in any field) must have one year of full-time work experience.

- Academic achievement without work experience. Candidates with a bachelor's degree (a B.A. or B.S. in any field) and a cumulative grade point average (GPA) of 3.0 or higher (on a 4.0 scale) or its equivalent, or an advanced degree (J.D., M.A., M.S., or Ph.D. in any field) are eligible under this skill track.

Drug Policy

The U.S. Postal Inspection Service is committed to a drug-free workplace. The unlawful use of drugs by employees is not tolerated, and those who apply for employment and illegally use or sell drugs are considered unsuitable for employment.

The Postal Inspection Service drug policy balances the need to maintain a drug-free workplace and the integrity necessary to accomplish its mission with the desirability of affording employment opportunities to the broadest segment of society, consistent with those needs. The policy is as follows:

- Candidates who have illegally used drugs while in a law enforcement or prosecutorial position, or while in a position with a high level of responsibility or public trust are considered unsuitable for employment.

- Candidates who have misrepresented their drug history in their application are considered unsuitable for employment.

- Candidates who have illegally sold a drug are considered unsuitable for employment.

- Candidates who have illegally used any drug (other than cannabis*) within the past 10 years are considered unsuitable for employment, absent compelling or mitigating circumstances.

- Candidates who have used cannabis within the past three years are considered unsuitable for employment absent compelling or mitigating circumstances.

* Cannabis may include marijuana, hashish, hash oil, and tetrahydrocannabinol (THC).

Candidates not in compliance with the Postal Inspection Service drug policy will not be considered for employment. Postal inspectors are randomly tested for illegal drug use throughout their careers.

Candidate Application Process

The applicant process for most postal inspector applicants consists of the following phases:

Phase One

- Completion of application. Applications may be completed online only during open seasons.

- Completion of a two-part on-line entrance examination. Part one of the exam is unproctored and may be completed anywhere the candidate can gain access to the Internet. (Candidates who fail part one may be eligible for one retest, provided they meet the job qualifications at the time of the retest.) A selected number candidates that are successful on part one will be invited to complete part two, as a part of an information exchange, at a designated facility.

- Participation in an information exchange. A Postal Inspection Service representative will meet with a group of invited candidates and facilitate an information exchange which includes the completion of the part two of the entrance exam, submission of paperwork to complete the comprehensive application package, a video presentation, and a question-and-answer session.

- Completion of the Comprehensive Application Packet, including forms used to initiate the National Agency Check for obtaining the Top Secret security clearance required for all postal inspectors.

- Language proficiency test, if applicable.

- Assessment center evaluation of knowledge, skills, and abilities: simulation of exercises used to assess core competencies needed by successful postal inspectors. (Candidates who fail the evaluation may be eligible for one reassessment, provided they meet the job qualifications at the time of the reassessment.)

- Polygraph examination to validate information obtained during the application process, including illegal drug use, criminal history, and integrity issues.

- Background suitability investigation.

- Management interview.

- Drug screening.

Phase Two

- Medical examination: An employment physical will be administered only to candidates who have received a contingent offer of employment. Successful completion of the employment physical is the final step in the selection process.

- Once an official appointment date has been established, the candidate begins:

- Residential Basic Inspector Training program at Potomac, Maryland. Graduation from the training program is a condition of employment.

- Six-month probation period for nonpostal candidates.

Current qualified Federal Law Enforcement Criminal Investigators (Occupational Code 1811), or equivalent, may be permitted to participate in an abbreviated applicant process, consisting of the following steps:

- Online application.

- Comprehensive application packet.

- National agency check (unless documentation is provided indicating the agent has a Top Secret security clearance).

- Polygraph interview.

- Background investigation and management interview.

- Employment physical and drug screening.

- Six-week residential Federal Investigator Orientation course. (This is an abbreviated version of the Basic Inspector Training course listed below.)

Basic Inspector Training Process

Basic Inspector Training at the Career Development Division (CDD) covers academics, firearms, physical fitness and defensive tactics, and practical exercises. Each candidate must participate fully in all program areas and achieve specific minimum academic and performance levels to graduate. Graduation from basic training is a condition of employment. Failure to meet the minimum academic and performance levels will result in the termination of the appointment.

Academics

Classroom instruction is divided into courses, or lesson blocks, which address the major areas of investigation and administration that postal inspectors are expected to perform. Three examinations will be given during training to evaluate a students understanding of the subject matter.

Firearms

Rigorous firearms training provides beginning through advanced students with the skills needed to handle firearms safely and develop shooting proficiency.

Firearms proficiency is tested twice during the program. Students must meet the standards set by the National Threat Management Committee and qualify on the Postal Inspection Service Practical Pistol Course, using the service-issued weapon. Students must also qualify on the shotgun course. The shotgun qualifications course consists of demonstrated safety, proper loading and unloading of the weapon, and firing rounds from various positions.

Physical Fitness/Defensive Tactics

All student inspectors must participate fully in both the physical fitness and defensive tactics programs.

The physical fitness program familiarizes students with various exercise options designed to improve their physical condition. Classroom time is set aside for physical fitness workouts, but students are responsible for additional workouts outside of class.

The defensive tactics program requires that students demonstrate the techniques taught and practiced through a practical exam and dynamic practical exercises. Students must develop the ability to use a level of force appropriate to the threat. After each course of instruction a students abilities to perform assigned maneuvers are evaluated by the instructors.

Practical Exercises

Practical exercises allow students the opportunity to perform the lessons learned during classroom activities and defensive tactics in a real-life simulation.

Compensation

Postal inspectors are exempt from the Fair Labor Standards Act (FLSA) and do not qualify for overtime compensation. Salaries are based on the Inspection Service Law Enforcement (ISLE) pay scale, which corresponds to the General Schedule (GS) pay scale for law enforcement officers. Minimum-entry base pay levels range from the equivalent of a Grade 9, Step 1, to Grade 12, Step 10. The entry-level salary for transferring 1811s range from a Grade 9, Step 1, to Grade 13, Step 10. Go to www.federaljobs.net to review the federal pay scales for all major metropolitan areas.

A candidate's qualifications and current pay–excluding overtime, premiums, night differential, higher-level details, and second incomes–are considered when entry levels are established.

In addition to basic pay, postal inspectors receive locality pay and law enforcement availability pay. Inspectors in the Contiguous United States (CONUS) receive locality pay based on the cost of living in various parts of the country. Inspectors domiciled in Hawaii, Alaska, and the U.S. territories receive a territorial cost-of-living allowance (TCOLA), which is a percentage of salary that is determined and published by the Office of Personnel Management.

Candidates start earning locality pay when they begin training at the academy. Overtime pay increases annual salaries by 25% and is applied upon graduation from the academy. Transferring GS-1811 investigators, attending the Federal Investigator Orientation, receive overtime pay compensation while at the academy.

Relocation Expenses

Mobility is an important component of the postal inspector position. Inspectors who are required to relocate to their first duty station will receive a paid move, which includes but is not limited to the following:

- Transporting household goods

- An advance round trip to visit a new duty location to find housing

- Temporary living quarters, if necessary.

Student inspectors learn about relocation benefits while attending the training academy. Students who initiate relocation before completing training will lose relocation benefits. Postal inspectors who move later in their careers under various components of the transfer policy or as the result of a promotion are eligible to receive relocation benefits.

Additional Information

Contact one of the Postal Inspection Service division offices for additional information and to find out when jobs will be advertised in your area. A divisional office list is provided on the next page. Visit www.postalinspectors.uspis.gov frequently for updated information and new job announcements. Visit this book's companion web site at www.postalwork.net for additional assistance and direct links to the official postal service sites. Explore federal law enforcement occupations, including positions with the Department of Homeland Security, at www.federaljobs.net.

Visit www.postalinspectors.uspis.gov for additional information and to locate open position announcements. The majority of the information provided in this chapter was excerpted from postal inspector job announcements, their website and from related occupational descriptions from the Department of Labor's Occupational Outlook Handbook.

U.S. Postal Inspection Service Division Offices

Miami 3400 Lakeside Dr 6th Fl Miramar FL 33027-3242 (877) 876-2455	**New Jersey / Caribbean** PO Box 509 Newark NJ 07101-0509 (877) 876-2455	**Denver** 1745 Stout St Ste 900 Denver CO 80299-3034 (877) 876-2455
Houston 650 N. Sam Houston Pkwy Houston TX 77067-4336 (877) 876-2455	**Boston** 495 Summer St Ste 600 Boston MA 02210-2114 (877) 876-2455	**Charlotte** PO Box 3000 Charlotte, NC 28228-3000 (877) 876-2455
Detroit PO Box 330119 Detroit MI 48232-6119 (877) 876-2455	**San Francisco** 2501 Rydin Rd., FL 2S Richmond, CA 94804-9712 (877) 876-2455	**Los Angeles** P.O. Box 2000 Pasadena CA 91102-2000 (877) 876-2455
Chicago 433 W Harrison St. Rm. 50190 Chicago IL 60669-2201 (877) 876-2455	**Fort Worth** 251 W. Lancaster Ave. 2nd Floor Fort Worth TX 76102 (877) 876-2455	**Philadelphia Metro** PO Box 3001 Bala Cynwyd, PA 19004 (877) 876-2455
Pittsburgh 5315 Campbells Run Rd Ste. 300 Pittsburgh PA 15277 (877) 876-2455	**Seattle** PO Box 400 Seattle WA 98111-4000 (877) 876-2455	**Washington Metro** 10500 Little Patuxent Pkwy Columbia MD 21044 (877) 876-2455
New York Metro PO Box 555 New York NY 10116-0555 (877) 876-2455		

Chapter Ten
Civil Service Job Options

The majority of jobs in the Postal Service are mail carrier and clerk positions. However, like most large corporations the Postal Service requires a broad spectrum of occupations, everything from janitors to engineers, inspectors, and administrative occupations of all types. Similar or related occupations exist in the federal Civil Service. There are over 900 occupational titles in the federal sector which provide abundant employment opportunities for those willing to seek them out.

Uncle Sam employs over 2.2 million full time equivalent federal civilian employees not counting the postal service, and half are now eligible for regular or early retirement. Over a million jobs must be filled as baby boomers retire from the federal civil service. There are many reasons to consider federal employment. The average annual federal worker's compensation, pay plus benefits, in 2018 was **$123,049** compared to just **$70,081** for the private sector.[1] Student loan payoff, relocation, and cash incentives are now offered for hard-to-fill positions, and the benefits package is exceptional.

You need to know how to take advantage of the federal hiring system and recent changes to successfully land the job you want in government.

---

[1]   Bureau of Economic Analysis, Compensation Tables 6.2D and 6.5D, 2017.

Excellent job opportunities are available for those who know how to tap this lucrative job market. All government hiring is based on performance and qualifications regardless of your sex, race, color, creed, religion, disability, or national origin. Where else can you apply for a high-paying entry-level job that offers employment at thousands of locations internationally, excellent career advancement opportunities, plus careers in hundreds of occupations?

This chapter will help you understand and explore civil service job options. Much of this chapter was excerpted from *The Book of U.S. Government Jobs*, 11th Edition, by Dennis V. Damp.

LOCATING JOB VACANCIES

Thousands of federal jobs are advertised on any given day. Yes, thousands of jobs are just a few key strokes away if you know where to find them. With 50 percent of the federal work force eligible for either early or regular retirement, there are abundant opportunities for those who seek them out. Jobs are available nationwide and overseas. The Office of Personnel Management (OPM) maintains the largest government online jobs database at http://www.usajobs.gov, and you can take advantage of their free online résumé and automated job alert services. Visit http://federaljobs.net/federal.htm to link to hundreds of agency employment web sites to locate **ALL** available jobs.

Not all government jobs are advertised on **USAJOBS**. Agencies with direct hire authority may advertise vacancies independently.

Individual agency personnel offices should also be contacted to obtain job announcements. Visit http://federaljobs.net for job listings and for direct links to 141 federal agency recruiting sites.

NATURE OF FEDERAL EMPLOYMENT

The federal government's essential duties include defending the United States from foreign aggression and terrorism, representing U.S. interests abroad, enforcing laws and regulations, and administering domestic programs and agencies.[5] U.S. citizens are particularly aware of the federal government when they pay their income taxes each year, but they usually do not consider the government's role when they watch a weather forecast, purchase fresh and uncontaminated groceries, travel by highway or air, or make a deposit at their bank. Workers employed by the federal government play a vital role in these and many other aspects of our daily lives.

---

[5] The Career Guide to Industries, U.S. Department of Labor

Over 200 years ago, the founders of the United States gathered in Philadelphia to create a Constitution for a new national government and lay the foundation for self-governance. The Constitution of the United States, ratified by the last of the 13 original states in 1791, created the three branches of the federal government and granted certain powers and responsibilities to each. The legislative, judicial, and executive branches were created with equal powers but very different responsibilities that act to keep their powers in balance.

The legislative branch is responsible for forming and amending the legal structure of the nation. Its largest component is Congress, the primary U.S. legislative body, which is made up of the Senate and the House of Representatives. This body includes senators, representatives, their staffs, and various support workers. The legislative branch employs only about 2 percent of federal workers, nearly all of whom work in the Washington, D.C., area.

The judicial branch is responsible for interpreting the laws that the legislative branch enacts. The Supreme Court, the nation's definitive judicial body, makes the highest rulings. Its decisions usually follow the appeal of a decision made by the one of the regional Courts of Appeal, which hear cases appealed from U.S. District Courts, the Court of Appeals for the Federal Circuit, or state Supreme Courts. U.S. District Courts are located in each state and are the first to hear most cases under federal jurisdiction. The judicial branch employs about the same number of people as does the legislative branch, but its offices and employees are dispersed throughout the country.

Of the three branches, the executive branch — through the power vested by the Constitution in the office of the president — has the widest range of responsibilities. Consequently, it employed 96 percent of all federal civilian employees (excluding Postal Service workers) in 2017. The executive branch is composed of the Executive Office of the President, 15 executive Cabinet departments, including the recently created Department of Homeland Security, and nearly 90 independent agencies, each of which has clearly defined duties. The Executive Office of the President is composed of several offices and councils that aid the president in policy decisions. These include the Office of Management and Budget, which oversees the administration of the federal budget; the National Security Council, which advises the president on matters of national defense; and the Council of Economic Advisers, which makes economic policy recommendations.

Each of the 15 executive Cabinet departments administers programs that oversee an aspect of life in the United States. The highest departmental official of each Cabinet department, the secretary, is a member of the president's Cabinet. The 15 departments are listed below by employment size with a brief description and total employment as of January 2018 .

Defense: (733,880) Manages the military forces that protect our country and its interests, including the Departments of the Army, Navy, and Air Force and a number of smaller agencies. The civilian workforce employed by the Department of Defense performs various support activities, such as payroll and public relations.

Veterans Affairs: (383,172) Administers programs to aid U.S. veterans and their families, runs the veterans hospital system, and operates our national cemeteries.

Homeland Security: (202,559) Works to prevent terrorist attacks within the United States; reduce vulnerability to terrorism; and minimize the damage from potential attacks and natural disasters.

Justice: (115,407) Enforces federal laws, prosecutes cases in federal courts, and runs federal prisons.

Treasury: (87,168) Regulates banks and other financial institutions, administers the public debt, prints currency, and collects federal income taxes.

Agriculture: (84,392) Promotes U.S. agriculture domestically and internationally and sets standards governing quality, quantity, and labeling of food sold in the United States.

Health and Human Services: (84,506) Sponsors medical research; approves use of new drugs and medical devices; runs the Public Health Service; and administers Medicare.

Interior: (62,223) Manages federal lands, including the national parks and forests; runs hydroelectric power systems; and promotes conservation of natural resources.

Transportation: (54,734) Sets national transportation policy; plans and funds the construction of highways and mass transit systems; and regulates railroad, aviation, and maritime operations.

Commerce: (47,340) Forecasts the weather; charts the oceans; regulates patents and trademarks; conducts the Census; compiles statistics; and promotes U.S. economic growth by encouraging international trade.

State: (12,009) Oversees the nation's embassies and consulates; issues passports; monitors U.S. interests abroad; and represents the United States before international organizations.

Labor: (14,833) Enforces laws guaranteeing fair pay, workplace safety, and equal job opportunity; administers unemployment insurance; regulates pension funds; and collects and analyzes economic data through its Bureau of Labor Statistics.

Energy: (14,677) Coordinates the national use and provision of energy; oversees the production and disposal of nuclear weapons; and plans for future energy needs.

Housing and Urban Development: (7,798) Funds public housing projects; enforces equal housing laws; and insures and finances mortgages.

Education: (4,023) Provides scholarships, student loans, and aid to schools.

WORKING CONDITIONS

Due to the broad scope of federal employment, almost every working condition found in the private sector can also be found in the federal government.[6] Most white-collar employees work in office buildings, hospitals, or laboratories, and most of the blue-collar workforce can be found in factories, warehouses, shipyards, military bases, construction sites, or national parks and forests. Work environments vary from the comfortable and relaxed to the hazardous and stressful, such as those experienced by law enforcement officers, astronauts, or air traffic controllers.

The vast majority of federal employees work full time, often on flexible (flexitime) schedules, which allow workers to tailor their own work week, within certain constraints. Some agencies also have "flexiplace" programs, which allow selected workers to perform some job duties at home or from regional centers.

The duties of some federal workers require that they spend much of their time away from the offices in which they are based. Inspectors and compliance officers, for example, often visit businesses and work sites to ensure that laws and regulations are obeyed. Few travel so far that they are unable to return home each night. Some federal workers, however, frequently travel long distances, spending days or weeks away from home. Auditors, for example, may spend weeks in distant locations.

EMPLOYMENT

The federal government, including the U.S. Postal Service, employs about 2.7 million civilian workers, or about 2 percent of the nation's workforce. The federal government is the nation's single largest employer. Because data on employment in certain agencies cannot be released to the public for national security reasons, this total does not include employment for the Central Intelligence Agency, National Security Agency, Defense Intelligence Agency, and National Imagery and Mapping Agency.

---

[6] Career Guide to Industries, U.S. Department of Labor

Table 1-2

Percent distribution of employment in the federal government
and the private sector by major occupational group

Occupational Group	Federal Government	Private Sector
Total	*100*	*100*
Professional and related	32.8	19.9
Management, business, and financial	27.4	9.0
Office and administrative support	16.7	17.6
Service	10.6	19.3
Installation, maintenance, and repair	4.8	4.0
Transportation and materiel moving	3.1	7.2
Production	2.1	7.6
Construction and extraction	1.9	4.7
Sales and related	0.4	10.1
Farming, fishing and forestry	0.2	0.7

OCCUPATIONS

Although the federal government employs workers in every major occupational group, workers are not employed in the same proportions in which they are employed throughout the economy as a whole (Table 1-2). The analytical and technical nature of many government duties translates into a much higher proportion of professional, management, business, and financial occupations in the federal government, compared with most industries. Conversely, the government sells very little, so it employs relatively few sales workers.

Professional and related occupations accounted for about one-third of federal employment. The largest group of professional workers worked in life science, physical science, and social science occupations, such as biological scientists, conservation scientists and foresters, environmental scientists and geoscientists, and forest and conservation technicians. They do work such as determining the effects of drugs on living organisms, preventing fires in the national forests, and predicting earthquakes and hurricanes. The Department of Agriculture employed the vast majority of life scientists, but physical scientists were distributed throughout a variety of departments and agencies.

Many health professionals, such as licensed practical and licensed vocational nurses, registered nurses, and physicians and surgeons, were employed by the Department of Veterans Affairs (VA) in VA hospitals.

Large numbers of federal workers also held jobs as engineers, including aerospace, civil, computer hardware, electrical and electronics, industrial, mechanical, and nuclear engineers. Engineers were found in many departments of the executive branch, but they most commonly worked in the Department of Defense, the National Aeronautics and Space Administration, and the Department of Transportation. In general, they solve problems and provide advice on technical programs, such as building highway bridges or implementing agency-wide computer systems.

Computer specialists — primarily computer software engineers, network and computer systems analysts, and computer systems administrators — are employed throughout the federal government. They write computer programs, analyze problems related to data processing, and keep computer systems running smoothly. Many health professionals, such as registered nurses, physicians and surgeons, and licensed practical nurses, are employed by the Department of Veterans Affairs (VA) in one of many VA hospitals.

Management, business, and financial workers made up about 27 percent of federal employment and were primarily responsible for overseeing operations. Managerial workers include a broad range of officials who, at the highest levels, may head federal agencies or programs. Middle managers, on the other hand, usually oversee one activity or aspect of a program. One management occupation — legislators — are responsible for passing and amending laws and overseeing the executive branch of the government. Within the federal government, legislators are entirely found in Congress.

Others occupations in this category are accountants and auditors, who prepare and analyze financial reports, review and record revenues and expenditures, and investigate operations for fraud and inefficiency. Purchasing agents handle federal purchases of supplies. Management analysts study government operations and systems and suggest improvements. These employees aid management staff with administrative duties. Administrative support workers in the federal government include secretaries and general office clerks. Purchasing agents handle federal purchases of supplies, and tax examiners, collectors, and revenue agents determine and collect taxes.

Compared with the economy as a whole, workers in service occupations were relatively scarce in the federal government. About seven out of 10 federal workers in service occupations were protective service workers, such as detectives and criminal investigators, police and sheriff's patrol officers, and correctional officers and jailers. These workers protect the public from crime and oversee federal prisons.

Federally employed workers in installation, maintenance, and repair occupations include aircraft mechanics and service technicians who fix and maintain all types of aircraft. Also included are electrical and electronic equipment mechanics, installers, and repairers, who inspect, adjust, and repair electronic equipment such as industrial controls, transmitters, antennas, radar, radio, and navigation systems.

The federal government employed a relatively small number of workers in transportation, production, construction, sales and related, and farming, fishing, and forestry occupations. However, they employed almost all air traffic controllers in the country and a significant number of agricultural inspectors and bridge and lock tenders.

OUTLOOK

Wage and salary employment in the federal government is projected to increase by 10 percent through 2018. There will be a substantial number of job openings as many federal workers are expected to retire over the next decade, although job prospects are expected to vary by occupation.

Wage and salary employment in the federal government, not including the post office, is expected to increase by 10 percent over the coming decade, which is close to the 11 percent growth rate for all industries combined. Staffing levels in federal government can be subject to change in the long run because of changes in public policies as legislated by the Congress, which affect spending levels and hiring decisions for the various departments and agencies. In general, over the coming decade, domestic programs are likely to see an increase in employment.

While there will be growth in many occupations over the coming decade, demand will be especially strong for specialized workers in areas related to public health, information security, scientific research, law enforcement, and financial services. As a larger share of the U.S. population enters the older age brackets, demand for healthcare will increase. This will lead to a substantial number of new jobs in federal hospitals and other healthcare facilities for registered nurses and physicians and surgeons. In addition, as cyber security becomes an increasingly important aspect of national defense, rapid growth will occur among information technology specialists, such as computer and information research scientists, who will be needed to devise defense methods, monitor computer networks, and execute security protocol. Furthermore, as global activity in scientific development increases, the federal Government will add many physical science, life science, and engineering workers to remain competitive. Aside from these specific areas, numerous new jobs in other occupational areas will arise as the diverse federal workforce continues to expand.

As financial and business transactions face increased scrutiny, a substantial number of compliance officers and claims adjusters, examiners, and investigators will be added to federal payrolls. In addition, as the population grows and national security remains a priority, many new law enforcement officers, such as detectives and criminal investigators, will be needed.

Job prospects in the federal government are expected to vary by occupation. Over the next decade, a significant number of workers are expected to retire, which will create a large number of job openings. This may create favorable prospects in certain occupations, but job seekers may face competition for positions in occupations with fewer retirements, or for popular jobs that attract many applicants.

GETTING STARTED

The Book of U.S. Government Jobs by Dennis V. Damp is an excellent resource that will guide you through the job search. You will find up-to-date information on how the federal employment system works from an insider's perspective, how to locate job announcements, and complete a thorough application package. Also visit this book's companion web site at www.federaljobs.net for additional information and federal job listings.

This book will guide you step-by-step through the federal employment process, from filling out your first employment application to locating job announcements, networking resources and hiring agencies. Follow the guidelines set forth in this book to dramatically improve your chances of landing a federal job.

PAY AND BENEFITS

Job security, good pay, and an excellent retirement system are just a few of the top reasons most people seek federal employment. Others consider government careers because of desirable travel opportunities, training availability, diverse occupations, and the ability to locate jobs nationwide and overseas. There retirement system is very generous, visit http://federalretirement.net to review their Federal Employees Retirement System (FERS) benefits.

In an effort to give agencies more flexibility in how they pay their workers, there are several different pay systems in effect or planning to be implemented over the next few years. The Federal Aviation Administration (FAA) uses a core compensation pay band system. Their system incorporates fewer, but wider pay bands, instead of grade levels. Pay increases, under these systems, are almost entirely based on performance, as opposed to length of service.

There are eight predominant pay systems. Approximately half of the workforce is under the General Schedule (GS) pay scale, 20 percent are paid under the Postal Service rates, and about 10 percent are paid under the Federal Wage System (FWS). The remaining pay systems are for the Executive Schedule, Foreign Service, Special Salary Rates, and Nonappropriated Fund Instrumentalities pay scales, and Veterans Health Administration.

The majority of professional and administrative federal workers are still paid under the General Schedule (GS). New employees usually start at the first step of a grade. In an effort to make federal pay more responsive to local labor market conditions, federal employees working in the U.S. receive locality pay.

The average wage for full-time workers paid under the General Schedule was $86,365 in 2018. For those in craft, repair, operator, and laborer jobs, the Federal Wage System (FWS) is used to pay these workers. This schedule sets federal wages so that they are comparable to prevailing regional wage rates for similar types of jobs. As a result, wage rates paid under the FWS can vary significantly from one locality to another.

EDUCATION REQUIREMENTS

In the federal government, 59 percent of all workers do not have a college degree. The level of required education is dependent upon the job applied for. Each job announcement lists needed skills and abilities, including education and work experience. However, the more education and work experience you have, the more competitive you will be when ranked against other applicants.

SUMMARY

It took me two years to land my first competitive federal Civil Service job. I was not aware of the employment options available at that time and I simply sent written requests for job announcements every two weeks to the local OPM office. Today there are many options available through special-emphasis hiring, case and direct hire authority, student employment, and internships, to name a few. Also, use the many Internet sites that provide links to key job lists and informational resources such as http://federaljobs.net. Take advantage of as many of the programs and varied positions that you qualify for to expedite your career search. Don't give up or get frustrated with the paperwork that is required when applying for federal employment. Finally, I must add that it is unwise to get angry with the process; instead of getting mad, **GET INVOLVED.**

Appendix A
Job Hunter's Checklist

WHAT TO DO NOW

❑ Review Chapters One, Two, and Three to fully understand postal service recruiting, employee benefits, salary, and how they hire. Also review:

- ✔ Chapter Four for exam overviews (all tested occupations)
- ✔ Chapter Five for the **473 Postal Exam Study Guide**
- ✔ Chapter Seven for veterans hiring preference
- ✔ Chapter Ten for related federal civil service occupations

❑ Review the postal service occupations listed in Chapters Three and Eight. Also review Chapter Ten for other job options. These chapters provide lists of postal jobs that you may qualify for — including job descriptions for over 40 occupations.

❑ Visit the following websites to locate job vacancies for all occupations, including mail carrier and clerk positions in your area:

- ✔ http://about.usps.com/careers/welcome.htm/ *(job vacancy lists)* Apply online at this site. If tests are required, you will be scheduled for exams in your area within 14 days from application date.
- ✔ www.postalwork.net *(job vacancy lists)* This site provides lists of all USPS, private sector, and federal jobs in your area. The consolidated job listings provide abundant opportunities for you to explore.

NOTE: Visit these sites often to locate job vacancies.

❏   See Appendix C for a national list of Customer Service District Offices that you can contact if you run into problems or need assistance.

❏   Contact regional and local postal facilities including customer service district sales offices, general mail facilities, sectional center facilities, management sectional centers, or bulk mail centers in your area. Don't forget to talk with your local postmaster about job opportunities in your area. Also visit this book's companion web site for updated information and to search for related jobs in all sectors:

✔ www.postalwork.net/ *(Career Center)*.

❏   Locate your school transcripts, military records, awards, and professional licenses. Collect past employment history; salary, addresses, phone numbers and dates employed, for the application. Use the PS 2591 form available online on the resource page at www.postalwork.net to review and compile the information you will need when you apply online.

APPLYING FOR A JOB

❏   When you locate a job announcement on the Post Service's site, register and apply online to complete your initial application and assessment. If monitored exams are required, you will be notified via e-mail and directed to select a date, location, and time where you will take the exam in your area.

> Print the position announcement for all jobs that you apply for. Click on the job vacancy of interest and print it out for future reference. A contact email address or phone number is provided for each announcement and you will need this information to follow-up or possibly to reschedule an exam.

❏   If no vacancies are posted, visit http://about.usps.com/careers/welcome.htm frequently to check for updated postings. The postal service also advertises in local newspapers and at State employment offices. You can also call or write your local District Office's human resources department to find out when jobs will be announced for your area. Consider getting your foot in the door by taking a casual or transitional temporary position. (See page 26)

❏   Complete your online application and assessments. **ALL** requested information must be provided to rate as high as possible and to be considered for a position. Collect your employment and educational history before starting your online application and draft your work descriptions offline. You can copy and paste your work descriptions into the online résumé builder when you register. They will need previous employer addresses, phone numbers, salary, dates employed, and more. Be prepared and follow all instructions.

Note: Corporate job vacancy announcements require applicants to complete write-ups for required knowledge, skills, and abilities (KSAs). If you neglect to complete these statements, your application may be rejected. Review Appendix B for KSA examples. *The Book of U.S. Government Jobs*, 11th edition, by Dennis Damp, provides detailed guidance for writing federal style resumes and KSAs. This book is available at bookstores, Amazon.com, and libraries.

❑   Your application is submitted online, and you can save your profile and exam results so that you can apply for other jobs. Be sure to write down your user name and password that you establish online for future use. You must also keep a copy of your **Candidate ID Number** that allows you to apply for other jobs without retaking the exam.

❑   After applying online, you have 14 days to complete all assessments. You will be notified when and where to report for proctored exams, if required. Most exams are now in two parts, an online assessment and a proctored exam at a local testing facility. You must bring your user assessment ID and password with you to take the proctored exam.

ADDITIONAL RESOURCES

NOTE: Internet access is required to contact the following services. Many libraries offer online connectivity for their patrons.

❑   http://about.usps.com/careers/welcome.htm **Postal Service Employment Page** – This highly informative service offers job listings and general information about the USPS and includes recent press releases. Visit this page often to search for job vacancies in your area.

❑   www.postalwork.net **Post Office Jobs & Career Center** – A popular site for exploring postal service careers and for direct links to key employment information. This site also provides job listings for related job vacancies in the federal, state, and private sectors for your area.

❑   www.federaljobs.net **Federal Civil Service Jobs and Career Center** – One of the most popular federal employment sites on the Internet today. Visit this site to explore federal job options, including jobs with the USPS.

❑   www.usajobs.gov **Office of Personnel Management's (OPM's)** official Web site. This site posts thousands of federal government job vacancies. Visit this site to search for related civil service job vacancies in your area.

You can also register for e-mail notification for specific job titles and occupational group vacancies.

RESULTS

❑   Your application is processed when you first register, and you have 14 days to complete all assessments. You will receive an e-mail message with instructions on how to access your test results. You can check your results as part of your candidate profile in eCareer after you complete your exam. Go to http://about.usps.com/careers/welcome.htm to log into your eCareer account and review your assessment results. Selected applicants must:

     ✔ Meet basic qualifications
     ✔ Score high on the exam (if required)
     ✔ Successfully complete an interview
     ✔ Pass a drug screen

THE INTERVIEW

❑   Prepare for the interview. Review Chapter Six for guidance on how to present yourself and prepare for the interview. Most postal job books completely ignore the interview phase. If you don't impress the selecting officials, you may be passed over for the position.

CAUTION

Many postal job scams advertise toll-free job hotlines online and in newspaper classifieds. They charge fees ranging from $70 to over $200 to help you apply for jobs and include a study guide. Don't waste your money. The application process is free to all who apply, and this book provides a comprehensive 473 exam study guide in Chapter Five. This book is also available at many libraries.

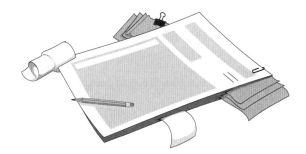

Appendix B
Corporate Positions

Corporate positions include management and supervision, administrative, professional and technical occupations. Jobs that are open to the general public are listed on the postal service's web site, http://about.usps.com/careers/welcome.htm. The jobs are advertised in the following categories, with a sampling of specific occupations:

- Engineering
  - Electrical
  - Electronic
- ERM/HR
  - Educational Psychologist
  - Training
  - Human Resources
- Facilities
  - Architect Engineer
- Finance
  - Accountant
  - Economist
  - Mathematical Statistician
- Information Technology
  - Business System Analyst
  - Information System Specialist
  - Systems Analyst
- Inspection Service
  - Security Architect/Engineer
- Marketing
  - Customer Service Support Analyst
- Network Operations
  - Transportation Specialist

When you apply for a corporate position with the postal services, recruitment is similar to the federal civil service application process. The applicant is rated on his/her work experience, education, special knowledge, skills, and abilities (KSAs). Job announcements are advertised on the USPS website, and the applicant must follow the job announcement application instructions precisely to be considered for the position. Any omissions can cause your application to be rejected. Many highly qualified applicants are excluded because of administrative errors or omissions.

This Appendix guides you through the application process so that you can complete your application or postal service style résumé that will get the attention of the selecting official. The PS Form 2591, "*Application for Employment*," was formerly required until the postal service initiated their eCareer online recruiting process recently. Applicants must prepare their résumés and applications in accordance with specific guidelines. The postal service has developed the following enhanced application services:

- ✎ Diverse methods to collect information from job applicants – written, telephone, and online techniques

- ✎ Applicant choices in how they submit applications

- ✎ Visit http://about.usps.com/careers/welcome.htm to search for job vacancies,

- ✎ Customer Service District Sales Offices (see Appendix C)

- ✎ Online applications for all job vacancies through eCareer

The application information is listed on the PS 2591 form. Download this form online at www.postalwork.net/resources.htm and use it as a guide to prepare your online application. Write your work experiences on your desktop using Word, WordPerfect or any word processor, spell and grammar check the document, and then copy and paste the write-ups into the online résumé builder after you register online. Use the form to collect your employment history and education so that when you go online you will have all the information needed to complete the application.

LOCATING JOB ANNOUNCEMENTS

Corporate jobs are advertised at http://about.usps.com/careers/welcome.htm. Search the listings and follow the links to the currently available job announcements. Jobs are listed in the categories noted on the previous page. The postal service posts announcements in federal, state, and municipal buildings open to the public; they advertise on the Internet, in local newspapers, and conducts and participates in job fairs, open houses, or other activities to reach the community.[1] I also suggest that if you visit the web site noted above and don't find jobs in occupations you are qualified, call the human resources department at your local Customer Service District Office (see Appendix C) and ask when they anticipate hiring for your occupation.

You may also wish to consider related occupations to get your foot in the door. For example, if you are interested in an administrative position and the postal service is hiring carriers and clerks, apply for these entry-level positions. If you are selected for the position you will have more opportunities within the system, since most administrative jobs are first advertised to current employees. If none meet the qualification standards for the position or there are insufficient bidders, the position is then advertised to the local public. You may also find related lower-paying jobs that will get your foot in the door as well. It all depends on what you can afford to do in this case. However, before deciding, look at target occupations and salaries to determine if it will be worth your while to sacrifice initial salary for greater future salary and upward mobility potential.

APPLYING FOR JOBS

Many talented job seekers are frustrated by the paperwork and give up prematurely. If you take the time to thoroughly complete your application and seek out all available job vacancies, your chances for employment will increase substantially. All forms and KSA statements listed in the job announcement must be submitted with your package. If you need forms, most can now be downloaded from the Internet.

Don't limit your search to applying for only one job vacancy. Seek out all available job vacancies and continue to send in applications with every opportunity. The more often you apply, the greater your chances.

COMPLETING YOUR APPLICATION

Previously, most postal job announcements, in the section titled "HOW TO APPLY," stated, *"Applicants must complete and submit a résumé or Form 2591, Application for Employment, plus a separate statement of qualifications for each knowledge, skill, or ability (KSA) to the application address on or before the closing date."* Now, online applications are required. Even though you typically submit an online application, I suggest using the PS Form 2591 to guide you through the data collection process. Download and use this form as a guide to collect required employment history and education. When you register and apply for jobs online you will have the information needed to complete the application. Complete your work histories on your desktop and copy and paste them into the online resume builder.

---

[1] Handbook EL-312, paragraph 223.12

Step One

Collect key data for your application. You will need the names, addresses, and contact phone numbers for previous and present employers. Locate or start compiling work histories, salary for each position, and starting and stop dates. You will also need transcripts from schools and the dates attended including major undergraduate subjects. Include special qualifications such as licenses, skills with machines, patents or inventions, publications, honors, awards, and fellowships received. Make up a folder and compile needed data for when you sit down and start your application.

You should also include volunteer work, temporary details, and other significant activities that were not work-related. For example, if you managed a Little League team you could capture management and organizational skills from that activity. Include this as a separate "Work History" entry under Section "C" on the application.

Step Two

Review the job announcement throughly before completing your online application. Highlight all keywords under the "Requirements" statements. Underline words that identify the key duties of the position. Do this with all job announcements and then incorporate relevant key words and duties in your "Work History" description of duties, responsibilities, and accomplishments in your work descriptions. If you have a skill or a related skill, include it in your application. The more you focus your application to key duties and responsibilities, the higher your rating will be. This will also help you complete required KSA statements.

Step Three

Complete your online application and assessments. Your work history should go back a minimum of 10 years or to your 16th birthday, whichever is earlier. Don't limit your work history to your last four employers. Expand it to include any and all related work history, relevant volunteer and community service experience or temporary details that showcase required knowledge, skills and abilities including military experience if applicable.

When describing your experience, use bullets to capture key KSAs. You have to show what you actually accomplished to achieve the stated skill or knowledge. Many who apply for federal jobs simply restate the skill, duty or accomplishment instead of describing how they attained them. If you don't provide specific examples, you won't receive points for those items. Take your time and be thorough.

Step Four

In most cases you will be required to submit a detailed description of how you achieved each knowledge, skills and abilities statement listed on the job announcement.

Understanding and Completing KSAs

Give a description of what you did to meet this KSA. Include in each KSA any of these relevant elements:

- Education
- Training
- Experience
- Volunteer work
- Outside activities
- Awards, licenses, etc.

You must include a narrative that indicates the degree to which you possess the KSA and include as many of the bullets listed above that apply in that narrative. For each work example or accomplishment listed, describe the situation, problem, or objective of the assignment, what was done, and the results obtained. Following the narrative, the applicant must indicate the duration (date) of the activity, and the name and telephone number of a person who can verify the information provided, if available. Applicants may attach copies of any relevant documents that will help substantiate their statements, such as performance evaluations, awards, or work products. The applicant's narrative must indicate exactly how these documents relate to the KSA.

Formatting Your KSAs

You can format your KSAs in a narrative form starting with "I" or use bullets that start with a forceful verb such as "organized, directed, managed, coordinated, analyzed, or conducted" to provide action to your statements. If you don't refer directly to an experience block, be sure to summarize the experience and provide the time and place where you performed that function. If you are applying for a supervisory position, mention the number of people you supervised, their status, such as part time or full time, and pay grade if applicable.

After writing your KSAs, review them a number of times, asking yourself "What did I do," "When did I do it," "Where did I perform these functions," and don't forget the proverbial question, "How often and how much did I do it." If you didn't answer these questions, edit your work until it is included. Add examples either in the narrative or by attaching an example, which is permitted in most cases.

Another factor many applicants overlook is the depth of training completed. Include correspondence study, online courses, seminars, classes, lectures, computer-based instruction, on-the-job training, every facet of training that you received, including software programs that you taught yourself.

Include special licenses, registration exams, or certifications that you obtained in your specialty. If you are a medical assistant and passed the Registered Medical Assistant (RMA) exam, annotate that on your application and in your KSAs. If you are in the trades and have various equipment operator's licenses, list items such as "Fork Lift Operator" certification; list whatever is relevant to the job announcement.

The following KSAs are provided as examples to show formatting techniques. Sample Supplemental Qualification Statements are provided for two elements.[2] If special forms are not provided or if specific formats are not specified on the job announcement, you can follow the sample outline to submit your narratives. Notice the use of bullets and short concise statements. You want the selecting official to focus on your key qualifications and good formatting techniques. The use of bullets, bold and underlined type will focus the reader's attention to your information. If you run everything together, it is difficult for the selecting official to identify key elements that you accomplished to satisfy the rating factors. Include all required information, and be sure to add your name, job announcement number, and position title at the top of each page.

Sample KSAs

The following samples were excerpted from *The Book of U.S. Government Jobs*, 11th Edition. They present a format that you can use to draft your KSAs. Note that each KSA is on a separate page and that on each page you can address related knowledge, skills, and abilities from multiple employers. You can use multiple pages for each KSA if needed. It is important to note that a rating of "no demonstration"on any of the KSAs will exclude an applicant from consideration for that position.[3]

Many applicants wonder why KSAs are needed when they already addressed their work experience in the application. KSAs are used by selecting officials to differentiate among the best qualified for the position. They present specific strengths and can point out weaknesses between candidates for the same position. It is important to take the time to draft clear and concise descriptions to improve your chances for the position. To keep the KSAs to one page, you can change the formatting and font size. However, don't use a font size of less than 10 points because it is too difficult to read. I like to use a 11 or 12 point font size when writing applications. If you have significant accomplishments to add to a description, include them even if the KSA is more than one page.

---

[2] KSA examples excerpted from *The Book of U.S. Government Jobs,* 11th Edition, with permission.

[3] Handbook EL-312, paragraph 754.41

Job Title: Administrative Officer

Announcement Number: XX-178A

Applicant's Name: John Smith

SSN: XXX-XX-XXXX

KSA #1 *Demonstrated ability to organize and coordinate work within schedule constraints and handle emergent requirements in a timely manner.*

I performed the following duties in my current position (Block C1):

- Managed the office suspense lists for all office supervisors. Transcribed meeting minutes and compiled action item lists, annotated due dates, and listed responsible parties. Sent reminders to responsible parties, kept list current and reported accomplishments to the office manager weekly.

- Planned and coordinated two annual shareholder meetings for over 700 stock owners, key management and staff. Drafted the itinerary, set up the registration booth, arranged for morning breakout sessions, planned lunch and the shareholders meeting from 1:00 to 3:00 p.m. Also staffed the shareholders information booth after the meeting.

Award: Received an award for exemplary service for planning and organizing the 2001 meeting, copy attached.

- Required to frequently complete short notice work assignments including reports, transcribing meeting minutes, and payroll accounting tasks. I am the chief headquarters payroll clerk and I provide backup to 12 field offices. If any of the field office clerks or supervisors are not available, I complete their payroll reports prior to the cutoff time.

- Responsible for notifying management of pending funding shortfalls and providing justification for additional fund requests. I analyzed budget reports for trends, calculated spend rates, and recommended reallocation of funds to satisfy pending or potential shortages.

Training:

1. Certificate: 24-hour Meeting Preparation and Planning seminar, March 2010

2. 40-hour Time Management Course, RMC Services, April 2008

Job Title: Administrative Officer

Announcement Number: XX-178A

Applicant's Name: John Smith

SSN: XXX-XX-XXXX

KSA #2 *Demonstrated ability to monitor important and complex projects concurrently.*

Performed these duties in my present position from 1/1/2004 to the present (Block C1):

- Budget analyst duties – Trend tracking, monitor, and control of the Office's annual budget of $350,000. Performed budget data entry, compiled reports, tracked trends, anticipated fund shortages in various program areas, and drafted requests for additional funds for management's signature. Audited program areas to ensure fund expenditures were justified and properly classified.

- Payroll chief clerk – Ensured timely submission of all payroll data before the cutoff date each pay period, entered amendments, and researched pay problems for 37 employees. I advised management of problems and notified them when to review and approve the attendance for each pay period.

Training: 80-hour accounting software class, by Peachtree, January 2002.

Performed the following duties in my previous position as Administrative Officer, GS-0341-7, with the USDA from 10/4/2006 to 12/31/2008 (Block C2):

- Organizational Charts & Staffing – Processed revisions to and generated complex organizational charts based on input from the management team. Reviewed proposed changes to ensure they conformed to authorized levels and that positions were properly classified. Concurrently, prepared, and tracked personnel actions for 124 employees and provided support in various program areas including payroll, benefits, staffing, and budget.

- Office of Workmen's Compensation Program (OWCP) Program – Conducted annual (OWCP) seminars for managers and supervisors. Seminars included guidance on procedures, claims processing and post-accident interventions. Provided guidance to immediate supervisors of injured employees and maintained the OSHA 200 log for all accidents.

Award: Cash award, June 2008, for managing the OWCP program, copy attached.

Training: 60-hour Position Management and Position Classification Course, 012-V-933, Graduate School, USDA, Washington D.C., June 2005.

Job Title: Administrative Officer

Announcement Number: XX-178A

Applicant's Name: John Smith

SSN: XXX-XX-XXXX

KSA #3 *Knowledge of Microsoft Word, Excel, Powerpoint, and Lotus Notes/other e-mail software.*

Performed these duties in present position from 1/1/2004 to the present (Block C1):

- Proficient in Microsoft Office, Word, Excel, Powerpoint, Lotus, and I use Lotus notes for office e-mail. Developed a 34-page Powerpoint presentation (copy attached) for our CEO to use at the 2005 annual stockholders meeting in Memphis. The presentation received rave reviews and I was asked to develop similar presentations for other meetings. Worked closely with accounting to compile the data and then integrated it into a succinct visual presentation. I use Microsoft Word for corres-pondence.

- Conducted Microsoft Word and Excel mini-training sessions for those less proficient in the office. Typically sessions ran 1 to 2 hours in length. Attended various software system seminars including Microsoft Office, Peachtree Accounting, and our new Lotus Notes e-mail program.

Volunteer Work: Performed these duties while working as a volunteer for United Way over past 6 years. Approximately 12 hours a week. (Block E):

- Developed our chapter's web site (http://www.xxxxxxxxxx.org) using Microsoft Expression Web. I consider myself very proficient in web site de-velopment, and I learned Expression Web through self study and experi-mentation. This web site consists of 48 pages and two databases. We used a secure server for confidential requests. I'm the webmaster. Contact the United Way Chairperson, Ms. Mary Jones, for verification at XXX-123-4567.

Performed the following duties in my previous position as Administrative Officer, GS-0341-7, with the USDA from 10/4/96 to 12/31/2003 (Block B):

- Proficient in VISO. I used VISO to generate ORG charts while at the USDA.

- Proficient in several payroll and T&A software systems including IPPS, the USDA's Integrated Personnel and Payroll System.

Training Certificates: 24-hour <u>VISO software course</u> and a 16-hour <u>IPPS software course,</u> both completed at our regional office, May 1998.

Job Title: Administrative Officer, GS-341-05/11

Announcement Number: XX-178A

Applicant's Name: John Smith

SSN: XXX-XX-XXXX

KSA #4 *Demonstrated ability to effectively communicate orally and in writing, to include writing and preparing memorandums, letters, and other official correspondence.*

Performed these duties in present position from 1/1/2004 to the present (Block C1):

- **Written Guidance** – Developed Standard Operation Procedures (SOPs) for program areas including payroll administration, office suspense tracking, monitor and control, and general procedures. Adopted by the regional office for use throughout the organization, sample attached. I also wrote numerous internal memorandums within my program areas that provided direction for specific functions and clarified company policy issues.

   Prepare transmittal forms for project files, letters to share holders, fax cover letters, e-mail messages to team leads and customers, flip charts for meetings, Power Point presentations, proof and edit management draft correspondence, and prepare replies to organizational reports.

- **Oral Communications** – In current capacity I teach office software to small groups, brief management team of progress at meetings, give presentations at inter-office meetings and to small groups of shareholders.

Volunteer Work

- I speak at various fund-raisers for our local United Way and prepare written presentations to our work group and chairperson. I organized and hosted a dozen fund raisers since 2004. Contact the United Way chairperson, Ms. Mary Jones, for verification at 890-123-4567.

Education: Completed 12 semester hours, three courses in communications, at Duquesne University in 2007; <u>Report Writing</u>, <u>Oral Communications I</u> and <u>Effective Writing Techniques</u>.

Training:

1) **Competent Toastmaster.** Joined Toastmasters International in 1999. Obtained Competent Toastmaster status in 2005. Chapter president, Dan McCormick, 321-654-0987. Certificate attached.

2) **Certificate;** <u>Constructive Communications with the Public</u>, USDA Course 01501, June 2005. <u>Interpersonal Communications</u>, Seminar 2008, sponsored by OPM.

KSA CHECKLIST

Use this list to ensure that you have included key information.[4] It's important to consider these areas when drafting your KSA statements. When you first start to draft your KSAs, don't worry about the specifics such as exact dates or contact information, etc. You can add that later. It is best to simply write down anything and everything, even the least significant events. After you get it all down, add specifics and put them in logical sequence. Review and rewrite your KSAs at least three times, and more if needed. Let your draft sit overnight and review it again the next day. You will be surprised at what you left out on the first draft.

❏ **Experience** – Include experience for all offices, departments or agencies that you worked for to show depth and range of experience. For example, include that you tracked inter-office correspondence at multiple locations, or that you tracked budgets for headquarters. Also show expertise in what you do well, such as having A++ certification, maintain LANS/WANS for several locations, thoroughly familiar with Peachtree accounting software, proficient at office organization, etc.

❏ **Supervision** – If you don't have a supervisory background, did you work independently with minimal supervision and make decisions for your program areas? If so, state that in your KSA. Were you assigned to be an acting supervisor on several occasions? Do you draft memorandums and letters for your supervisor's signature? Do you manage/supervise programs or projects?

❏ **Complexity factors** – Did you write reports or work on large projects, coordinating activities for various groups? Does your job impact the safety of others, and what standards do you follow and utilize in your present and past jobs? Do you have certifications, licenses, specific training, or accreditation that would help you land this job?

❏ **Achievements and Impact** – How did you show initiative and creativity in your office while working under adverse conditions? Were you responsible for major programs, products, or activities? If so list them. What did you do to save time, money and resources or to improve the work environment?

❏ **Awards/Recognition** – Include all awards, monetary rewards, letters of achievement, time-off awards, or write-ups in your office newsletter. Include scholastic nominations as well, and any service awards or recognition received from volunteer work.

❏ **Contacts** – If you dealt with headquarters staff, the general public, EPA or OSHA inspectors, local authorities, or government officials, list them in your KSAs.

❏ **Fashionable Trends** – Mention current trends such as "Business Process Engineering (BPE), Model Work Environment (MWE) initiatives, Management by

---

[4] Excerpted from *The Book of U.S. Government Jobs*, 11th Edition

Objectives (MBO), Partnership, Quality Work Groups," etc. If you have exposure to these and other initiatives list them in your write-up.

OVERVIEW

Now that you have your application and KSAs completed, you are ready to submit your package. Follow the instructions in the job announcement. Your application must reach the listed address on or before the specified closing date. If it is received after the closing date your application will not be considered.

If selected for the position, you will have to complete other forms such as the PS Form 2181-A, a "Pre-Employment Screening – Authorization and Release Form.

KEYS TO SUCCESS

There are three basic ingredients to successfully finding federal employment for qualified applicants:

- Invest the time and energy needed to seek out all openings.
- Correctly fill out all required application forms.
- Don't give up if you receive your first rejection.

You can learn from rejections by contacting the selecting official. Ask what training and/or experience would enhance your application package for future positions. If they specify certain training or experience, then work to achieve the desired skills.

NETWORKING

Networking is a term used to define the establishment of a group of individuals who assist one another for mutual benefit. You can establish your own network by talking to personnel specialists, contacting Customer Service District Office human resources departments, conducting informational interviews, and by bidding on all applicable job announcements. By following the guidelines outlined in the book and using your innate common sense, your chances of success are increased substantially.

Visit http://federaljobs.net to explore viable civil service options in the competitive sector and to use the many resources offered on this site, including direct links to hundreds of federal agency employment Web sites. You will also find updates to this book posted on http://postalwork.net as changes occur.

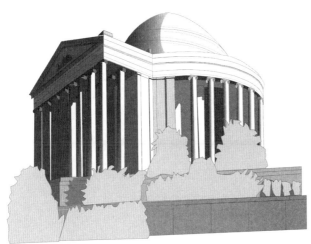

Appendix C
Customer Service District Offices

In addition to the national headquarters, there are sixty seven Customer Service and Sales District (CSSD) Offices supporting post offices, branches, and stations throughout the United States. The postal service has approximately 644,000 employees and handles over 200 billion pieces of mail annually, generating billions in operating revenues.

If you need to ask a question about a job vacancy or have to reschedule an exam you will find a contact email address or phone number on the job announcement. If you lose this paperwork contact your local CSSD office. They can direct you to the proper HR and staffing office.

The postal service offers abundant job opportunities in all 50 states and U.S. territories. With more than 35,000 postal facilities, individuals have an excellent opportunity to apply for positions in thousands of small towns and in all major metropolitan areas.

CUSTOMER SERVICE AND SALES DISTRICTS

The postal service recently consolidated nine Customer Service District Offices into seven. The sixty seven district offices are divided geographically into seven areas: Eastern, Northeastern, Capital Metro, Great lakes, Pacific, Southern, and Western.

The following District Office list provides the district manager's name, address, phone and fax numbers. If you see an (A) next to the manager's name that indicates that person is acting in the position. There are also a number of human resource, staffing and customer service numbers listed. Call the staffing or human resource specialist numbers first if you have an issue with your application. If a staffing specialist isn't listed ask the receptionist that answers the district managers line to forward your call to their staffing specialist.

The main reason for offering this information is to provide a central contact that you can call for help during the application and testing process. Many applicants misplace the job announcement and correspondence they receive from the postal service.

Job applicants should keep a copy of the job announcement for the position they applied and all correspondence including copies of email notifications for future reference. These documents include a contact name and number that you can contact for assistance. If you misplaced the job announcement, exam notification, or your Candidate ID Number the local staffing specialist will be able to provide assistance and the district manager's secretary can forward you to the proper office.

You can also contact the manager or post master at the facility where the vacancy is being filled. They can give you the number of the local human resource office that handles their recruiting.

To locate job vacancies in your area, visit the Postal Service's site at http://about.usps.com/careers/welcome.htm. You can also contact General Mail Facilities (GMF), Sectional Center Facilities (SCF), Management Sectional Centers (MSC), Bulk Mail Centers in your area, or the Customer Service and Sales District (CSSD) office nearest you, to inquire when jobs will be advertised in your area.

This list does not include testing centers. Proctored exams are conducted by third party contractors that are certified to administer computer based postal exams for that location. Examinations can be scheduled at designated testing facilities nationwide.

CUSTOMER SERVICE DISTRICTS

EASTERN AREA

Wendy L. English
District Manager
Appalachian
1002 Lee St. E
Charleston, WV 26350-9992
(304) 561-1200
(304) 561-1209 (FAX)

Samuel Jaudon
District Manager
Ohio Valley
1591 Dalton St
Cincinnati, OH 45234-9990
Customer Affairs Office (513) 684-5167 or 5452
District Manager (513) 684-5360
(513) 684-5197 (FAX)

Melvin J. Anderson
District Manager
Northern Ohio
2200 Orange Ave., Rm 210
Cleveland, OH 44104-9005
(216) 443-4573
(216) 443-4577 (FAX)

David J. Dillman
District Manager
Tennessee
525 Royal Pkwy.
Nashville, TN 37229-9998
(615) 885-9525
(615) 885-9317(FAX)

James Lentz
District Manager
Western New York
1200 Williams St.
Buffalo, NY 14240-9990
(716) 846-2532
(716) 846-2407 (FAX)

Dale Walker
District Manager
Central Pennsylvania
Postmaster's Office
3000 Chestnut St.
Philadelphia, PA 19104-9998
(215) 895-8818

Elizabeth Schaefer (A)
District Manager
Kentuckiana
PO Box 3100
Louisville, KY 40231
Field Staffing Specialist (502) 454-1642
Customer Affairs Office (502) 454-1642
District manager (502) 454-1814

Troy Seanor (A)
District Manager
Western Pennsylvania
1001 California Ave., Rm 2001
Pittsburgh, PA 15290-9996
Staffing Specialist (412) 359-7135
Consumer Affairs Office (412) 359-7845
District Manager (412) 359-7771
(412) 321-3373 (FAX)

Chu Falling-Star
District Manager
Philadelphia Metro
3190 S 70th St., Rm 100
Philadelphia, PA 19153
(215) 895-8607
(215) 895-8611 (FAX)

Sharon M. Rogers
District Manager
South Jersey
PO Box 9001
Bellmawr, NJ 08099-9998
HR Staffing Specialist (856) 933-4288
Consumer Affairs: (856) 933-4419
Finance: (856) 933-4331
District Manager (856) 933-4400
(856) 933-4440 (FAX)

GREAT LAKES AREA

Peter Allen
District Manager
Central Illinois
6801 West 73rd St
Bedford Park, IL 60499-9998
(708) 563-7800
(708) 563-2013 (FAX)

Gregory Johnson
District Manager
Chicago
433 West Harrison, Rm 2036
Chicago, IL 60607-9998
(312) 983-8030
(312) 983-8010 (FAX)

Lee Thompson
District Manager
Detroit
1401 W. Fort St
Detroit, MI 46233-9992
(313) 226-8605
(313) 226-8005 (FAX)

David F. Martin
District Manager
Gateway
1720 Market St., Rm 3027
St. Louis, MO 63155-9900
(314) 436-4114
(314) 436-4565 (FAX)

Bernice Grant
District Manager
Greater Indiana
3939 Vincennes Road
PO Box 9850
Indianapolis, IN 46298-9850
(317) 870-8201
(317) 870-8688 (FAX)

Krista A. Finazzo
District Manager
Greater Michigan
PO Box 999997
Grand Rapids, MI 49599-9997
HR Staffing Specialist (616) 336-5328

Consumer Affairs (616) 776-6157
District Manager (616) 336-5300
(616) 336-5399 (FAX)

Debra Woodrum
District Manager
Lakeland
PO Box 5000
Milwaukee, WI 53201-5000
HR Staffing Specialist (414) 287-1802
(District Manager (414) 287-2238
(414) 287-2296 (FAX)

CAPITAL METRO OPERATIONS

Scott Raymond
District Manager
Atlanta
P.O. Box 599300
North Metro, GA 300026
(770) 717-3736
(770) 717-3735

Darryl Martin (A)
District Manager
Baltimore
900 East Fayette St., Rm 309
Baltimore, MD 21233-9990
(410) 347-4314
(410) 347-4289 (FAX)

Kelvin L. Williams
District Manager
Capital
900 Brentwood Road, N.E.
Washington, DC 20066-9998
(202) 636-2210
(202) 636-5301 (FAX)

District Manager
Greater SC
PO Box 929998
Columbia, SC 29292-9998
(803) 926-6469
(803) 926-6470 (FAX)

Russell D. Garbner, Jr.
District Manager
Greensboro
418 Gallimore Dairy Road

P.O. Box 27499
Greensboro, NC 27498-9900
(336) 668-1201
(336) 668-1366 (FAX)

Angela Curtis (A).
District Manager
Mid-Carolinas
2901Scott Futrell Drive
Charlotte, NC 28228-9980
(704) 424-4400
(704) 424-4489 (FAX)

Kevin McAdams
District Manager
Northern Virginia
8409 Lee Highway
Merrifield, VA 22081-9996
(703) 698-6464
(703) 698-6609 (FAX)

Jeffrey Becker
District Manager
Richmond
1801 Brook Road
Richmond, VA 23232-9990
(804) 775-6365 or 6364
(804) 775-6058 (FAX)

NORTHEAST AREA

Michael Rakes
District Manager
Albany
30 Old Karner Road
Albany, NY 12288-9992
(518) 452-2201
(518) 452-2309 (FAX)

Lisa Ojeda (A)
District Manager
Caribbean
585 FD Roosevelt Ave.,
San Juan, PR 00936-9998
(787) 662-1800
(787) 622-1803 (FAX)

Kimberly J. Peters
District Manager
Connecticut Valley

141 Weston St.
Hartford, CT 06101-9996
(860) 524-6137
(860) 524-6199 (FAX)

John W. (Mike) Powers
District Manager
Greater Boston
25 Dorchester Ave.
Boston, MA 02205-0098
(617) 654-5007
(617) 654-5816 (FAX)

Lorraine Castellano
District Manager
Long Island
PO Box 7800
Islandia, NY 11760-9998
(631) 582-7410
(631) 582-7413 (FAX)

William Schinaars
District Manager
New York
421 8th Ave., Rm 3018
New York, NY 10199-9998
(212) 330-3600
(212) 330-3934 (FAX)

John T. Godlewski
District Manager
Northern New England
151 Forest Ave.
Portland, ME 04104
(207) 482-7109
(207) 482-7105 (FAX)

Steven Hernandez (A)
District Manager
Northern New Jersey
494 Broad Street, Rm 307
Newark, NJ 07102-9300
(973) 468-7111
(973) 468-7215 (FAX)

Frank Calabrese
District Manager
Triboro
1050 Forbell St., Rm 2011
Brooklyn, NY 11256-9996

(718) 348-3991
(718) 348-3992 (FAX)

Elizabeth A. Doell
District Manager
Westchester
PO Box 9800
White Plains, NY 10610
(914) 697-7104
(914) 697-7128 (FAX)

PACIFIC AREA

Mark A. Martinez
District Manager
Bay-Valley
1675 7th St.
Oakland, CA 94615-9987
(510) 874-8222
(510) 874-8301 (FAX)

Gregory Wolny
District Manager
Honolulu
3600 Aolele St.
Honolulu, HI 96820-3600
(808) 423-3700
(808) 423-6060 (FAX)

Ed Ruiz
District Manager
Los Angeles
7001 South Central Ave.
Los Angeles, CA
    90052-9998
(323) 586-1200
(323) 586-1248 (FAX)

Barbara Plunkett
District Manager
Sacramento
3775 Industrial Blvd.
Sacramento, CA 95799
(916) 373-8001
(916) 373-8704 (FAX)

James P. Olson
District Manager

San Diego
11251 Rancho Carmel Dr.
San Diego, CA 92199-9990
(858) 674-0301
(858) 674-0405 (FAX)

David Stowe
District Manager
San Francisco
PO Box 885050
San Francisco, CA 94188
(415) 550-5591
(415) 550-5327 (FAX)

Larry Munoz (A)
District Manager
Santa Ana
3101 W. Sunflower
Santa Ana, CA 92799-9993
(714) 662-6300
(714) 557-5837 (FAX)

Kerr Wolny
District Manager
Sierra Coastal
28201 Franklin Parkway
Santa Clarita, CA 91383
(661) 775-6500
(661) 775-7184 (FAX)

SOUTHERN AREA

Timothy Costello
District Manager
Alabama
351 24th St., N.
Birmingham, AL
    35203-9997
(205) 521-0201
(205) 521-0058 (FAX)

David Camp
District Manager
Arkansas
420 Natural Resources Dr.
Little Rock, AR 72205-9800
(501) 228-4100
(501) 228-4105 (FAX)

Charlie Miller
District Manager
Dallas
951 W. Bethel Road
Coppell, TX 75099-9998
(972) 393-6787
(972) 393-6192 (FAX)

Brenda Baugh
District Manager
Fort Worth
4600 Mark IV Parkway
Fort Worth, TX 76161-9100
(817) 317-3301
(817) 317-3320 (FAX)

Yul Melonson
District Manager
Houston
600 N. Sam Houston Pkwy
West Houston, TX 77202
(713) 226-3717
(713) 226-3755 (FAX)

Bruno Tristan
District Manager
Louisiana
701 Loyola Ave.
Rm T11001
New Orleans, LA
   70113-9800
(504) 589-1950
(504) 589-1432 (FAX)

Gregory Gamble
District Manager
Mississippi
PO Box 99990
Jackson, MS 39205-9990
(601) 351-7350
(601) 351-7504 (FAX)

James Nemec
District Manager
Gulf Atlantic
PO Box 40005
Jacksonville, FL 32203-0005
(904) 858-6605
(904) 858-6610 (FAX)

Julie Gosdin
District Manager
Oklahoma City
4025 W. Reno Ave.
Oklahoma City, OK 73125
(405) 815-2101
(405) 815-2010 (FAX)

Kim E. Quaule
District Manager
Rio Grande
One Post Office Drive
San Antonio, TX 78284
(210) 368-5548
(210) 368-5511 (FAX)

Jeffery A. Taylor
District Manager
South Florida
PO Box 829990
Pembroke Pines, FL 33082
(954) 436-4466

Nancy Rettinhouse
District Manager
Suncoast
2203 N. Lois Ave., Ste. 1001
Tampa, FL 33607-7101
(813) 354-6099
(813) 877-8656 (FAX)

WESTERN AREA

Ronald S. Haberman
District Manager
Alaska
3720 Barrow St.
Anchorage, AK 99599-0001
(907) 261-5418
(907) 273-5866 (FAX)

John Diperi
District Manager
Arizona
4949 E. Van Buren St.
   Rm. 211C
Phoenix, AZ 85026-9900
(602) 225-5400
(602) 225-3286 (FAX)

Rick Pivovor
District Manager
Central Plains
PO Box 199500
Omaha, NE 68119-9500
(402) 930-4400
(402) 930-4434 (FAX)

Selwyn D. Epperson
District Manager
Colorado/Wyoming
7500 East 53rd Place,
Rm 1131
Denver, CO 80266-9998
(303) 853-6160
(303) 853-6099 (FAX)

William J. Herrmann (A)
District Manager
Dakotas
PO Box 7500
Sioux Falls, SD 57117-7500
(605) 333-2601
(605) 333-2777 (FAX)

William J. Herrmann
District Manager
Hawkeye
PO Box 189800
Des Moines, IA 50318-9800
(515) 251-2601
(515) 251-2050 (FAX)

Gail. M. Hendrix
District Manager
Mid-America
300 W. Pershing Rd.,
Ste. 210
Kansas City, MO 64108
(816) 374-9105
(816) 374-9487 (FAX)

Brenda L. Olson (A)
District Manager
Nevada-Sierra
1001 E. Sunset Road
Las Vegas, NV 89199-9998
(702) 361-9300
(702) 361-9508 (FAX)

Anthony C. Williams
District Manager
Northland
100 South lst St.,
Rm. 409
Minneapolis, MN 55401
(612) 349-3505
(612) 349-6377 (FAX)

Kim Anderson
District Manager
Portland District
P.O. Box 3609
Portland, OR 97208-3609
(503) 294-2500
(503) 276-2020 (FAX)

Jimmy Wolf
District Manager
Salt Lake City
1760 W. 2100 S.
Salt Lake City, UT
    84199-8800
(801) 974-2947
(801) 974-2339 (FAX)

Don Jacobus
District Manager
Seattle
34301 9th Ave., South #205
Federal Way, WA 98003
(253) 214-1701
(253) 214-1824 (FAX)

Index